CHRISTIAN SCIENCE:
Its Encounter With Lesbian/Gay America

CHRISTIAN SCIENCE:
Its Encounter With Lesbian/Gay America

Bruce Stores

iUniverse, Inc.

New York Lincoln Shanghai

CHRISTIAN SCIENCE: Its Encounter With Lesbian/Gay America

iUniverse, Inc.

For information address:
iUniverse, Inc.
2021 Pine Lake Road, Suite 100
Lincoln, NE 68512
www.iuniverse.com

ISBN: 0-595-32620-X (pbk)
ISBN: 0-595-66658-2 (cloth)

Printed in the United States of America

*...[T]he soul of Jonathan was knit to the soul of David, and Jonathan
loved him as his own soul...*
*I am distressed for you, my brother Jonathan; very pleasant have you
been to me; your love to me was wonderful, passing the love of women.*
                                    —I Samuel 18:1; II Samuel 1:26 RSV

*I recommend that Scientists draw no lines whatever between one person
and another, but think, speak, teach, and write the truth of Christian
Science without reference to right or wrong personality in this field of
labor. Leave the distinctions of individual character and the discrimina-
tions and guidance thereof to the Father, whose wisdom is unerring and
whose love is universal.*
                         —Mary Baker Eddy, *No and Yes* page 7, lines 21–2

Judge not, that ye be not judged.

                                                        —Matthew 7:1

This book is dedicated to my son, David Bruce Stores.

Contents

Acknowledgements

Many thanks are given to those who generously contributed to this book with their time, detailed information, logistical support, computer skills, and just plain encouragement.

The extensive personal interviews that were granted provided by far the bulk of the information for *Christian Science: Its Encounter with Lesbian-Gay America*. All the main players in the narrative showed a willingness and great patience to provide extensive background material. In some cases several follow-up interviews were necessary to get the full story. In this regard deep gratitude is extended to Ernest Barnum (Little Rock, AR), Robert Mackenroth (New York, NY), Christine Madsen (Freeport, ME), Robert McCullough (New York, NY), Carol Pierson (San Francisco, CA), Craig Rodwell (New York, NY-deceased), Ray Spitale (New York, NY) and David Stores (Washington, MO). Also helpful were Jim Bradley (Washington, DC-deceased), Chandler Burr, Amy Duncan (Rio de Janeiro, Brazil), Dr. Stuart Grayson (New York, NY—deceased), Jim Heuer, David Hosely (San Francisco, CA), Kathelen Johnson (Oakland, CA), Hugh Key C. S. (Sugarloaf Shores, FL), Laura Matthews C. S. (Framingham, MA), Katherine Triantafillou (Boston, MA), Earl Welther (Chicago, IL), David White (Washington, DC), and Dell Yarnell (Chicago, IL). Thanks to Michael K. Hughes (Seattle, WA) for permission to re-print his letter from the "Reader's Write" column in the *Christian Science Monitor*. Thanks also to Diego Flores Cortés (Puebla, Mexico) for technical help with the cover design, Glen Hunt (Seattle, WA-deceased) for valuable logistical help, and Tim Mayhew (Seattle, WA) for his untiring assistance in sharing his computer expertise.

Special appreciation goes to National Public Radio station KQED-FM, San Francisco, for making available its extensive files covering the five-year history of its negotiations with Monitor Radio. Thanks to Ann Beals, Founder of the Bookmark, for permission to quote from her talk, "*The Spiritually Organized Church*," and Dr. Gillian Gill for use of excerpts from her biography, *Mary Baker Eddy*. Thanks also to the following publications for permission to quote from articles:, *Bay Area Reporter* (San Francisco), The *Boston Globe, Christian Century, Christian Science Monitor* (Boston), *The Nation, National Review, U. S. News and World Report, The New Republic, Newsweek, Time*, and *San Francisco Chronicle*.

And finally, thanks to the women and men in Emergence International whose words of encouragement from the beginning and along the way helped provide the incentive to see this project through.

The naming of individuals in this work does not connote sexual orientation or sexual preference, except where such orientation or preference is specifically indicated.

The author accepts full responsibility in the event of errors or omissions in the text. He would appreciate hearing from readers should they want to send corrections and/or comments. This could prove helpful in the event there is a second edition. He can be reached through the publisher or directly by electronic mail: <rbstores@hotmail.com>

Abbreviations

KJV   King James Version of the Bible

RSV   Revised Standard Version of the Bible

Misc.   *Miscellaneous Writings*, by Mary Baker Eddy

S&H   *Science and Health with Key to the Scriptures*, by Mary Baker Eddy

EI   Emergence International

LGBT   Lesbian, gay, bisexual, and transgender/Sexual minorities

Preface

The present flux in religious faith may be found to be a healthy fermentation, by which the lees of religion will be lost, dogma and creed will pass off in scum, leaving a solid Christianity at the bottom—a foundation for the builders.

—*First Church of Christ, Scientist and Miscellany,* page 301, lines 5–9

Some American churches are in crisis. Defining the place of sexual minorities (lesbian, gay, bisexual, and transgender persons or LGBT) in their ranks has caused the most painful upheaval since slavery. We may yet see churches split, with new denominations formed. These conflicts in many denominations have not gone unnoticed in the national news media.

In some denominations, particularly the Episcopalians, Methodists, and Presbyterians, the media have given intense coverage to their divisions. This was especially true when the first gay Episcopalian Bishop was ordained. By contrast, the change from blatant discrimination of sexual minorities to a degree of acceptance by Christian Science Church officials occurred quietly. So quietly, most members didn't know it was happening. The reform that took place in the decade of the 1990's was never discussed in the Church's religious periodicals. Not even the *Christian Science Monitor* mentioned it. It was all but unnoticed in the wider media. Only when the Christian Science Church seemed to backpedal and relieved a teacher of her position in 2004 after she legally married her long-time partner, did some media coverage occur. The narrative that follows will try to identify and describe some of the events and forces behind the Christian Scientists' quiet revolution.

This book, however, is not about religion. Its purpose is to chronicle a segment of the age-old conflict between freedom of conscience and ecclesiastical authoritarianism. The pursuit of freedom in one religious denomination is set against the background of the wider lesbian/gay movement for equality and civil rights.

Positive acceptance by sexual minorities of their sexual orientation in the wake of the Stonewall rebellion in 1969 resulted in deep conflict with society. Much of this conflict arose in ecclesiastical arenas. This resulted in the flowering of les-bian/gay support groups throughout the spectrum of America's religious denom-inations. This book narrates these developments among lesbian/gay Christian Scientists and their Church. The narrative is not limited to the struggle of LGBT people to achieve fairness within their denomination. Their story is intricately locked into the wider lesbian/gay movement for equality. Therefore, it was deemed necessary to include in this work some of the major events in the history of the modern lesbian/gay movement. From this context the dedication of les-bian/gay Christian Scientists can be better understood. What follows is a segment of sexual minority history. Some of this history has never been told. It is at the same time a slice of recent denominational history that has been all but unknown to the wider (non-LGBT) Christian Science community.

Let the reader be warned. What follows is not a neutral history of sexual minorities in Christian Science. As an active player in this arena since 1980, the author admits to a bias in favor of the lesbian/gay groups. Beyond that, it may be helpful to identify the prejudices that will be found throughout this book.

To the extent the Church of Christ, Scientist has been an authoritarian entity, I have opposed the organization. This includes telling members how they must enhance their spirituality, what members can/cannot read to further their spiri-tual awareness, defining members social conduct, and especially by prescribing with whom they can and cannot share physical love in their human experience.

On the other hand, a church that upholds "…man's individual right of self-government" (S&H page 447, line 2), which treats "all believers" as "kings and priests unto God" (Revelation 1:6 KJV; quoted in S&H page 141, lines 20–21), and champions Christ Jesus admonition, "Judge not," (Matthew 7:1) is worthy of respect and support.

I believe spiritual growth can come entirely through one's own efforts. It can also come from a teacher and/or with others through informal groups. It can also come from a highly structured organization such as a church. In that context, Mrs. Eddy's counsel "organization has its value and peril" (Retrospection and Introspection, page 45, line 6) is still valid in our spiritual and human journeys. Her counsel is a signal for us to have the utmost caution in how we handle orga-nizations of all kinds including the governing of political jurisdictions, academic and social groups, as well as churches.

History is replete with "perils" of organization. A case can be made that the Christian Science Church has been as much a victim of power and love of organi-zation for its own sake, as was the Hebrew religion in the time of Jesus, and Christianity itself, a few centuries later. Out of autonomous communities of spiritually equal believers, early Christians developed a sophisticated hierarchy demanding special privileges as intercessors between congregants and the Holy Spirit. A similar proclivity emerged in the twentieth century. Here, the Christian Science Board of Directors (Board) saw themselves as ultimate arbiters in defining exact meanings of the Bible and Mary Baker Eddy's writings, by defining correct literature for members to read (i.e. authorized) and legislating behavior for Church members in highly personal areas. Some Christian Scientists have found that for them to yield total allegiance to the Board, or any ecclesiastical authority, on spiritual matters, would be inconsistent with their Church's sixth tenet: "…[W]e solemnly promise to watch, and pray for that Mind to be in us which was also in Christ Jesus;…."(1)

Dissidents have always been part of the greater Church scene. Up to the last quarter of the 20th century, a shell of invincibility protected the Board from "disloyalty" and competition for the conscience of rank and file members.

Nearly solid support for the Board began to crack when Reginald Kerry's letters to the Church field made their shocking debut in 1975. Yet, it would take many events to cause what *U. S. News and World Report* 14 years later called, "a crisis of confidence that could threaten the faith's very survival."(2) The events, in addition to the Kerry revelations, included loss of the coveted copyright once given as an act of Congress to the denomination's basic text, *Science and Health with Key to the Scriptures*;(3) losing in court its legalized monopoly on the very words "Christian Science" to an excommunicated congregation;(4) and an intense internal dispute resulting from Board imposed changes in the *Christian Science Monitor*. This was seen by critics as a downgrading of the *Monitor* in favor of vastly increased use of radio and television. The dispute resulted in numerous protest resignations. These included three top editors and some of its most distinguished writers.(5) Confidence was further eroded following a decision to carry a number of previously "unauthorized" books in Christian Science Reading Rooms. *Time* magazine noted,

> Official publication of [one] volume has led to a rare outburst of protest from within the ranks, with critics charging that apostasy has resulted from both a bizarre bequest [$90 million from the author's family tied to Church acceptance of the book as 'authorized' for members to read] and the faith's financial crisis.(6)

The Church was also involved in courtroom trials over the rights of parents to withhold medical treatment for their children. Some of the trials were heavily spotlighted in the national media. Accompanying the turmoil has been a steady attrition in membership resulting in an average of twenty-five branch churches dissolved in the United States per annum since 1970. By the 1990's the number of lost churches in America had soared to forty or more a year.(7) But as far-reaching as these quandaries have been, they were only symptomatic of a much larger problem.

The overriding dilemma in the Boston-based Church has been a membership asleep to the injustices of an unresponsive hierarchy. Injustice was manifested by a Board seemingly unable to tolerate criticism. Constructive and even healing-based criticism were often equated as treason. A perception arose by a number of church members and employees, as well as dissidents and free thinkers, that the Board was fearful of new ideas, and felt threatened by others' opinions. This was manifested by the Board's reluctance to dialogue with any group that suggested tinkering with the status quo, not just sexual minorities.

There will be, no doubt, readers who would love to see strong condemnations of the Church's leadership for what they believe are former discriminatory policies, and other injustices. They might also point out the policies were usually accompanied with harsh judgmental overtones insisting, for example, on "healing" as the only adequate response to a same-gender sexual orientation.

Others would take the opposite view. They would have Church authorities seen only in a light that would absolve them from the slightest suspicion of wrongdoing. Conflicting viewpoints such as these no doubt cause a predicament for anyone writing about Church history.

A constructive way to approach the issue came from a Church authorized practitioner. Learning of this book in progress, she said,

> Please try to love both sides as you write. This is the only way to be balanced and to really educate. There is no "enemy" here, just a bunch of people doing their best as the moment presents itself.

The advice is practical. In the absence of evidence to the contrary, it must be pointed out that the author assumes all players in this narrative are acting out of sincere convictions. Then, what we are left with are sincere, albeit profoundly divergent views.

The question may also arise as to the appropriateness of discussing past errors. The answer to that is to point out it would not do justice to record United States history by omitting the slavery years, the injustices of the reconstruction era, factory sweathouses, child labor, the oppression of women, legalized racial segregation, the Vietnam war, Watergate, being caught off-guard on September 11,

2001, for some, the "error" of invading Iraq coupled with wide-scale prisoner abuse, and a Presidential condemnation of same-gender marriage as a result of entrenched homophobia, even in 2004. Through all this, Americans for the most part, including lesbians and gays, love their country. The same is true when we record mistakes by the Christian Science Church. Another reason to bring up ecclesiastical *faux pas* is that it may make it less likely for past errors to be repeated.

Part of the uniqueness of Christian Science is its claim that it is not just another religion. This is because it takes issue with foundational premises of physical science, medical science, and orthodox theology. It also claims its teachings to be the very Comforter promised by Jesus, "that he may abide with you forever" (John chapter 14, verse 16 King James Version; hereafter John 14:16 KJV). If this is true, one wonders how the Church could have been infected by racism, homophobia, and especially, authoritarianism. Sadly, the Church of Christ, Scientist has largely followed others by becoming mired in these ills.

Perhaps the most appropriate guideline for writing was laid down nearly a century ago by Mary Baker Eddy. Her motto for the international daily newspaper she founded is, "To injure no man, but to bless all mankind." What a shame it would be to limit this to the domain of the *Christian Science Monitor!* It is indeed a sound basis for all writing in all times. Lesbians and gays, however, do not feel Mrs. Eddy's motto has been extended to include them by many writers in the Church periodicals. For this reason, many sexual minorities believe their Church has violated the Golden Rule many times over.

In the decades of the 1960's, 70's and 80's, LGBT people were spoken of derisively in the Christian Science publications. The harshly judgmental vocabulary included such pejorative words as "aberration," "abnormal," "bizarre," "cursed," "deviates," "immoral," "outcasts from society," "perverted," "promiscuous," "second class," "unhealthy," "unnatural," "unseemly," and "vile."(8) Of course, it wasn't just the Christian Science Church (Church) that was throwing stones.

An old cliché among sexual minorities is that they were called "sick" by the medical establishment, "criminal" by the legal profession, and "sinners" by theologians. Among this triad are the religious communities which have consistently been the most intractable when it comes to acknowledging the inherent dignity of LGBT people and granting them basic human rights.

The vast majority of lesbians and gays in the 1950s, '60s, '70s, and to a lesser extent the '80s, were deeply closeted. The narrative that follows looks at several personalities in those years. These activists defied conventional wisdom. They not only disagreed with the pervasive homophobia in their Church and society-at-large, but they felt it to be a personal mission to confront and destroy the erroneous thought. In so doing, they helped make the world a better place for the generations of GLBT people who followed.

This work has its limitations. Chief among them is the scant attention paid to the Church perspective. Nearly every event is seen from the viewpoint of outsiders alone. No doubt the debate among top-ranking Church officials over their position with lesbian/gay people in their ranks was, at times, intense. But complicating its documentation is a deep reluctance by officials to make internal conflict known. A well-placed "deep throat" from the Church's top echelon would have brought greater perspective with more insight as to how policy evolves. Unfortunately, that did not prove possible for this work.

A second limitation comes from not expressing the full depth of personalities. Sexual minorities have personalities as diverse and complex as heterosexuals. In the interest of brevity, their complexities and divisions were not fully explored. So it is that LGBT people may be shown at times as being one-dimensional, both in their individual and collective conditions.

It is hoped this narrative will be useful to non-Christian Scientists as well as those within the denomination. This is because same-gender sexuality has become the most divisive issue within many Christian and Jewish faiths in the past 140 years. My desire is that this work will provide new frameworks in defining the place of sexual minorities in ecclesiastical institutions. Foremost among these perspectives is that sexual orientation may be responsible for one's attraction, but never one's behavior. This is as true for sexual minorities as it is for heterosexuals. Another is the fallacy that certain sexual orientations need to be healed and replaced by a different sexual orientation. Yet another, is the misguided perception that an individual can choose her or his sexual orientation.

In recent years the Board has to be commended for reaching out in dialogue to other religious denominations and especially the medical profession. It is also hoped its quiet revolution as to the place of LGBT people in the Church will extend to all constituencies among students of Mrs. Eddy's writings. If "all believers are made 'kings and priests unto God,'" as she confirms(9), then shouldn't they all have a place at the table?

Bruce Stores
City of Puebla,
MEXICO

Introduction

The origins of the modern lesbian/gay political and religious movements can be traced to the late 1960's. They began less than nine months apart. The religious movement came first.

The first organized church for supporting sexual minorities began in Los Angeles in 1968. Founded by Rev. Troy D. Perry Jr., a defrocked Pentecostal minister, Metropolitan Community Church was a unique response to treatment of sexual minorities by traditional churches.

Rev. Troy Perry fulfilled his childhood dream of becoming a Pentecostal minister only to see that dream shattered due to his intense sexual feelings toward other men. After five years of preaching, he felt compelled to come to terms with these feelings. He began to read books about homosexuality. These books convinced him he was indeed homosexual. He relayed this to his superiors and was relieved of his ministry. He then separated from his wife and two sons. He went to work for Sears until he was drafted in the Army. Following his military discharge, Troy Perry returned to the Los Angeles area and set up home in Hollywood. Once settled, he began to take account of his situation and the LGBT communities. He had not yet discovered his niche in life, but felt a deep desire to help his fellow gays. He had no idea how this "help" might take form, but, like Moses, "…he went out unto his brethren and looked on their burdens." (Exodus 2:11 KJV) He met someone in a club with his own sexual orientation arbitrarily arrested by the police. Troy Perry was able to bail the man out of jail, but calming him down was a different story. The man told Rev. Perry he believed no one cared about him because he was a homosexual. Not even God.

In that instant, Troy Perry discovered his calling. He would minister to lesbians and gays by organizing a church to support them.

By today's standards such an act would seem a natural step in the development of an emerging lesbian/gay consciousness, but in 1968 it was a revolutionary thought. No church service had ever been held for a group of people who by their very being were considered a perversion by society. The thought of a church ministering to people of such inclinations was blasphemous to the consciousness of 1968, *even* among homosexuals. Nonetheless, Rev. Troy Perry persisted. He began his ministry by placing a small display ad in the *Advocate* (a gay newspaper based in Los Angeles, which later became a national magazine). He met resistance. One neighbor told him he would be raided on the first Sunday. Another said no one would attend a church like that. Such was the prevailing mood when the first church service, by and for gay people was held, October 6, 1968 in Rev. Troy Perry's living room. Twelve persons were present.

What followed was not just a new church. The idea soon spread to other cities and a new denomination was born: Metropolitan Community Church (MCC).(1) Its theology was that of mainstream Protestantism, with an eclectic flair. Not only does it combine liturgies of ceremonial churches such as Lutheran and Episcopalian, it brings in elements of hand-clapping, foot-stomping, Pentecostals. Its emphasis varies from city-to-city, depending on predominate local religious sentiment. More importantly, MCC is the only major denomination in the world comprised almost entirely of sexual minorities. Its wings kept spreading. Proof that its time had come, MCC also developed within a brief span of 18 months, congregations in Chicago, San Diego, and San Francisco. Perhaps the best indicator that MCC was having an effect was how much the rising denomination irritated traditional churches. Evidence of this came from *Christianity Today*, a national magazine for evangelical Christians. The magazine felt it necessary to denounce the upstart Church that dared to say "gay is okay." Its issue for April 26, 1970 included an attack on MCC doctrines in an article titled *"Metropolitan Community Church: Deception Discovered."* But in spite of the concern among evangelical Christians, MCC kept on growing and spreading its message throughout the country and abroad. By the mid-1980's, most major cities in America and many small ones had at least one MCC church. By the century's last decade, some metropolitan areas could boast several MCC churches. Among its many accomplishments: it has knocked on the door of the National Council of Churches as a credible applicant, almost gaining admission, and may yet become a full member of that ecumenical body.(2)

In its development, MCC has served as a role model for many lesbian/gay denominational groups that followed. These include: Affirmation (Methodist), Affirmation (Mormon), American Baptists Concerned, Axios (Eastern and Orthodox Christians), Brethren/Mennonite Council for Lesbian and Gay Concerns, Dignity (Roman Catholic)(3), Evangelicals Concerned, Friends for Lesbian and Gay Concerns (Quaker), GLAD (Disciples of Christ), Honesty: Lesbian/Gay Southern Baptists, Integrity (Episcopalian), Interweave (Unitarian-Universalist), Kinship International (Seventh Day Adventist), Living Streams (evangelical/charismatic), Lutherans' Concerned, National Gay Pentecostal Alliance, Presbyterians for Lesbian and Gay Concerns, Reformed Church in America-Gay Caucus, United Church of Christ Coalition for LGBT Concerns (Congregational), World Congress of Gay and Lesbian Jewish Organizations, and the list goes on to also include *EMERGENCE International* for LGBT Christian Scientists.

MCC was one of very few efforts supporting sexual minorities as the decade of the sixties neared its end. This would soon change. An event outside a New York City club catering to African-American and Hispanic homosexuals, as well as transgendered persons, was about to dramatically transform the movement and the collective consciousness of sexual minorities everywhere.

PART I
PIONEERS

o o o o o o o o o o o o o o o o o o o o o o o o o o o o o o o o o o o

It is the task of the sturdy pioneer to hew the tall oak and cut the rough granite. Future ages must declare what the pioneer has accomplished.

—*S&H, page vii, lines 23 to 26*

1

Craig Rodwell

1950s to 1973

In every age, the pioneer reformer must pass through a baptism of fire.

—*Misc.* page 213, lines 17–18

Craig Rodwell and his partner at the time, Fred Sargeant, were playing cards in a friend's apartment on a certain Friday evening/Saturday morning. The apartment looked out over Manhattan, high above New York's Greenwich Village. It was Craig's turn to deal the cards. The hand would be the last in the evening/morning hours of June 27th/28th, 1969.

Craig enjoyed his neighborhood and his friends. Greenwich Village was as comfortable and stimulating a place as he might find in the 1960's—relative tolerance and many who shared his lifestyle. In spite of this, he wanted more. Much more.

Craig craved a world where gays and non-gays would live in harmony. He wanted everyone to view homosexual love as equal to heterosexual love. Craig's yearning for the world he envisioned helped make him a leading, or quite possibly *the* leading, activist in the early homophile movement of the 1960's.

Craig's other passion was Christian Science. The idea of bringing his two interests together had intrigued him ever since he first learned the two were thought to be incompatible.

Craig's background in religion was intense. From the age of six to fourteen he was raised in a small Christian Science boarding school, the Chicago Junior School in Elgin, Illinois. Craig recalls,

> We lived, played, ate, and thought Christian Science from sunup to sundown. We even had to say the 'Scientific Statement of Being'(1) in football huddles.

3

The school provided a close-knit environment for the forty-five boys living in three dormitories out in the woods year-round. In this atmosphere, sexual play was something that came naturally.

> We freely expressed our adolescent sexuality with each other in a very healthy way. In the seventh and eighth grades we were going steady, although we didn't call it that. We used to hold hands, and had one best friend. We had sex too, usually in the woods, or in the dorm, after the housemothers went to bed. When they saw us holding hands, the housemothers used to make us stop and we couldn't understand why.(2)

Craig's innocence also surfaced when he first learned of a gay subculture. This awareness came as a result of a sexual encounter he had with an adult when he was only thirteen. The man was later arrested for having sex with the boy, but Craig insists, "I picked *him* up." The man went to prison for three or four years. This is something that completely baffled Craig. "It made no sense whatsoever to me at the time."(3)

After he graduated from boarding school, Craig attended public high school in Chicago. He also enrolled in Sunday School at 16th Church of Christ, Scientist. It was there that one Sunday School class would have a major impact on Craig's life. This class was one of those times that became a defining moment for the young Craig Rodwell. Possibly it was his most defining moment.

> It was there, I learned from my Sunday school teacher that the official Church stance on homosexuality was negative. I knew then [1957] that someday, somehow, I would help challenge the false teachings in the Christian Science movement.(4)

Learning of their Church's disapproval for same-gender love is a painful blow for most lesbian/gay Christian Scientists as one aspect of their life suddenly comes in conflict with another. As a reaction to this discovery, some try to ignore their sexual orientation. Others hope their "feelings" will go away. Others yet, sought "healing." Craig would do none of these. In that way, he represented a tiny minority in the 1950's who were certain their Church was wrong. Craig further removed himself from most homosexual Christian Scientists by going far beyond just believing the Church was wrong. Craig developed a strong desire to confront his denomination and challenge its "false" teachings. He wanted to help the Church heal itself of this "enormous error." He decided this when he was barely sixteen years old. In spite of his tender age, not to mention the pervasive homophobia of the period, there was no uncertainty for him that his commitment was set to "someday, somehow…challenge the false teachings in the Christian Science Church." Twenty-two years would elapse before Craig's promise to himself would be realized. In the interim, Craig went on to become a foremost activist in the early homophile (term used by sexual minorities to identify themselves in the 1950's and '60's) movement.

After high school, Craig accepted a scholarship to study at the American Ballet School in New York. The scholarship looked all the more attractive when someone in Chicago referring to Greenwich Village, but not intending to portray it in a kindly way, told him, "That's where all the queers are!" This was big news to Craig. He also had a desire to be in New York so he could volunteer for the Mattachine Society, then the leading gay political organization in America.

Craig did move to New York City. Once there, it didn't take him long to become immersed in the embryonic homophile movement. This was "my main consuming interest in life." After some disappointment with the Mattachine Society, Craig was finally able to change its purpose to a more activist approach. He did this by sheer force of his personality.

Meanwhile, he joined other organizations. Through one new group, he helped organize and participated in, what was later recognized as the first known public gay demonstration ever held in the United States. The year was 1963.

Whithall Street Induction Center was picketed to protest the loss of confidentiality of draft records of homosexuals. Less than a dozen demonstrators marched. They sent out press releases to the New York City media. Unfortunately, the activists represented a segment of the population not yet credible with society. As historic as the demonstration was, it received no publicity whatsoever.

For a long time Craig felt sexual minorities needed a focal point where they and others working to promote the same goals could find resources for learning more about, and expanding on, their activism. He felt even homophile activists didn't understand their community very well, but the need was apparent. It took him years to realize this goal. By working in various jobs, Craig was able to save enough money to realize his dream. It would be a bookstore. The bookstore would mirror homophile life and with it the aspirations of sexual minorities. After exhaustive searching, he found a suitable location at 291 Mercer St.

The Oscar Wilde Memorial Bookshop opened its doors on Thanksgiving Day, 1967. It was later seen to be the first bookstore established in the United States devoted exclusively to lesbian/gay concerns. As such, Craig felt it unique in many ways.

My general policy was to have a shop where gay people didn't feel they were being exploited either sexually or economically...It was not a porn shop. There were no drawn blinds or 'Adult only' signs or 'peep shows' in the back. Young people and women were welcome. About one-fourth of the clientele were women. The bookshop also became a social gathering place for lesbians and gays in the neighborhood, [as] notices, and bulletins of community events helped bring many inside.(5)

Opening the bookshop was eventually seen in a historic sense. By all accounts, it was a major contribution by Craig to an emerging homophile consciousness.(6)

The bookshop, together with his involvement in innumerable causes for LGBT people, gave Craig the reputation of being a tireless, unrelenting activist. He would do most anything he could to advance the cause of fairness and respect for sexual minorities. Now, quite unexpectedly, events were about to overtake Craig Rodwell and all the sexual minority communities. In the process, Craig's mettle would be greatly tested. He would come through the experience shining as the activist star he was.

The last game completed, the men put down their cards. Craig began thinking of the weekend ahead. Summer had come full force to New York. The warm humid air permeated city life even in the middle of the night. Now the hour was late. It was time to go. A little more talk, a hug to their hosts, and the men were gone.

The three-day period, Friday, June 27 through Sunday, June 29, 1969 saw middle and upper class lesbians and gays leave New York City in droves. This was their custom on warm summer weekends. Many opted for Fire Island, a sexual minority enclave offshore from Long Island's Cherry Grove community.

Craig and Fred rode down the elevator and were soon out on the street. The night was warm, almost hot, with a humid tinge. New York City has a reputation of staying awake all night, especially on weekends. This night was no exception. The men were long accustomed to the usual noise of city life, even at this late hour. Yet in a few moments they would hear sounds that didn't seem quite normal. They could hear not only the blare of sirens, but screaming and perhaps some rage. The clamor came from Sheridan Square, a focal point for sexual minority hangouts. Instinctively, the men quickened their step.

While neither of them could have possibly imagined it, just blocks away, the singular most important event for sexual minorities in the 20th century had started to unfold. While its impact couldn't possibly be imagined at the time, the event would dramatically transform LGBT communities, not only in New York

City, but throughout the country. Recalling this many years later, Craig said, "we immediately went over there. We saw the beginning of the Stonewall riots."

That evening (or early morning), the New York police raided one of the most flamboyant sexual minority bars in Greenwich Village—the Stonewall Inn. It was, at the time, illegal for clubs in New York to identify themselves as a homosexual bar. It was even a greater crime for men to dress as women. That didn't deter clubs in Greenwich Village from having both. These clubs on society's fringe were places where "respectable" (closeted, middle-class) homophile men and women would never be seen. Now times were changing. Earlier in the decade other minorities had begun clamoring for their rights. Unease swept the country first with the African-American civil rights movement, then by anti-Vietnam war protests and a counter culture "hippie" movement. Until now, homosexuals accepted their lot in silence.

The raid started as routine. About 200 patrons were inside the Stonewall. After checking ID's, the police allowed all to leave except "drag queens" (cross gender dressers). The "drag queens" were forced into police paddy wagons. The other patrons left the premises, but for unknown reasons, they didn't scatter as usual. Watching police "escort" the "queens" into the waiting vans, the crowd slowly became unruly and started to shout obscenities. Sensing "she" had an audience, one of those being "escorted" put up a fight with police who had to struggle to get "her" aboard. This prompted the leaderless crowd to start throwing anything they could get their hands on at the police, including garbage—even coins. The confrontation was heard by patrons from nearby clubs. They too, spilled out into the street. With the crowd growing every minute, things soon got too heavy for the police. They were forced to barricade themselves back inside the Stonewall Inn.

In addition to throwing whatever they could find at the police, the crowd was somehow able to pull a parking meter from out of its place. They would use it as a battering ram. They would try to force open the doors in the Club where the police had taken refuge. They almost succeeded, but reinforcements soon arrived. Then the police came out of the bar. Still, the crowd remained.

Now with even a greater show of force from New York's Finest, the crowd would not stop harassing and pelting them. Then, what started as name-calling and object throwing, turned into a game of cat and mouse. Gays were run off in one direction only to turn up once again behind the same Tactical Patrol Force chasing them.

About five months later, *Newsweek* magazine would report on these events.

> …As the police evicted patrons, hundreds of angry young men gathered outside and began hurling stones, coins, garbage, and shrill obscenities. [They shouted] *'Gay power! Gay power! Gay, gay power to the gay, gay people!'*"

The hour was portentous for sexual minorities. While these LGBT men and women could not have known it at the time, their act of defiance would accomplish for their movement what Rosa Parks' refusal to give up her seat on a Montgomery bus did for African-Americans a little over a decade before. *Newsweek* continues:

> Inside the bar, Deputy Inspector Charles Smyth and ten patrolmen exchanged incredulous looks as they bolted the heavy wooden door. Suddenly a brick shattered the plate-glass window, showering the inspector's head with slivers. Another brick struck a policeman's eye. Seconds later a firebomb exploded inside the room. Now the door was beginning to buckle under the mob's weight. Methodically, Smyth and his men drew their revolvers and formed a defensive line. They pointed their guns at the door.
>
> At exactly that moment, the wail of patrol-car sirens punctured the uproar. The trapped policemen lowered their guns and, within minutes, beefy reinforcements from the Tactical Patrol Force were dispersing the squealing protesters. "I was still shaking an hour later," Smyth recalled last week. "Believe me, I've never seen anything like it."(7)

Few people at the scene were better prepared to understand the meaning and context of the riot than was Craig Rodwell. In the movie documentary *Before Stonewall,* and the book of the same name, he recalled:

> There was a very volatile political feeling, especially among young people. And when the night of the Stonewall riots came along, just everything came together at that one moment. People quite often ask, 'What was special about that night, Friday, June 27, 1969?' There was no one thing that was special about it. It was just everything coming together, one of those moments in history where, if you were there, you just knew that this is IT. This is what we've been waiting for.(8)

While Craig didn't throw objects at the police, he believes he was the first to holler *"Gay Power."* He yelled it with all his might.

One of Craig's strengths was to see events in perspective even as they were happening. So while he was emotionally a participant, Craig all-at-once realized, "Hey! This is news!" But would it make a difference? He fretted over the fact that no one apart from the protesters may ever know what's happening. So Craig ran to find a phone booth. When he found one, he called newsrooms across Manhattan's towering skyline and pleaded with them to send someone to cover the melee.

In spite of Craig's efforts, most New York newspapers did not cover the riot, or at least not in its immediate aftermath. A notable exception was the *Village Voice*. The neighborhood tabloid carried the message to homosexuals under a front-page banner headline: "**GAY POWER COMES TO SHERIDAN SQUARE.**" Right beside it was the same story as taken from interviews with members of the police department telling the story from their point of view, headlined: "**FULL MOON OVER THE STONEWALL: A View From Inside.**"

In the context of the times the riot was almost unimaginable as up to this point, homosexuals had never fought back in a significant way for anything. They generally accepted the stereotypical image that they were the pansies and pushovers everyone thought them to be. Certainly the police believed they had nothing to lose by raiding their bars. It was this sudden, decisive, break with the past that created news in the early morning hours of June 28, 1969. As Lucian Truscott IV wrote in the *Voice*:

> Sheridan Square this weekend looked like something from a William Burroughs novel as the sudden specter of 'gay power' erected its brazen head and spat out a fairy tale the likes of which the area has never seen.(9)

The next night crowds again thronged the area. Gay graffiti all over the neighborhood bore testimony to the awakened consciousness. Police had to break ranks to stop the protesters; those who didn't escape were shoved and clubbed to the ground. From the demonstrators came repeated shouts of *"gay power, gay power..."*

Crowds would gather again on Sunday night, and the next night, and the next. Craig showed up all five nights of the riots. He recalled the events of Sunday evening:

> ...police "chased people away they would just go around the block...and come in another way...[G]ays started taking over the street and stopping cars from coming through"-unless driven by homosexuals. Shouts of "Christopher Street belongs to the queens!" "Liberate Christopher Street!" One car of newlyweds was half lifted, then gays relented and the open-mouthed bride and groom were permitted to drive on...(10)

The Stonewall Inn may not have been the most ideal place for the beginning of the modern lesbian/gay movement. Craig recalls having been inside the Stonewall Inn, though not on the night of the riots.

> I hated the place. It was typical Mafia, exploitative. [Their idea was to] sell the queers as many drinks as you possibly can. They had go-go boys on the bar in their underwear dancing—a disgusting place.(11)

Nevertheless, more than anything else, it was "Stonewall," that came to represent the lesbian/gay movement.

The time was right. If the late 1960's which saw racial ghetto riots, anti-war demonstrations, and a flourishing counter-culture on an unprecedented scale, could not cradle the birth of the modern lesbian/gay movement, then one could argue, it might never happen. As *Newsweek* reported in its discussion of the Stonewall uprising,

> In summers past [a police raid on a gay club] would have stirred little more than resigned shrugs among the Village's homophile population but in 1969, the militant mood touches every minority.(12)

Years later when the modern lesbian/gay movement wanted to understand its roots, many of those trying to chronicle its history would call on Craig Rodwell. They were looking for explicit reasons that caused the spontaneous riots. Craig said,

> I found over the years that researchers, reporters, what have you—the main question they ask is, "What was it that actually caused the Stonewall riots?" They're all looking for one specific act or something. That's not what happened. It was an accumulation of decades and centuries of repression of our people. It just all came together that one night, that one moment in Sheridan Square that hundreds realized, "This is it! This is the beginning of the end. Its over. We're going to fight back." That's what happened.(13)

The most significant element of the Stonewall uprising, however, was not the violence. It was the birth of a discovery: the discovery that in spite of heaps of volumes to the contrary, and centuries of repression notwithstanding, *gay is good!*, and the challenge to bring that idea to the world is more than worthy of the struggle.

The impact of Stonewall was so far-reaching that its dawning on homosexual sensibilities could be compared in some ways to Mary Baker Eddy's remarkable healing from a fall on an ice-covered sidewalk in 1866 which set the Christian Science movement in motion.(14) While the former was the catalyst for a minority group discovery, and the latter a metaphysical discovery, both events had much in common:

- Both discoveries, in their own way, created a movement profoundly affecting a sizable segment of America and the world.

- Central to each discovery was a change in consciousness about the very nature of women and men. Mrs. Eddy saw the tide of humanity as poor counterfeits of a higher, truer selfhood. This true selfhood she saw as able to image God in innumerable expressions of unlimited perfection, goodness, and potential. Thus sin of every sort, disease of every kind, even death itself, must yield to the understanding Mrs. Eddy would come to call "Christian Science."

For homosexuals it would mean the beginning of the end of seeing themselves as "sick," "perverted," "degenerates," "unworthy" of a decent place in life. This change in consciousness liberated lesbians and gay men to begin overcoming major obstructions to their rightful place in society. Another part of this discovery was their acquired sense of their inherent equality as fellow citizens with heterosexuals. As these discoveries became sealed in consciousness, LGBT people began to free themselves from negative images and stereotypes. This revolution of thought allowed them to assert themselves in the greater society with a political agenda. This would begin to give them equality in employment, in social and religious institutions, and other areas of life without having to pretend they are who they are not. One of the first enemies that had to go was the myth perpetuated by the medical establishment that homosexuals are sick. The force of their discovery "gay is good" proved so powerful that in just a few years following the Stonewall riots, the American Psychiatric Association (APA) came to agree with the lesbian/gay communities. Following an intense internal struggle, the APA in 1973 removed their negative stigmatizing labeling of same-gender sexuality or orientation to that of a "normal variation."(15)

- Another common feature in both discoveries is that regardless how well the true facts were presented to the individual, each adherent must re-discover them for her/himself. As individuals, Christian Scientists and sexual minorities alike came to the conclusion that society has foisted on them a lie which has been universally accepted as truth. Only by increased understanding of who they really are and with it a new perspective, can true freedom be found. What both the Stonewall demonstrators and Mrs. Eddy struggled against was a lie about God's creation, and every adherent of these movements must learn the truth about themselves as well.

To be sure, there were differences between the two movements. Following her momentous discovery, Mrs. Eddy isolated herself for three years to search "…the solution of this problem of Mind-healing,…"(16)

Stonewall, on the other hand, was a collective discovery. News traveled fast. Lesbians and gays began asserting their newfound awareness almost immediately. By the second night of the Stonewall riots, gay graffiti was widespread in the neighborhood. "Gay power" became an instant slogan.

The Stonewall riots were followed by an infusion of heretofore unimaginable numbers of people and energy pouring into the seemingly instantly created LGBT organizations. The Stonewall uprising did more than force New York City police to come to an understanding with LGBT communities. It began a dialogue with authorities. This dialogue would spill over into nearly every governmental jurisdiction in the country. In just a few years towns, cities, states, eventually, the United States Congress, would begin to consider inclusion of the words "sexual orientation" in their civil rights codes. These efforts were no doubt stimulated by the civil rights act of 1964, which ended the "Jim Crow" laws in employment, housing, credit, public accommodations and other areas for racial minorities.

The Stonewall rebellion led directly to the formation of the Gay Liberation Front (GLF) in August 1969. The GLF held public meetings, published a gay newspaper, and organized gay demonstrations. What was happening affected how every American would come to view lesbians and gay men. The uprising at the Stonewall Inn caused the lesbian/gay movement to reverberate everywhere, and in nearly every conceivable way, challenge the status quo. Included were some immediate and noble victories.

> …[H]istory was made in the annals of American scholarly and professional societies when the annual business meeting of the American Sociological Association…in San Francisco adopted the first resolution on the rights of Homosexuals and other Sexual Minorities ever adopted by such a body."(17)

The American Sociological Association adopted the resolution less than three months following the Stonewall riots. The last sentence of the resolution reads:

> Be it resolved that the American Sociological Association condemns the firing, taking economic sanctions, and other oppressive action against persons for reasons of sexual preference.(18)

A year and five days after the Stonewall riots, the American Library Association created a task force on Gay Liberation on July 3, 1970. One of its announced goals was,

> the revision of library classification schemes to remove homosexuality from the realm of sexual aberration, to encourage all libraries to build objective collections on homosexuality, and to make these collections easily available to all.(19)

The single most significant way in which the status quo was upset, and never to be reversed, was its effect on homosexuals themselves. This new feeling of inner-liberation would come to be known as "gay pride." Sexual minorities would acknowledge lesbian/gay pride through continued protests as well as celebrations of who they are.

It was this time period that had particular meaning for Craig Rodwell. In the immediate aftermath of the riots he came to full bloom as an activist. What Craig did prior to the watershed events at Stonewall was more than enough for his memory to be enshrined forever in the annals of sexual minority history. But his contributions in the immediate aftermath of Stonewall may be where his record shines the brightest. Seeing the unprecedented energy pouring into the movement, Craig simply seized the opportunities and took charge.

As a respected activist in leading lesbian/gay organizations, Craig Rodwell had much to do with major decisions affecting the lesbian/gay communities. Only a few days following the riots on July 4, 1969, Craig attended what was called the "Annual Reminder" in Philadelphia. Lesbians and gays had gone to Independence Hall for several years to bear witness of their second class status in America. In sensing the enormity of the riots on the collective lesbian/gay consciousness, Craig became aware the time had come to go beyond this event. Clearly, it was time for the communities to proceed to bolder action. In place of the annual trips to Philadelphia, Craig felt the movement had arrived to the point where it should come out of the closet in a bold way. This led Craig Rodwell to become the father of the lesbian/gay pride marches that now take place in nearly every major community in the United States and in many countries abroad. Activists, he felt, should make their work a permanent way of life. The way to do it, he believed, was for lesbians and gays to take to the streets again. This time legally. He knew any major decision affecting all the sexual minority communities would not be effective without the backing of women as well as men. Therefore, for what may have been the most far-reaching proposal he ever made to the GBLT communities, Craig teamed up with lesbian activist Ellen Broidy. Ellen and Craig together proposed the following resolution to the Eastern Regional Conference of Homophile [lesbian/gay] Organizations assembled in Philadelphia, November 1 and 2, 1969:

> We propose that a demonstration be held annually on the last Saturday in June in New York City to commemorate the 1969 spontaneous demonstrations on Christopher Street and that this demonstration be called CHRISTOPHER STREET LIBERATION DAY.(20)

The resolution passed easily. Then Craig exhorted his fellow activists to encourage these marches in other cities, especially those far from New York City.

During the ensuing year, much of the planning for the first lesbian/gay pride march was carried on at Craig Rodwell's bookstore.

The first lesbian/gay pride march did take place, just as planned, Sunday, June 27, 1970. This coincided with the first anniversary of the Stonewall riots, just as Ellen and Craig proposed.

One can only imagine the euphoria that came from being part of the first large effort of lesbians and gays to portray publicly their cause in an open display of who they are. Donn Teal in *The Gay Militants* records part of that day:

> The sun a blowtorch in a sky bluer than any New York had boasted since the horseless carriage—no gay would remain in the shadows that day—Sheridan Square was gay militant at 12:30. Placards to be hosted or worn declared: GAY PRIDE—LESBIANS UNITE!—FEM and BUTCH—HI MOM!—HOMOSEXUAL IS NOT A FOUR LETTER WORD—ME TOO [on a dachshund]-WE ARE THE DYKES YOUR MOTHER WARNED YOU ABOUT—EVERYTHING YOU THINK WE ARE, WE ARE!—SMASH SEXISM—SAPPHO WAS A RIGHTON WOMAN—FREE OSCAR WILDE—GAY POWER—I AM A LESBIAN AND I AM BEAUTIFUL...(21)

Whereas the media was nearly silent following the Stonewall riots, considerable coverage was given to the March commemorating the first anniversary of that uprising.

Michael Brown, one of the March leaders, provided the *New York Times* with its quotation of the day, Monday, June 29th, 1970:

> We're probably the most harassed, persecuted minority group in history, but we'll never have the freedom and civil rights we deserve as human beings unless we stop hiding in closets and in the shelter of anonymity.

From New York City, lesbian/gay marches and festivals have become commonplace throughout the United States. In time, Christopher Street Liberation Day would become known as Pride Day. By century's end, the ubiquitous Pride Marches had even come to many small conservative communities throughout the country and abroad.

Christopher Street and Sheridan Square would become even gayer after Stonewall. Many clubs and business catering to those with a same-gender orientation moved in. One of them was Craig Rodwell's bookstore. In 1973, Craig Rodwell relocated his Oscar Wilde Memorial Bookshop to 15 Christopher Street.

By 1974, only five years after Stonewall, lesbians and gays had made irreversible progress on several fronts. Perhaps the most significant was the decision described earlier by the American Psychiatric Association to consider same-gender sexuality as a normal variation among sexual orientations, instead of an illness. But the period between 1969 and 1974 also marked unprecedented development of lesbian/gay subcultures. The sexual minority press came of age. Lesbian/gay newspapers were established in major cities. They came into being largely because the mainstream media often ignored or distorted their issues. Now sexual minorities had first hand knowledge of national and local events on issues important to their lifestyle, written from a lesbian/gay perspective. The sexual minority press made a significant contribution to a developing sense of community consciousness. In the civil rights area, elected officials were forced for the first time to consider measures outlawing discrimination based on sexual orientation. As individuals, lesbians and gay men were leaving the closet in unprecedented numbers. As a result, more and more Americans were waking up to learn they had lesbian/gay neighbors, lesbian/gay co-workers, lesbian/gay children, lesbian/gay brothers and sisters, and lesbian/gay parents. Even husbands and wives were coming out to their legally married spouses.

The ferment created by the emerging lesbian/gay consciousness extended also to theological arenas. Synagogues and churches of all denominational stripes were exploring the issues, sometimes with painstaking difficulty with so few guidelines to interpret God's will on this, to them, a delicate issue. In some cases there was a lesbian/gay organization within the church or synagogue to either spearhead deliberations or at least serve as a resource. More often than not, however, sexual minority groups were not at all recognized by the religious body. Gays and lesbians were then forced to work from outside official sanction.

In the Christian Science world, The Mother Church had been responding for years to the lesbian/gay lifestyle as well as special demands put upon it by the emerging lesbian/gay movement.

Homosexuality had been mentioned in the Church's periodicals for many years going back at least to the early 1960's as a condition in need of healing.

An article in the *Christian Science Sentinel* (February 17, 1962) may have underscored not only the denomination's revulsion of same-gender sexuality, but society's as-a-whole. Under the title *"A Timely Warning,"* *Sentinel* Editor, Helen Wood Bauman wrote,

> There is alarming evidence that the world is letting sexual depravity rob it of the only true security humanity has—the security of obedience to God's demand for moral purity. Statistics on the vile, Scripturally condemned practice of homosexuality, on vicious sex crimes, marital infidelity, and the like, are appalling.

The first article devoted exclusively to the topic appeared in the April 27, 1967 *Christian Science Sentinel* titled, *"Homosexuality Can Be Healed"* by Carl Welz. Welz, an editor of the periodicals, backed his claim of same-gender sexuality as deviant behavior on the same basis as do fundamentalist Christians by citing the Hebrew Holiness Code.

> That homosexuality is a deviation from the moral law, is made plain in the Bible, where it is recorded that the Lord spoke to Moses saying, "If a man...lie with mankind as he lieth with a woman, both of them have committed an abomination: they shall surely be put to death, their blood shall be upon them."(22)(23)

The same verse from Leviticus was occasionally included in the weekly Bible Lessons during the 1970's and 80's from the *Christian Science Quarterly.* This is a collection of Bible verses and citations from *Science and Health* on a single subject. The Lesson is studied by Christian Scientists around the world on a daily basis. Lesbian/gay Christian Scientists were astounded that a Bible verse demanding they be stoned to death could be portrayed as inspired. But there it was! enshrined in their Bible Lesson, and studied daily by Christian Scientists everywhere for six consecutive days. On the seventh day, Sunday, it was read aloud in every Church of Christ, Scientist in the world.

During church services, Bible verses are read by the second reader. What feelings might this verse have brought to those second readers who themselves happened to be lesbian or gay? If not gay themselves, some second readers might have a child or other relative or close friend with a same-gender sexual orientation. Regardless, all second readers had no choice but to read aloud the offending verse to their congregations.

> "...[Homosexuals] shall surely be put to death; their blood shall be upon them." (Leviticus 20:13)

Other articles on homosexuality occasionally made their way onto the pages of the *Christian Science Journal, Sentinel,* and *Herald.*

Still, the Christian Science Church had not yet come out with a position on the rights of sexual minorities to live in society free of discrimination from employers and landlords as had some other denominations.

A goal of lesbian/gay activists in this period was to have all churches declare their positions on the appropriateness of lesbian/gay lifestyles as well as civil rights for lesbians and gay men. If the denomination had no viable lesbian/gay component, then the larger sexual minority community might confront the institution. This situation faced the Church of Christ, Scientist in 1974.

2

Ernest Barnum

1974

The prophet of to-day beholds in the mental horizon the signs of these times…

—*S&H* page 98: lines 4–5

Ernest Barnum was in shock. With the telephone still in his hand, he called his partner, "Come here!"

"What's wrong?" his partner asked. When he finally looked at Ernest, he noticed his arm was trembling. Something happened.

Ernest replied emotionally, "Would you believe they told us to live in separate houses?!"

"What are you talking about? Who told us to do what!?"

"The Church!"

"*The Church!???* But why!? They've sorta known about us for years. Why *now?*"

Ernest placed the phone back in its receiver. "I don't know" he said, "but I think it's that new practitioner [in his local Church]. She wants to be the greatest of all."

"How brazen of them!…So what are you going to do?"

With a resolute look on his face, Ernest, still staring at the telephone, said, "I'm going to resign my membership. There's nothing else I can do."

Eager to support his life mate anyway he could, his partner said emphatically, and with the barest of pauses, "If you resign, I'll resign!"

Ernest and his partner removed sheets from their writing pad and began to pen their resignation letters. They would address them to the Clerk at First Church of Christ, Scientist, Little Rock, Arkansas. The year was 1974. They have not been members of a branch (local) church since.

Ernest was not born into Christian Science. His parents gave him no Church upbringing. In late childhood, he turned to the Church of God. "They built a church in our community, and that was the church for me for awhile."

In his growing up years he discovered he had a gifted talent in music. He had a good voice and found music a natural for him. He decided early on to make it his career. He majored in music both at Southeastern Louisiana College and Louisiana State University.

After his college years he took various trips to Los Angeles staying sometimes several months at a time. When he was about 30, he had a music teacher in the city of the Angels who impressed him greatly. Not only did Ernest look up to her for her music ability; he was in awe of the way she lived. "I noticed there was a difference about her. She was living what other people talked about." One day Ernest learned that she was a Christian Scientist. Immediately he began to investigate his music teacher's religion. What Ernest learned about Christian Science impressed him greatly. He discovered, "It's a now situation. We don't have to put our good off to the future. It's a present reality." He also thought highly of the unique format of the Christian Science Bible lesson sermon that is read Sundays in all churches. This was the way he wanted religion presented. "It was impossible to scold somebody through the sermon," he said.

> You didn't get a lesson on politics. It was always the same sermon [in all Christian Science churches in the world]. Even if the Governor showed up, it was the same sermon.

Since coming into Christian Science, Ernest held a wide range of positions in various local branch churches. "I read, I sang, I played the piano." He really thought his new religion could fill all his needs.

Later on Ernest located for awhile in the Boston area. He worked for The Mother Church as a greeter at the Church-owned sanatorium in Chestnut Hill, just outside Boston. He was also employed for a spell as a night watchman at The Mother Church.

In time, Ernest became aware of a darker side of his Church. This was reflected by homophobic articles in Church periodicals and policies. The anti-gay articles instilled in Ernest a determination to do whatever he could to get the Church to overcome its lack of understanding on sexual minority issues. It was necessary, he felt, for the Church to enter into a dialogue with the lesbian/gay communities. He decided he would try to make that happen.

The odds appeared overwhelming against Ernest being able to do any activism toward his Church of a significant nature. He had no political experience whatso-ever. At the time there was no organized movement among lesbian/gay Christian Scientists. He had no important connections in the wider lesbian/gay communi-ties. Neither did he have money set aside to spend on such a project. His sole resource was a genuine desire to create change. Ernest felt strongly he must stand up for his convictions even if they went against the present positions of his Church. He knew both Christ Jesus and Mary Baker Eddy acted in accordance with their convictions even when they were at odds with their own religious insti-tutions. "I was taught to live as they did," Ernest said. He was also comforted in the knowledge that the Bible provides countless examples of right prevailing in spite of seemingly insurmountable odds against it.

The phone call from his Church, asking him and his partner to live separately, instilled in Ernest how pervasive homophobia is in the Christian Science move-ment. He knew that the tenor of the anti-gay articles in the religious periodicals contributed to the bias in local branch churches. This led him to a deep desire to do whatever he could to overcome what he considered to be false teachings in the Christian Science Church.

After praying for direction, he got to work. He decided his first step would be to write a letter to a weekly newspaper he remembered from his Boston days: *Gay Community News* (*GCN*). In his letter he asked for addresses of leading lesbian/gay organizations in the Boston area. Once he received the addresses, he mailed copies of anti-gay articles published by the Church with the following letter to six organizations in the Boston area including *GCN*.

May 13, 1974

Dear [name of organization]
    Enclosed find copies of [the articles] *The Bible and Homosexuality* and *The Christian Science Standard of Morality*. These are crude creations that should never have been written. But they are the *official* position of the Christian Sci-ence organization and need to be dealt with.
    The annual meeting of The Mother Church is June 3 & 4, 1974 and would afford a great time to protest their position on gay rights. The Blacks successfully protested there one year. They were given time to speak.
Sincerely,
Ernest Barnum

If Ernest was hoping for a confrontation that resulted, as did the 1969 Annual Meeting, when Black militants were given the right to speak from the First

Reader's podium, he did not get his wish.(1) But his simple request to lesbian/gay organizations did result in a modest confrontation that produced local publicity focusing on the Church's biased attitude towards sexual minorities. This would be a first for LGBT people in the many years spent confronting that homophobic institution.

The possibilities for positive action stemming from Ernest's letter, however, were nearly nil. The lesbian/gay organizations had their own agendas. Prior to receiving his letter, no lesbian or gay activist in Boston ever heard of Ernest Barnum. Almost certainly, his request to sexual minority organizations for a confrontation at The Mother Church would have gone unheeded if it hadn't been for an amazing coincidence.

Within days after Ernest sent his letter to lesbian/gay community groups, a gay organization in Boston was evicted from a building owned by The Mother Church. The group was told it could no longer meet there. The *Boston Globe* reported at the time that a group called "Fengay" is a two month old organization said to have 25 members who live and work in the Fenway [neighborhood]." One of its members told the *Globe*,

> Fengay was organized "to get the Fenway community to recognize there are gays with similar problems as their own, as housing and urban renewal." But taking on churches was not part of Fengay's agenda. The Mother Church got the organization's attention when Fengay held a meeting at the Boston Center for Older Americans (BCOA), 236 Huntington Avenue, in Boston. The building happened to be one of the vast real estate holdings in the neighborhood belonging to The Mother Church.(2)

A more detailed description of Fengay's ouster was published in Boston's *Gay Community News* (*GCN*).(3)

It was an indirect result of the ouster of Fengay from a Mother Church owned building that precipitated a leafleting demonstration. The fact that the Church refused in the press to commit itself one way or the other on the issue of lesbian/ gay rights, Fengay apparently felt it had a chance to force the Church's hand. This proved to be the first collective attempt to affect the denomination's position on concerns to sexual minority communities.

This was also a clear example how the lesbian/gay press had come of age. This newly emerging press was contributing significantly to a sense of unity in lesbian/ gay communities. It was itself responsible, directly and indirectly, for much of the activism then taking place among sexual minorities. Boston was one of the few

American cities that had a lively, sophisticated lesbian/gay publication dating from the early 1970's.(4)

Due to Ernest Barnum's letter, Boston's sexual minority communities were alerted to the fact that thousands of the denomination's faithful would descend on Boston in a few weeks for the Church's Annual Meeting. Fengay, therefore, hastily planned a leafleting demonstration for the Tuesday evening meeting, June 4, 1974.

It was a small group that leafleted the Annual Meeting, but their message got across. Both the mainstream press via the *Boston Globe*(5) and the lesbian/gay press via *GCN*(6) covered the event, bringing with it statements from Church officialdom.

One of the demonstrators passing out leaflets was Elaine Noble. Noble was then an openly lesbian candidate for the Massachusetts state legislature. Her candidacy was being watched closely. No candidate with a same-gender sexual orientation had, at this point, ever been elected to state-wide office anywhere in the United States.

Unfortunately, the first serious attempt to engage Church members in a dialogue was frustrating. Besides focusing attention in Boston's lesbian/gay communities on the Church's anti-gay position, little was gained. This was the only demonstration at The Mother Church by sexual minorities until lesbian/gay Christian Scientists themselves would confront their Church's homophobia six years later.

Among those who read the *GCN* articles about the Fengay demonstration in Boston was Craig Rodwell in New York City. Craig was understandably thrilled. It meant much to him to learn The Mother Church was beginning to be educated, if only in a small way, that a same-gender sexuality was neither sick nor sinful. He eagerly shared this information with other gay Christian Scientists he had by this time come to know. Much more importantly, perhaps, the articles served to maintain in Craig's thought his own date with destiny at The Mother Church. That date with destiny was now but six years away.

Meanwhile, back in Little Rock, Ernest Barnum was a model of patience. He would not learn of the demonstration at The Mother Church that he proposed until more than three months after it happened. It wasn't until September 27, 1974 when one of the organizations let him know a demonstration took place and he was responsible for it.

Dear Ernest,

    I don't recall writing to thank you for the info about the Christian Science convention here in June. Because of your letter, the gay community here was able to get together a modest confrontation, which received coverage in the Boston *Globe.*

Sincerely,

Laura Robin for DOB [Daughters of Bilitis]

Shortly afterward Ernest was sent copies of the *Globe* and *GCN* articles reporting the event. Ernest felt he was doing the right thing when he contacted lesbian/gay organizations in Boston the previous June. Now, he believed he must build on what the sexual minority activists did at The Mother Church. He decided to pursue the dialogue with Church officials any way he could.

Ernest Barnum's correspondence with the Church was no doubt one of the first attempts to dialogue with ecclesiastical authorities over their homophobic positions. In his first letter he reminded the Board that Douglas Russell, the church's communication supervisor was quoted in the news articles: "The Church does not take positions period."

Ernest wanted to know if these quotes from a denominational spokesperson were official Church policy. He asked if the remarks about not taking positions on social issues would "invalidate" the Carl Welz *Sentinel* article "*The Abortion Question,*" August 4, 1973, and Naomi Price's *Sentinel* editorial, "*The Bible and Homosexuality,*" November 18, 1972.

If Ernest was one of the first to communicate with the Board about its homophobic policies, he was also one of the first to receive letters that dismiss or trivialize these concerns.

Weeks went by and Ernest did not receive an answer from the Board. Undaunted, he sent the same letter again. This time it went by certified mail "so I will know if you receive it or not."

This time, he got an answer. Lloyd G. Marts, Assistant Executive Administrator, writing for the Board, told Ernest in part:

> ...It should be obvious to all regular readers of the *Christian Science Monitor* and the other periodicals of The Mother Church that The Mother Church does not seek to impose on its members partisan positions on political, economic, or social issues. However, these publications do uphold the standard of morality that is inherent in the teachings of Christian Science. Moral blindness or laxity find no encouragement or sanction in the teachings of Christian Science or in the publications issued by The Mother Church.

There is no need or basis for anyone to look to such diverse publications as the *Boston Globe* or the *Gay Community News* for authoritative statements on the subject. The spokesman for The Mother Church was obviously misquoted, as should be evident to all those who are well acquainted with Christian Science teachings.(7)

Future letters were written to and from Arthur P. Wuth, a member of the Christian Science Board of Directors. The letters found little common ground between the two men. The last letter Ernest received from Wuth (June 17, 1977) closed with the words,

You are wasting your time, Mr. Barnum. You have far from convinced me, and I apparently have made no impression upon you. It is my feeling that we should discontinue this exchange. I love you as God has made you, but I do not love the evil with which you have identified yourself. I know that you can be healed through Christian Science, but there must first come the humble desire for it.

The frustration Ernest felt would be shared years later when locally organized groups of lesbian/gay Christian Scientists and non-Christian Scientists would initiate major letter writing campaigns to the Church. These letters would protest firings of gay people employed by the Church and vent frustration over a discriminatory policy that did not allow for the simple courtesy of the Board of Directors (Board) to meet with those directly affected by their exclusionary policies.

The cold manner in which the Board kept its distance was not limited to lesbians and gays. Any person or group who tried to influence Church policy or merely attempt a dialogue with its officials in this period received the same treatment. The Board was accountable to no one. Therefore, they could and did sit atop a high perch of inaccessibility to those who had contrary ideas. The result was a stagnant Church. The Board's fear of new ideas caused many fine thinkers to leave the organization. What was left was increasingly becoming a chorus of "yes" people, those with neither the imagination, nor the desire to think for themselves. Therefore, the Board could afford to ignore anyone who appeared to threaten the status-quo. With loyalty and obedience superseding original thinking and spirituality, the denomination's attrition continued, losing members, practitioners, teachers and churches. To turn things around, it would take something far greater than the audacity of a Craig Rodwell, the concern of an Ernest Barnum, or an activist group like Fengay. Something far greater than the Church had ever seen would be required just for its officials to sit up and take notice. As unlikely as that might have seemed, something of that magnitude was actually in the making.

The moment was drawing near when a "bombshell" of major proportions would catch an unsuspecting Board and Church far off-guard. The resulting fall-out would create a rippling effect throughout the movement. It would bring about the most disruptive stir in the denomination's history in over 50 years. Unfortunately for lesbians and gays the upheaval did not seek to heal the relationship with their Church. Its chronically homophobic instigator sought instead to widen the rift between them through sensationalism and character assassination. As this ferment is so important in tracing the history of lesbians and gays in the Christian Science movement, the next chapter is devoted to this development.

If thought was stagnant within the Christian Science Church in 1974, there was progress for lesbians and gays going on in many other places. Even voices within the politically conservative community were pleading for laws "to ensure constitutionally guaranteed rights" for sexual minorities.(8)

Probably the single most important event for LGBT people in 1974, and a highlight of the decade, was Elaine Noble's election to the Massachusetts State Legislature. In November 1974, she became the first elected, openly lesbian or gay person to attain statewide office in the United States. She won with 59% of the vote. Noble went on to serve two terms in the Massachusetts State House. She then ran a losing campaign for the United States Senate.(9) Interestingly for this history, was Noble's district. It took in Boston's fashionable Back Bay neighborhood. Here one finds the 14-acre Christian Science Center. Dominating the Center is a Byzantine/Renaissance temple built in 1906. The temple is the largest and most conspicuous religious edifice in Boston and quite likely all of New England. The Church, seating some 3000 congregants, forms the centerpiece of the worldwide headquarters and administrative offices of The Mother Church, The First Church of Christ, Scientist, in Boston, Massachusetts.

PART II

THE STIRRING UP

○ ○
The muddy river-bed must be stirred in order to purify the stream.

—S&H, page 540, lines 9–11

3

The Reginald Kerry Letters

1969 to 1977

The human heart, like a feather bed, needs often to be stirred, *sometimes roughly, and given a variety of* turns *else it grows hard and uncomfortable...*

—*Misc.* pages: 127–128, lines 31–2

Tuesday, June 2nd 1969 was a warm day in Boston, as thousands of believers from around the globe descended on the international headquarters of the Christian Science Church. The theme for their Annual Meeting was, "What Can We Do For Our World?"

After opening the conclave, Board of Directors' Chairperson, Inman H. Douglas told attendees, "In all our meetings this week we shall in one way or another turn our attention especially to the welfare of mankind." These words rang unusually true that day, but not at all as Mr. Douglas and the assembled congregation might have imagined.

The Church had just begun its largest construction project since the extension of The Mother Church was completed in 1906. It would include a twenty-two story administration building, a colonnade building, a Sunday school building, a large underground garage, and a plaza replete with fountain and reflection pool. What had already been a highly conspicuous landmark in Boston's Back Bay neighborhood, would now become even more visible. Signs of construction were seen on all sides of Church property.

Other than the physical disarray created by the onset of construction, the situation appeared normal. The well-dressed, largely affluent, mostly middle-aged population had filed themselves into the Church in an orderly fashion. The Annual Meeting was being conducted as planned and there was no apparent reason anyone might expect anything out of the ordinary. Who could imagine the most unsettling drama ever to take place in an annual meeting was about to occur? But if it were to happen, this was a militant time. Not only was this the 1960's. It was, interestingly, the same month, June 1969, in which riots by sexual minorities at New York's Stonewall Club were only 25 days away. Still, the denomination's headquarters was hardly an imagined setting for militant activity. As it was, the first sign of something unusual came shortly before 3:00 p. m.

A small crowd of about 15 African-American activists, accompanied by the media, gathered outside a main entrance to the Church. They were demanding admission to join the Meeting.

Aghast at this confrontation, Church leaders immediately sent representatives to mollify the group.

The militants identified themselves as the Metropolitan Committee of Black Churchmen and repeated their demands to participate in the Annual Meeting. They had singled out this Church before taking their demands to other congregations, because the Christian Science Mother Church was the largest and most conspicuous religious edifice in Boston. The men, sporting wide Afro hairdos, symbolic of the new African-American militancy, were unyielding in their demands.

For their part, Church leaders were adamant that the would-be intruders did not enter. Their representatives tried hard to pacify them and work out an alternative arrangement. They even told the militants they could have a private meeting with the Board of Directors when Annual Meeting was over.

The militants held their ground. Their position was a refusal to meet with "any appropriate official" except the entire membership.

When it appeared no other recourse was possible, Church leaders backed down. David Sleeper, Church Manager of the Committee on Publication told the group's chairperson, Hayward Henry, he could read his statement to the congregation. The militants were then ushered inside the large domed temple. They walked briskly down the aisle. Representatives from the media followed after them.

What a sight! Hardly ever in Church history had non-members and journalists been allowed entrance to an annual meeting. When they reached the front of the auditorium and climbed the few steps leading to the readers' platform, they gathered behind the readers' podiums. Board of Directors chairperson Inman Douglas immediately introduced Hayword Henry to the assembly.

If Church leaders were dismayed, members were dumbfounded. One can imagine many in the congregation looking at each other in wide-eyed disbelief. If members felt the one place on earth most immune to the upheavals of the 1960's was the serene, stately edifice of their Mother Church, then this must have come as profound a shock as might be imagined.

Once introduced, Henry came right to the point. He recited a list of demands the Black churchmen were giving the Christian Scientists. These included full public financial disclosure by the Church, $100 million dollars from area churches and synagogues, that Second Church of Christ, Scientist in Roxbury (a part of Boston) be donated to Boston's African-American community, and that all Black employees of The Mother Church be upgraded.

Despite their understandable consternation, the members gave polite applause to the militants.

For their part, Church officials never gave into their demands.

Was the confrontation over? No one was sure. As Henry stepped down from the platform area, Church leaders were perplexed. They wondered what might happen next. It appeared the militants might want to stick around. Perhaps they wanted to talk with members on a one-to-one basis. What would Church leaders do now? Plainly, they were at a loss as how to handle the situation.

From out of nowhere, it may have seemed, an ad-hoc group of Church members appeared on the scene. The group engaged the militants in conversation. As they kept talking, one member of the group captivated the militants with his reason and charm. Using his powers of persuasion he was able to convince the militants to leave the sanctuary and retire to the Publishing house. Then they all left together.

What a relief!

Church leaders were extremely pleased the militants left without further confrontation. They also felt indebted to the Church member who came to their rescue. But who, they couldn't help but wonder, is this helpful member? It wasn't long before they learned his name is Reginald G. Kerry.

After the drama at the 1969 Annual Meeting unfolded, the Board of Directors decided they would like to get to know Kerry. They soon did. It didn't take them long to become impressed with the man from Santa Barbara. They felt he could be a great asset to the Cause.

At this time the Directors were about to enter into negotiations with the Carpenter Foundation regarding their collection of memorabilia relating to the earliest days of the Church. It was a collection of considerable scope concerning the life and teachings of Mary Baker Eddy. The situation was regarded as sensitive. Gilbert Carpenter was a student of Mrs. Eddy. He recognized the value of preserving notes of Mrs. Eddy's class instruction, association addresses, memoirs by her students, and her letters. Together Gilbert Carpenter and his son Gilbert, Jr.

compiled the largest collection of unpublished material by Mrs. Eddy outside The Mother Church. While the Carpenters were very loyal to Mrs. Eddy, they were among the first to resist what they felt were authoritarian dictates of the Board of Directors. They were gradually ostracized by the movement and forced out of the Church. It was of more than passing importance to the Board that the Carpenter collection would fall into the "right" hands but it would take a skilled negotiator to obtain them on the Church's terms. Reginald Kerry seemed the perfect one to negotiate on behalf of The Mother Church. He was offered the assignment and agreed to take it on.

Again, Kerry showed his skill in negotiation. On June 20, 1973 the Board of Directors thanked him for his efforts on behalf of the Church in negotiating a successful transfer of the Carpenter Foundation's literary and historical collections. Not only did the Board write him that,

> We are deeply grateful to you for your part in the successful completion of these negotiations and the transfer of property, [but], in addition [to expenses] we would like you to accept the enclosed check for $3,000.00 as an honorarium in recognition of your services in the Carpenter matter as evidence of our sincere appreciation for what you have done.

Interestingly, Kerry was not born into Christian Science. He came into it as a result of a healing from cancer when he was a teenager. Thus the idealism and zeal of a convert may have played a role in his becoming a tireless, diligent Church worker. On the branch (local) church level he claims to have held every position: Chairman of the Board, first reader, Sunday school teacher, etc. Professionally, Kerry had two careers: law enforcement and restaurant management. He was a parole officer and served as police commissioner in Santa Barbara, California. He also owned one of the largest restaurants in that city. He served on the boards of trade associations as well as state and national restaurant hotel associations. When he came to the Board's attention, he was considered by everyone who knew him as a highly loyal and esteemed Christian Scientist.

Kerry continued to get assignments from the Board. He handled them well. For this work, he was highly rewarded. He was a speaker at an annual meeting and at a Christian Science youth meeting in Los Angeles. The Board also gave him permission to address Christian Science college and university organizations. These were favors bestowed on only the most loyal Christian Scientists. He was juggling his work for the Board while also taking on patients as a Christian Science practitioner. At about the same time he received an offer to be a teacher and lecturer for the denomination, but turned it down.(1) But he did continue his

Board assignments. At the same time, he began to consider how long he wanted to stay in this role. Perhaps the time had come to move on to other things. The Board, however, had other ideas.

One day, quite unexpectedly, Kerry received a startling memo. In it he was asked to meet with the Board of Directors on a matter of "extreme importance." Of course, this piqued his curiosity. He had no way of imagining what this might be.

When they were all together, it was explained to Kerry that the Board wanted him to conduct an extensive survey of all departments in the Church. This would be no ordinary assignment. The Directors said they believed he was uniquely qualified to be entrusted with overseeing a major project: a study of the inter-workings of every department. It was a task so large in scope it would reveal for him (and eventually the world) a number of serious problems. The assignment was a major security investigation.

Kerry did not decide immediately. He asked for time to consider the Board's request. He knew it could last two years or more—a long time. In reviewing the Board's proposal, he could see its potential value for his Church. The scope of the new project was so vast he would be able to learn about every department in the Church in stunning detail. This, he came to believe, would greatly aid the Church to fulfill its mission: "...to commemorate the word and works of our Master, which should reinstate primitive Christianity and its lost element of heal-ing."(2) After deliberating the pros and cons with much care, Reginald Kerry decided to accept the assignment.

Kerry dove into his new job right away with his usual gusto, tenacity, and per-severance. In this new assignment, he would investigate every department, one department at a time. He interviewed everyone. As he gained new information, he expanded his questions and re-interviewed each employee as often as he felt necessary. He also studied vast amounts of church documents, financial records, letters, and memos. As his authority from the Board to look into everything was carte blanche, he would leave no stone unturned. In this way, he amassed an enormous amount of data. In time, he began to sense there were serious flaws in the management and operations of many departments. He kept his findings to himself while continuing to work and unearth information. Eventually, Kerry came from having only a sense things were out-of-hand, to having made detailed documentation of serious underlying problems at Church headquarters. Still, he kept working. As long as there were unanswered questions, he would persevere until he could document everything. The project would require two years before he could compile all his findings.

Everyone knew the organization was going through a difficult period. The attrition in members and churches, which had begun in the early 1960's, was steadily increasing. This led many members to think there may be serious problems in Boston, but few had anything in the way of concrete information. For most members there was no clear way to learn about the day-to-day inner workings at the Church Center. The only information members had was what Church officials decided to tell them. So Kerry's findings went far beyond what most members knew. There were serious problems in the financial affairs of the Church. He unearthed a number of personnel problems he felt had to be solved. As his work neared an end, he felt the seriousness of the problems he uncovered were of such magnitude the denomination could not survive another decade if his findings were not dealt with immediately.

Kerry had no reason to imagine the Board would not review his findings. After all, they commissioned his work. He was eager to share his knowledge with the Board. He no doubt planned his presentation to them with great care. He was comfortable in his belief the Directors would be alarmed. He was sure they would undertake whatever remedial steps were necessary to correct the difficulties. Clearly, he was not prepared for the Board's reaction after he brought his findings to their attention.

They didn't care!

What a shock! Kerry's two years of research was treated as trivia. The very Board of Directors who commissioned his investigations now dismissed them. Their indifference to his findings was a stunning blow. Kerry had become convinced the very survival of the denomination depended on the Board taking immediate action on the information he turned up. But now his work was shunned. To them it was totally irrelevant. In this atmosphere, it didn't take him long to see the Board as the problem, not the solution.

For Kerry, the problems he uncovered were far too encompassing, too important, not to be heeded. So relevant were his findings to the future well being of his Church, he would do anything necessary to get the Board's attention. Later Kerry would write about this period and his tenacity in trying to reach the Board:

> I have endeavored for over two years to work with the Board of Directors and am still endeavoring to do so. I had conferences with the individual Board members and tried to tell them what was going on at the Church Center. Twice I met with the entire Board. Even then I could not reach them. They would not believe me or investigate to determine if I was right or wrong. I told them of the immorality and dishonesty at Headquarters that was destroying our Cause. I told them of the plight of the branch churches. I said that the

Cause could not go forward until these problems were faced and resolved. But they did not listen to me.(3)

It appears Kerry did everything reasonable to get the Board's attention. When these efforts failed, his options were few. The idea of resigning in protest and retiring to sunny California must have passed through his thought. If so, he must have felt that to be out of the question. He loved the spiritual mission of his Church. He also believed no one else could, or would, be in a position to bring needed change to his Church. Therefore, it was at this juncture that Reginald Kerry made what was almost certainly the most far-reaching decision of his life. Whether or not the decision was agonizing for him, or a result of deep prayer, he doesn't tell us. What we do know is, he would become a rebel. He would resort not only to unorthodox means to get his way; he would go far beyond the boundaries of discretion in his Church to highly unapproved actions. In doing so, he forever changed the way many Christian Scientists look at their denomination and its officials. The full impact of Kerry's decision may not be fully appreciated or understood even today.

The action he decided on was a series of lengthy tell-all letters he would mail to *all* Christian Science churches in the world. He would mail them also to *every* practitioner listed in the *Christian Science Journal*. His letters would outline, in detail, gross mismanagement, and other problems at the Church headquarters. Possibly, he thought he might never have to go through with the letter writing project. Just threats at doing so might be enough to bring the Board around. What he wanted above all was for the Board to have a sense of the magnitude of the problems facing the denomination and act on them. Instead of playing his cards close to his chest, however, Kerry revealed his plans to the Board. He told them he would correspond directly with the field if they did not act on his findings, and act on them soon.

But the Board still did not take Kerry seriously.

Kerry continued the threat to write letters to the greater Church community "many times" hoping such action would not be needed. When he felt nothing else could save the day, Kerry penned his first draft of a proposed letter. It seems likely he didn't want to send it. He made one last-ditch attempt to reach the Board. He forwarded Board members a copy of the letter he wrote for the Christian Science world. Kerry tells us they received it two days before he mailed it out. He said they received it on December 9, 1975, but they "did not bother to read it."

Then it happened.

Exactly two weeks prior to Christmas day, 1975, Reginald Kerry gathered up the thousands of copies of the multi-page letter he wrote and took them to the post office. Then and there, he released not only the letters, but with them, his future standing in the Church, and much more importantly, the beginning of the end of members' complacency towards their ecclesiastical officials. His message would soon find its way to branch churches and practitioners offices throughout the world.

There was no way for Kerry to anticipate reaction to what he had done. The days he had to wait for the field to react must have seemed forever. But in a few days his letters began to land in mailboxes at branch churches and offices of *Journal*-listed practitioners worldwide.

Unfortunately for Kerry, most recipients were ill-prepared to receive his message. Few had prior knowledge of serious problems at headquarters. For Kerry, there was an additional problem. Although he had been highly revered by Church officialdom, he was virtually unknown outside Church headquarters. Further compounding his troubles, it was not uncommon for churches and practitioners to receive all kinds of dissident mail, which they tossed away with regularity. Wasn't Kerry running the risk his letter would be rejected as just one more dissident with an axe to grind?

Kerry must have known no one before him with grievances fared well when they strayed from established channels. Moreover, he knew members were conditioned to look at all who dissent publicly with the Board of Directors as enemies of the Cause. On the other hand, no dissident appeal had ever come to the field's attention with the detail and scope of the situation at Church headquarters as Kerry conveyed. All things considered, the letter was a gamble of major proportions.

Novelist Madge Reinhardt suggested, "such a letter would, at first, mainly serve to bring Kerry into disrepute with the majority of Christian Scientists."(4) But as Kerry must have felt, from a mailing of this magnitude, there would certainly be those with whom the letter would strike a responsive chord. It would begin a dialogue.

So it did. Wherever there was a practitioner, a clerk, executive board member or other church official who had courage and independence of thought, Reginald Kerry's letter, written under official Church letterhead, just might be read:

To our beloved Journal-listed Practitioners and Executive Boards of Branch Churches of The First Church of Christ, Scientist
Boston, Massachusetts 02115

Friends:

I am writing to you as a loyal Christian Scientist who feels a great concern for the future of our Cause. During the past three years I have worked in various capacities at the Church Center in Boston, including being responsible for conducting a comprehensive security survey. This work has brought me in direct contact with the actual condition of things, both here at Headquarters and throughout the Field.

I came to Headquarters at the request of The Christian Science Board of Directors and the Legal Department with an unblemished church record of over 40 years. While you may not be aware of the problems facing our cause at this time, those like myself who know the true picture, realize that there looms a very real possibility that the Cause of Christian Science will be lost to the world in the near future, unless some positive action is taken to prevent this from happening...

The letter continues by going into explicit detail over financial conditions. Kerry contends: "...a lack of fiscal responsibility and good business practices [have created] a financial crisis that is becoming chronic and will in time put the Church into bankruptcy unless it is corrected."

The letter said the high cost of the construction at the Church Center was nearly ten times its original estimate.(5) He gives figures of the decline in Church reserves and discusses serious financial problems.

In all probability, no one else was in a position to document first hand such precise explanations to the Christian Science field. Kerry's grasp of the Church's financial situation could be considered breathtaking. He proves himself to be highly competent in money matters and demonstrates a keen ability to fathom their long-term implications. But he does not continue this line of reasoning.

After carefully laying out these concerns in front of his readers, Kerry abruptly changes course. This would prove highly unfortunate. His new concern would not only cause unnecessary damage to the future of his already beleaguered Church. Its personal toll would be devastating. Letter number one and future correspondence would send promising careers down the drain, destroying the lives of countless, devoted Church workers. The letter continues:

...I was called in by a department head to investigate the charge "the [Church] Center was a hotbed of homosexuals and lesbians." I very reluctantly accepted the assignment. After investigating, I had a list of 18 names that included individuals from the Board of Directors, Speech and Editorial Department, Committee on Publication, General Services, Department of Branches and Practitioners, Music, and other workers throughout Headquarters. When I saw how far-reaching and out-of-hand the problem appeared to be, I felt this investigation should be discontinued and so advised the department head. Later I was blamed for conducting a "witch hunt." "Uncover error, and it turns the lie upon you." (*S&H* page 92, line 21)

This moral problem is known to the Board of Directors. In fact, they know many others in positions of authority who are either homosexuals or lesbians. Yet nothing is done at all levels of The Mother Church.

As damaging as Kerry's revelations may have been, the matter remained very much an internal one for Christian Scientists. Kerry's letter got scant attention outside the denomination. *Time* was one of the few publications that mentioned the letter. This must have prevented, from the Board's point of view, a bad problem from getting worse. Probably very few branch church boards shared the Kerry letters with their membership, much less the media. It is likely, therefore, Kerry would have had a lot to gain by going to the public media and making his allegations more widely known. By not going to them he may have helped his credibility in the movement, but by ignoring the press, he kept a lot of members in the dark. With respect to the *Time* article, Kerry said,

> I did not contact *Time* magazine to give them any information for the article…In fact, their reporters were after me for several days to give them a statement and I absolutely refused to talk to them.(6)

For reasons that may never be known, Kerry did not want greater publicity than that generated by his letters alone. Perhaps from Kerry's point of view, there may have been no need to involve the world outside the flock, as his first letter to the field was an "overwhelming success."

> Thousands of letters were received by me and the Christian Science Board of Directors from you demanding that a positive effort be made to save the cause of Christian Science…
>
> In addition to the letters of support, voluntary contributions of several thousand dollars to help defray the cost of these letters to the Field were received…Offers to assist by donating their services were received from attorneys, certified public accountants, stenographers, and workers in other callings…

There is no question that Kerry's letter came as a shock to the Christian Science world. It was a stunning blow in a Church community that believed all was well. Reflective of the nerve touched by Kerry, the denomination's headquarters was besieged with calls and letters.

Following the mailing of Letter no. 1…phone calls and letters poured in to the Church Center, resulting in a considerable stir. The confusion was such that I was asked by a Board representative if I would agree to a 'cease fire agreement with the Board'—that was their choice of words—so they could enjoy the holiday season, as they had not slept since Letter No. 1 went out.

Things were now so far out-of-hand, the Church had no choice but to react. Reaction came both from headquarters in Boston and numerous localities. In local areas, the Committee on Publication (somewhat like a church media rela- tion's office with a Mother Church appointed manager in every state and foreign country) was the center for most reaction. In several states, the Committee on Publication (COP) sent a letter to their representatives in every branch church in their state, assuring them all is well. Kerry contends that one state COP manager called all his representatives to watch incoming mail, to seize the dissident letter in their churches before anyone saw it, and destroy it unread. Of this, Kerry said,

> I ask, is this the reaction of people who have been conducting their affairs properly and who have nothing to hide? How does this differ from Mr. Nixon's initial reaction to Watergate?

Probably the most convincing proof the letter was having an effect, was the extent the Board tried to persuade Kerry not to send another one. Among these efforts, the Board gave him a list of ten changes that have been accomplished.

Kerry believed the list only included "surface changes which could be reversed overnight at the whim of the Board of Directors," so that didn't deter him.

As a last resort, a letter was sent to Kerry from the Board only thirteen days before his second letter was mailed. With no small desire to silence his work, the Board resorted to saber-rattling with the weapon used so effectively by popes and church hierarchies for nearly two millennia. They would excommunicate Regi- nald Kerry *unless* he agreed not to send more letters. "If you will now give us the assurances we are asking for," read the ecclesiastical intimidation,

> you can preserve your membership in The Mother Church…But if you are unwilling to give us these assurances, our Board would be compelled to place you on probation under Article XI, Section I, of the *Church Manual,* subject to such further disciplinary action under this or other provisions as may be required by your subsequent conduct.…

Whatever were the other long and short-term effects of his first letter to the field, one thing was clear: Reginald Kerry finally had the Board's attention.

In addition to threatening Kerry himself, the Christian Science Board of Directors counterattacked his letters in various ways. First, they sent out their own communications. Their first letter went out December 15, 1975.

According to Kerry:

> The Board's letter raises a smoke screen by falsely alleging that Letter No. 1 is "an unusually detailed attack on The Mother Church and the Movement." This is a deliberate lie. Letter No. 1 is an attack on immorality, dishonesty, political ambition, love of money, confusion, and chaos. It is not an attack on The Mother Church. The mismanagement and immorality at the Church Center are no part of the real Mother Church, and in attacking these I am by no means attacking The Mother Church.

So great was the Board's desire to forestall another letter by Kerry, the Board even agreed to meet him, although it would have to be after the first of the year. The Board went so far as to ask Kerry if he would be willing to compose a joint letter with them "assuring the field that an investigation and clean-up were taking place."

The idea sounded wonderful to Kerry. But what did it mean? Could it mean the beginning of a real dialogue? Might it be the Board saw the writing on the wall and felt the time had come to be open and candid with the membership? There was no immediate way to tell. Kerry felt maybe, just maybe, there was reason for hope. It was a faint possibility. If the Board's gesture was in good faith this could mark a beginning. Answering the request, he said he "was more than willing" to meet as the Board suggested. Reason for hope increased when a date for the "meeting" was set. It would take place January 29th, 1976.

But Kerry's short-lived hopes were dashed again. Unbeknownst to him, the Board had been working on a very detailed letter of its own to the field. A fifteen-page letter would discuss many of the charges and announce the convening of an investigative task force to look into the charges made by Kerry's letter.

When the Board's letter went out, Kerry did not hide his frustration and anger over its timing. He called the letter,

> An action comparable to Japan's sneak attack on Pearl Harbor, while peace talks were in progress…They made every attempt to discredit my character, distort the facts stated in Letter 1, and whitewash the entire situation. This is just like what happened in the Washington Watergate.

So much for working it out with the Board.

It is difficult to ascertain what results Kerry anticipated from his letters. It is possible he had no idea where they might lead other than a general stirring up. When the Board made a conciliatory offer of a joint letter he no doubt entertained a ray of hope he was finally getting through. Then hope was lost. Perhaps the Board's dashing his hopes after giving him reason for optimism fueled his desire to pursue his efforts. No doubt with increased vigor Reginald Kerry went on "disclosing to the Field…conditions troubling our movement and preventing it from making the demonstrations necessary to further the healing of mankind." So he persevered in documenting malfeasance as he saw it.

Kerry's second letter went out March 24, 1976.(7) This 30-page letter (plus 20 exhibits) went deeper into charges made in the first letter, particularly in the area of financial affairs. He also discussed in detail efforts of the Board to "cover up" charges in letter number one.

> Disappointingly, but not unpredictably, the Christian Science Board of Directors reacted to the statements in Letter No. 1 exactly as did former President Richard Nixon when confronted with charges of wrong-doing by himself and by members of his administration. He hid behind the dignity of his office…He denied all wrongdoing.

Letter two sought to answer the Board's criticisms of letter one and described how his charges of malfeasance were whitewashed. The thirty-page letter delves deeper into financial affairs of the Church. The section *"Periodicals, lectures, and archive materials"* is an eloquent discourse on Church treatment towards exponents of free expression. Also, Kerry goes into detail on the character and background of individual Board members. He explains how they got where they are and why he feels they are totally unqualified for the position. In addition to the thirty-page letter, he adds twenty-seven pages of supporting exhibits.

It is difficult to assess the effect the letters had on the greater Church community. There was no forum where views could be exchanged. Church officialdom had control of all Church publications. There has never been room for dissenting views in the periodicals apart from the *Monitor*, which does not normally deal with Church affairs.

Given how hard it is to get the Church's ear, one can ascertain that Kerry must have been highly motivated in order to bring to its attention what he did. In so doing, he was on his own schedule. No one knew precisely when his letters would appear, or their content.

It took seven months following letter two for Kerry to issue his third letter to the Church field.

Letter number three begins with Kerry's assessment of the results from letters one and two.

> Many constructive changes are coming about in our precious Movement...From all fifty states—Alaska to Florida, Maine to Hawaii—and from overseas—England, France, Canada, Belgium, Switzerland, Australia,—letters, telegrams, phone calls and personal contacts assure me that thousands of Christian Scientists are awakening to realize that all is NOT well in Boston.

But letter number three also marked a serious turning point. Here Reginald Kerry shifted markedly from concerns about finances, incompetent personnel, abuse of power, and declining membership. It is this letter that distances him so much from lesbian/gay Christian Scientists, some of whom may have cheered him on up to now. True, he did touch on "immorality" in letters one and two and said the Church Center was "a hotbed of homosexuals and lesbians." One could argue he tried to gain more adherents by appealing to many sentiments. Now these arguments were baseless. In letter number three he became vicious. He practiced what would come to be called "outing" (the act of pushing individuals out of the closet by revealing their sexual orientation without their permission).

Midway through the 29-page letter is a section titled "Expose and Denounce." This, together with Exhibit L, is where Kerry reached the heights of homophobia. He first discusses an incident that took place at the Annual Meeting, June 1976. As this was the first meeting of the membership since the first Kerry letter went out, there must have been a sense of drama. Thousands of the faithful descended on Boston to listen to reports from Church leaders. No doubt many members hoped there would be a full-scale accounting of Kerry's charges. It did happen that many charges were discussed. Unfortunately, Church officials talked about them in a general, superficial way, with few specifics given. Kerry contended many of their statements were outright lies. They even chose to respond to the charge that the Church Center was "a hotbed of homosexuals."

Dewitt John, a member of the Board of Directors, announced to the assembly gathered at Annual Meeting, "There are no known homosexuals working at the Church Center."

In letter number three, Kerry said of DeWitt John that he "deliberately, consciously, and with malice aforethought told a bare-faced lie." Kerry said because "the first four speakers at the Annual Meeting [names mentioned] are alleged homosexuals, as is...The Mother Church organist." The speakers included a member of the Board of Directors, a well-known biographer of Mrs. Eddy, and the Treasurer of The Mother Church. Then Kerry discussed individually, five other highly prominent officials at the Church Center who he alleged were homosexual. In addition to the speakers at Annual Meeting, his list of names included the Second Reader in The Mother Church, and the Manager of the Practitioner's Division. He went into great length on what he knew about their personal life, lovers, and other details.

> One well known Christian Scientist [name mentioned] was allegedly in a serious homosexual offence at a boys' school...Charges were brought against him but the case did not come to trial. It is alleged The Mother Church paid to have this situation covered up.

At the conclusion of the section "Expose and Denounce" in letter three, Kerry lamely gives reason for his viciousness:

> My motive is not to harm individuals, but to protect our movement...

Gossip about the sexual orientation of various church officials, however, did not begin with Kerry. There was considerable discussion about sexual minorities in the Church, well before Kerry's letters went out. As one employee in the Church Center in those years put it,

> Both before, during, and after the Kerry letters...the general feeling I got was that gays were not welcome as employees, that they were "sick" and needed to be "healed." Even before the Kerry letters came out, all kinds of rumors were going around about officials in high places having intimate relations with members of the same sex in the bathrooms at the Church Center, etc.

Interestingly, letter three went out only about two years before lesbian and gay Christian Scientists themselves would begin to organize. Those sexual minorities who read letter number three could have been understood for feeling betrayed. Kerry wrote a number of things in letters one and two which many of them felt were excruciatingly important for the Christian Science field. When letter three appeared, it seemed as if the cause for lesbians and gays in an already homophobic Church was about to take a giant leap backwards.

It is one of the saddest ironies of this history that the one individual who has done more than anyone to waken the Church community to blatant mismanagement in Boston is at the same time chronically and uncompromisingly homophobic. How much Kerry influenced the Church to harden its line against lesbians and gays can only be surmised. The depth of Kerry's disdain for sexual minorities can be seen in the following excerpt from a letter given him by the wife of a former law officer. This he uses as "Exhibit L" in letter number three to illustrate his perception of lesbians and gays.

> To have homosexuals in a considerable number, I am told on good authority is like a rotten apple in a barrel. Get rid of them. If I were faced with the choice of rattlesnakes or boa constrictors or a homosexual, I would choose the former...In private life they prey like a vulture on the weak and helpless to perform sadistic acts for them, like men from prison who cannot find a job, dope addicts, people with a past and down and outers...
>
> That is why Chief Davis of the L. A. P. D. has fought having any homosexuals in his police department. He fears for the safety of his young men, whom they will threaten, coerce, frame or worse, and he knows it. Our Church is not a mental hospital. Such people will ruin it. Quit alibis and get rid of them!

Kerry uses the above letter to describe the danger of hiring lesbians and gay men. But what these statements illustrate the most is the extent of his homophobia.

An understanding of the time period that Kerry released letter three brings a degree of perspective to his prejudice. Lesbian and gay sexuality was not yet a subject for general discussion, at least at the dinner table in suburban America. It was rarely discussed among major candidates for public office except to lump it with crime. This was about to change. The first initiatives and referendums in the United States over the issue of civil rights for sexual minorities would take place only seven months after letter three was mailed. But as it was, there was probably little opposition to Kerry's intensely anti-gay attitude, except from sexual minorities themselves.

Homophobic as they were, Kerry's letters have to be seen as a watershed in the development of the independence movement in Christian Science. Unlike previous Church dissidents, Kerry seems to have been heard by a significant number of rank and file members. By proving the Church hierarchy was vulnerable and in need of reform, an argument can be made that the letters gave an enormous boost to future dissident groups. Notable among them are the Plainfield, New Jersey Independent Christian Science Church, David Nolan's United Christian Scientists, and possibly even organized efforts by lesbian/gay Christian Scientists. Discussion groups and/or classes were also being held by followers of those who believed the Church had misled its members with respect to Mrs. Eddy's teachings and/or amplified her teachings in certain areas. Noted independent Christian Scientist, Ann Beals said:

> The [Kerry] letters have stirred the field and awakened Scientists to the serious possibility that Christian Science could be lost. This has resulted in the development of the work of the independent Scientists.... As he persisted in sending these letters to the field he has broken the control of the Board over the movement.(8)

One of Kerry's major obstacles was apathy among rank and file members. While membership had steadily declined since the early 1960's, Church members weren't alarmed. Church dissidents had been present since Mrs. Eddy's day. The common belief was there are those who are working to destroy the Church, so we must not heed them attention. With branch church and practitioner addresses so easily accessible in the *Christian Science Journal,* mailings are received from many with an axe to grind. For these reasons the majority of recipients of Kerry's letters probably ignored them. The author personally witnessed a local branch church board chairperson toss a Kerry letter unread and unopened in the trash can saying, "He just wants to destroy the Church."

There is little doubt the letters caused no small amount of anxiety among employees at The Mother Church and the Christian Science Publishing Society when each Kerry letter came out. One employee at The Mother Church recalled, "We as Church employees were not allowed to read them."

Chris Madsen, a reporter for the *Christian Science Monitor* who was fired in 1982 after admitting she was a lesbian, (see Chapter 6) said,

> When the Kerry letters came out, that is the first time I saw fear in the Christian Science Church. They would do damage control like tell people they didn't have to read them, but they had to deliver them because they were sent through the U. S. mail.(9)

No doubt the greatest fear generated by Kerry's letters came from lesbian and gay employees at the Church Center. One Church employee, a heterosexual, recalled,

> I had somewhat of an "inside track" because my best friend was a gay guy who...worked for the *Monitor*, and he kept me abreast of things. He feared for

his job after the Kerry letters came out, but no one ever approached him and he stayed on for many years until he decided to leave on his own.

On balance, the Kerry letters caused a furor of major proportions. But why in a Church where ostrich-like behavior is to obediently, but blindly, follow those in charge no matter what? The reasons he succeeded, to the extent he did, appear to be:

1. *Timing.* The first Kerry letter was sent in the aftermath of one of our nation's most convulsive periods: Watergate. Americans and other world citizens were shocked when our nation's highest leaders were proved liable for criminal activity. The Nixon administration included Christian Scientists at the highest levels of government. They included Bob Haldeman and John Erlichman, administrative assistants to Richard Nixon. They were proved to be co-conspirators with the President's cover-up. Kerry's first letter was mailed only fifteen months following Richard Nixon's resignation. Could this have made it easier for rank and file Christian Scientists to see top Church officials as also fallible?

2. *Access.* An incredible array of information was available to Reginald Kerry. Its scope was far beyond that available to almost any other Church member, dissident or not.

3. *Previous loyalty.* When he came to Boston, Kerry had an impeccable record as a competent, loyal, dedicated Church member of 40 years.

4. *Money.* Kerry was independently wealthy enough to print and send his letters to every church and practitioner listed in the *Christian Science Journal.*

5. *Honesty.* When Kerry was not sued for slander or libel, many believed he must have told the truth.

◆   ◆   ◆

Meanwhile, outside the Christian Science Church, the lesbian/gay rights movement surged ahead in the years following the Stonewall uprising. In time, the words "sexual orientation" were added to more and more local ordinances forbidding discrimination in city after city. This was largely due to intense work by sexual minority activists. All of a sudden, candidates for public office were being asked their position on lesbian/gay issues.

Miami, Florida was one city where the lesbian/gay rights cause advanced significantly in 1976. That summer, gay activist Jack Campbell invited representatives from twelve of the area's leading lesbian/gay organizations to his home. Out of this meeting the "Dade County Coalition of Humanistic Rights of Gays" (DCCHRG) was formed. One of its first activities was to write a questionnaire about issues of concern to lesbians and gays. That included questions about outlawing discrimination against sexual minorities in housing, public accommodations, jobs, and child-custody laws. The questionnaires were mailed to two hundred local candidates for public office. Based on responses, the coalition endorsed 49 candidates in the coming municipal/county election.

The success of the venture was stunning. The activists in DCCHRG could not have imagined that as many as 44 of their endorsed candidates would win.

Emboldened by their perceived strength, DCCHRG decided to pursue higher goals. They asked Ruth Shack, one of the winners backed by the Coalition, to introduce a proposal for an anti-discrimination ordinance to the Dade County Metropolitan Commission of which she was now a member.

Shack readily agreed.

In doing so, Shack and the DCCHRC could not have foreseen the Pandora's box about to be set loose on the nation. The introduction of the anti-discrimination ordinance was destined to precipitate the greatest backlash against the rights of lesbians and gays the United States had ever seen. The fury of the backlash would prove more costly than just the loss of Dade County's protective ordinance. It would, in a very short time, initiate a series of contests that would reverberate from coast-to-coast, dismantling legal protections for lesbians and gays, from Miami, Florida to Eugene, Oregon.

4

"Save Our Children"

1977–1978

Sweet are the uses of adversity;
Which, like the toad, ugly and venomous,
Wears yet a precious jewel in his head.
And this our life exempt from public haunt,
Finds tongues in trees, books in the running brooks,
Sermons in stones and good in everything.

—Shakespeare, *As You Like It,* Act II, Scene I

On January 18, 1977, Commissioner Ruth Shack introduced a resolution in the Dade County, Florida Metro Commission. It would amend Charter 11A of the County Code to include an ordinance prohibiting discrimination in the areas of housing, public accommodation, and employment against persons based on sexual orientation. (This was a scant three months after Reginald Kerry's notorious letter number three, with its homophobic poison, landed in Christian Science church and practitioner mailboxes worldwide.) Dade County's action was hardly unique. Over 30 similar laws had been introduced and became law in various communities around the country, beginning with Ann Arbor, Michigan in 1972. San Francisco and Seattle were among larger cities that by this time had codified rights for lesbians and gay men. As there had never been an historical precedent challenging such laws, the DCCHRG must have felt it had little to fear by introducing such a proposal.

Before the resolution could become law, a public hearing would be held allowing citizens to speak pro and con on the proposed amendment. Then a majority of Commissioners would have to vote in favor of the proposal.

The public announcement of the Dade County proposed ordinance coincided with a prayer revival by Reverend William Chapman at Northwest Baptist Church in North Miami. Revivals in Baptist churches include extended sermons given over a period of several days. Just before the revival began, Rev. Chapman was told about the proposed lesbian/gay rights ordinance by one of his parishioners. The revival couldn't have come at a better time to "teach" parishioners about the proposed ordinance. As there had never been significant community action in the past to thwart a proposed or actual lesbian/gay rights ordinance, Rev. Chapman's sermons may have been the first in the nation to enthuse parishioners to oppose such a measure. He apparently did a superb job. One of the church members attending the revival later recalled that her pastor discussed how the proposed ordinance could affect schools, public and private. Presumably this would mean the schools might be required to hire open lesbians and gays if they were otherwise qualified. Parishioners might have been concerned, in an averse way, that their children might be taught by a lesbian or gay person.

At least one of the parishioners felt the need to become more involved in local politics. She came to believe God wanted her to attend the Metro Commission hearing. The whole ordeal would reveal many stunning surprises.

> As our pastor spoke, he noted the effect this ordinance would have on private and religious schools. I suddenly started to realize what he was saying. The thought of known homosexuals teaching my children especially in a religious school bothered me…. During that revival period…the Lord showed me that a part of my own personal revival would be to take more of an interest in what was going on around me in my community. All this happened the first week of January 1977. Even in our wildest imaginations we could not have dreamed of what would come in succeeding months…I knew God was telling me to go with others from our Church to the Metro Commission hearing.(1)

When Anita Bryant learned who introduced the proposed ordinance, that was at least as shocking to her as the ordinance itself. But was it true? The individual who introduced it, Metro Commissioner Ruth Shack, was the wife of Bryant's booking agent, Dick Shack. In the past election, Anita Bryant not only voted in favor of Shack to become Commissioner, but she helped her campaign along by taping a radio spot and donating $1,000. Bryant said "At first I couldn't accept it, and I questioned my husband…" Anita Bryant originally didn't have trouble with Shack's candidacy. When she was a candidate, Dick Shack asked her to record a radio commercial which she did after she discussed the idea with her husband. Fellow congregants in Bryant's congregation became upset with her because Anita Bryant had asked them to vote for Shack. That fueled Bryant's desire to get involved in a more political way.

> Dick Shack had been my agent for many years. When he asked me to tape a radio spot for his wife in her bid to run for the Dade County Metro Commission, I agreed, after talking it over with [my husband] Bob [Green]. Ruth had some good ideas about different programs relating to the ecology, helping the elderly, and other issues. My mistake hit me full force when people from the church came to me and said, "I voted for Ruth Shack because you said to do it, and now look at the resolution she's introduced." I knew I had to do something of a public nature because of that earlier endorsement.(2)

When she recovered from her shock, Bryant first attempted to change Ruth Shack's position. She phoned her and talked "almost an hour."(3) When that failed she wrote each commissioner a long letter describing why he or she should cast a "no" vote against the proposed ordinance. Confidently, she went to the public hearings that preceded the vote.

Supporters for basic rights for lesbians and gays must have felt overwhelmed when the hearing began. Those wanting to deny them basic human rights outnumbered them by a ratio of eight-to-one. No one on the pro-rights side was particularly prominent in the community, much less nationally. Their opposition, however, could boast the support of two nationally famous attendees: Alvin Dark, former major league baseball player and the acclaimed singer and former Miss America runner-up, Anita Bryant. When the time for public testimony came, however, the numbers speaking pro and con were more even.

When it was Anita Bryant's turn to speak, no doubt all listened intently, as she was by far the best known personality at the hearing. In Bryant's words, one can sense the fear she felt that somehow lesbians and gays would be likely to corrupt her children if the ordinance became law. Bryant addressed the commissioners as one having.

> ...a God-given right to be jealous of the moral environment for my children.... God created us so our children would be dependent upon us as their parents for their lives. And I, for one, will do everything I can as a citizen, as a Christian, and especially as a mother to insure that they have the right to a healthy and morally good life....(4)

The same fear reflected by Bryant's testimony would do much to motivate other opponents of lesbian/gay rights around the United States in the next year and a half.

Finally the hearings were concluded. It was time for the Dade County commissioners to cast their vote.

Notwithstanding the best efforts by Bryant and those who agreed with her, the ordinance passed by a vote of 5 to 3.

Bryant had been close to the commissioners and thought she knew how they felt about the proposed ordinance. Obviously, she did not. Apparently she was hurt. In her own words:

> I was visibly stunned, as were the others. I couldn't believe it. I was devastated.

Within a few minutes the media present were looking for reactions. A TV newsperson asked Bryant how she was dealing with the events. "How do you feel? Are you disappointed?"

Bryant agreed she was disappointed, but that her resolve was strong. "Yes," said Bryant. "I'm disappointed and I'm shaken, but the flame that God put in my heart is becoming a torch. It will not be quenched. We have just begun to fight."

As soon as the opposition was able to pull themselves together from this defeat, they asked Anita Bryant if she would lead an organized effort to repeal the new ordinance by petition and referendum. She conferred with her husband, Bob Green, and agreed.

In so doing, Anita Bryant was declaring war against sexual minorities. Based on a belief that same-gender sexuality is intrinsically evil, it was warfare against the conviction "gay is good." Thus she was striking at the very heart of the lesbian/gay movement. The idea that one's sexual identity, no matter how cursed by society, is a positive force, was discovered by masses of sexual minorities in the aftermath of Stonewall. Just as African-Americans want to proclaim "Black is beautiful," lesbians and gays feel a deep desire for society to affirm "gay is good." Therefore, the referendum campaign in Miami would not be just about the rights of lesbians and gays to be free from legal discrimination, or even rights of employers to hire and fire whoever they choose. Ultimately, it was a public referendum over the public's attitude on lesbian/gay sexuality itself.

In Miami, the battle lines were drawn. An intensely emotional campaign ensued. "Before I yield to this insidious attack on God and his laws," Bryant proclaimed, "I will lead such a crusade to stop it as this country has not seen before."(5)

No one can doubt that she kept her word. Within weeks, Bryant and her cohorts collected over 64,000 voter signatures to force a countywide referendum on the new ordinance. Although its boundaries were those of Dade County, Florida, a referendum on lesbian and gay rights would have intense national implications. No test of lesbian/gay rights had ever been put to the polls. For this reason, the local campaign in Dade County soon exploded onto the national stage. And right in the middle of it was the orange juice saleswoman, the famous singer who toured with Bob Hope overseas and as Miss Oklahoma was a runner-up in a Miss America pageant. Anita Bryant Green soon emerged as the number one anti-lesbian/gay spokesperson in America. But she did a lot more than that. By challenging the rights of lesbians and gay men to have legal protection, Bryant did what sexual minorities could never do for themselves, despite their best efforts. She made the issue of political rights for lesbians and gay men a concern for the average person. She forced churches, politicians, and organizations of all kinds, to take a stand on the issue. As odd as it seems, she, more than anyone else, gave credibility to the idea of lesbian/gay rights. Discrimination based on sexual orientation became, thanks to Anita Bryant, a legitimate topic for the media and dining room conversation alike.

Once the issue hit the center of the national spotlight, both sides brought in their heaviest artillery. Large sums of money and expertise came from all 50 states.

Millionaire Jack Campbell led the lesbian/gay communities. Their campaign raised over $350,000. Their strategy was to emphasize individual freedom and civil rights. They felt their best chance was among others who had also been singled out for less than equal rights. They specifically targeted Miami's African-American, Cuban, and Jewish communities with this approach.

The opposition used fear as its main weapon. Save Our Children stressed that deviant behaviors such as child molestation would increase with the new ordinance as law.

On the surface, Anita Bryant would seem an improbable figure to lead a referendum campaign to repeal a city/county ordinance. She had nothing in the way of political background, whether by experience or education. She admitted,

> Never before had I taken a public stand on any controversial issue…I have chosen to live a very private life…(6)

Her inexperience and naiveté in the rough and tumble of politics became fully apparent in the nearly five month long campaign. Yet, she may have been the first to galvanize the conservative Christian element in our country, proving the religious right had significant political clout. Only three years later, this awakened knowledge among Christian fundamentalists would play no small part in the election of President Ronald Reagan.

In spite of her devoted following and credibility at home, supporters of lesbian and gay rights were quick to capitalize on Anita Bryant's lack of political skill. She became the laughing stock of stand-up comedians. Worse yet, her lack of savvy in dealing with media kept her from getting her message across. Constantly in the press, and on talk shows, Anita Bryant was goaded into implying what she did not wish to infer. She came to believe the media were unfair to her and often controlled by a liberal agenda.

The naiveté of their leader, and the inconsistencies of their campaign notwithstanding, "Save Our Children" struck a sympathetic cord with the voters of Dade County. Those deeply committed to Bryant's cause worked for her with undying loyalty.

> Bryant's Save Our Children, Inc. rallied some 3,000 volunteers who rang bells, sent out mailings, manned phones, and chauffeured the elderly to the polls. The association won the support of a key conservative rabbi, fundamentalist Protestant clergymen and Roman Catholic Archbishop Coleman F. Carroll who wrote an anti-statute message that was read to the faithful at Masses. In addition the local TV stations, the Miami *News* and the *Miami Herald* opposed the ordinance.(7)

On June 7, 1977 Dade County voters went to the polls and by a two-to-one margin, repealed the ordinance outlawing discrimination against lesbians and gays in housing, employment, and public accommodations.

Sexual minorities throughout the United States felt the full intensity of the heartache produced by this setback. But they were, nevertheless, quick to respond with spontaneous street demonstrations in San Francisco, New York, Chicago and elsewhere.

> Across the country, gay communities responded to the Miami defeat with angry marches. In San Francisco, 5000 activists staged a noisy, impromptu three-hour parade downtown after hearing of the loss. In Chicago, about 175 men and women held a candlelight vigil at midnight. In New York, hundreds of homosexuals marched through Greenwich Village for two straight nights shouting "Gay Rights now!"
> At [Miami] election-night rallies in the fashionable Fontainbleau and Dupont Plaza hotels, gay leaders were defiant and angry in defeat. Some homosexuals hugged and kissed in front of the cameras.... [Former Air Force Sergeant Leonard] Matlovich led a crowd of followers singing a version of

"We Shall Overcome" and launched into Anita Bryant's favorite tune, "Battle Hymn of the Republic."(8)

While gay rights supporters were still licking their wounds and Christian fundamentalists still gloating, there arose in both camps intense speculation as to what Anita Bryant might do next. Some thought she would capitalize on her status as an effective politician and run for public office. Others saw her sticking with her work in opposition to codification of laws protecting sexual minorities. What Anita Bryant might do next became a concern in fundamentalist churches as well as lesbian/gay communities from Maine to Hawaii.

The suspense was short-lived.

"Save Our Children" announced its intention to become a national organization and help other communities defeat existing ordinances protecting lesbians and gays from discrimination. Anita Bryant remained its titular leader.

Meanwhile "Save the Children, Inc.," a Connecticut-based organization that raises money for starving children overseas, ordered an injunction against Anita Bryant's organization from using their name. Rather than face a lengthy, expensive lawsuit, Bryant and company backed down. They changed their name to "Protect America's Children, Inc."

The first call to Anita Bryant from another community didn't take long in coming. By early February 1978 a fundamentalist preacher in St. Paul, requested help. With a small group in the Minnesota Capitol, he was able to get over 7,000 petition signatures, enough to force a vote for repeal of non-discrimination laws for lesbians and gay men. "Protect America's Children" sent Rev. William Chapman, Anita Bryant's pastor, to St. Paul. His visit attracted much attention. Local stations granted TV interviews. More importantly, an over-all campaign strategy was developed with Bryant's organization supplying initial seed money.

In many ways, it might have been difficult finding a friendlier testing place for lesbian and gay rights than Minnesota's Capital city. The state's fourth congressional district, which includes St. Paul, had sent liberals to Congress the likes of Eugene McCarthy with large majorities for over a generation. The anti-repeal forces garnered the support of Catholic, main line Protestant, and Jewish clergy, labor and political leaders. Polls two weeks before Election Day showed 38 percent opposing repeal, 30 percent for, and the rest undecided. Yet when Election Day came, pro-repeal forces garnered 54 thousand votes in favor to only 31 thousand opposed to repeal. Even those on the side of repeal were shocked at the size of the vote to end legal protection for lesbians and gays.

For the average voter, deciding pro or con on lesbian/gay rights was something new. It was not a clear-cut choice for the person-in-the-street as it was for sexual minorities and Christian fundamentalists. To the average voter, image and implications of protective ordinances had everything to do with whether it was correct or not. In this regard, there were elements of the St. Paul vote that may have relevance for all such contests:

1. As long as the vote seemed to imply social approval for gay/lesbian life styles, that may have had more importance to voters than civil rights for homosexuals.

> It seems…likely that people voted for repeal for a specific reason…they simply refused to believe there was no connection between writing homosexuals into the human rights ordinance and social approval for the gay life style.

2. The radial groups within the larger lesbian/gay rights movements had to be reigned in.

> …The St. Paul Citizens for Human Rights were led by homosexuals who fully believed in the politics of coalition and practiced it with considerable skill. Inevitably, however, they were outflanked by a splinter group of gay rights activists who…accused the larger organization of secretly plotting to sabotage the human rights ordinance, and who, owing to perverse notions of equal time, got more media attention than they deserved. Their idea of effective campaigning was to stage a dance in a hall next door to the Bryant rally. When the ten o'clock news flashed a scene of young men with no shirts on, dancing with each other, one could have ticked off several thousand votes for [pro-repeal].
>
> For its hour-long debate on the subject, a local TV station chose as spokesman for the human rights ordinance a second-term [state] Senator…who [is openly gay]. Sen. [Alan] Spear made the usual argument that the ordinance constituted no endorsement of homosexuality, but with the aid of a liberal Protestant theologian, he also made a different argument which in effect undercut the first point, viz, that even the Bible does not permit one to conclude that homosexual behavior is immoral. Whatever Scripture scholars may think of this claim, it was not calculated to reassure voters worried about the implications of the ordinance…
>
> …People voted for repeal not because they wished homosexuals to be persecuted, but because they wished to thwart the aims of the radical gay rights minority riding in the wake of civil rights…(9)

The defeat in this liberal city cut deep. Lesbians and gays rightfully began to wonder what the future would hold for them. Would political backlash occur everywhere that protection existed? Would lesbians and gay men have to return to the closet? Had the McCarthy era returned? Jean O'Leary and Bruce Voeller, co-directors of the National Gay Task Force said,

> We are outraged that a majority of misinformed voters have once again denied civil rights to a group of American citizens....

As the national campaign against the rights of gays and lesbians became more intense, individual differences in their communities were put aside. Lesbians and gays knew in their hearts there would be many battles ahead. They began to get scared.

If lesbians and gays were feeling uncomfortable, those on the other side did not necessarily feel jubilation. Pat Buchanan, the national syndicated darling of the ultra-conservatives, may have spoken for many voters who were uncomfortable with what they believed were the implications of the gay rights movement.

> [C]onstitutional rights are not what the homosexuals are demanding. Nor are they asking a measure of compassion and understanding. What the National Gay Task Force seeks is to unfurl and elevate a banner of homosexuality—and force the rest of us to fire a 21-gun salute. They ask not acceptance or tolerance, but approbation and celebration of gay pride. [Lesbians and gays] wish to flaunt what their fellow citizens consider to be depraved or sick or sinful behavior—and then be exempt, by law, from any social or economic sanction. They want to flout the customs, mores and standards of society—and remain immune from social reprisal.(10)

The light at the end of the tunnel seemed non-existent for supporters of lesbian and gay rights, as once again a call came to Anita Bryant for help in knocking down yet another anti-discrimination law. Attention now focused on Wichita, Kansas.

Probably from the beginning, supporters of lesbian/gay rights knew they didn't have a chance in this Midwest community, so entrenched as it was in the Bible belt. What they were not expecting, however, was such an overwhelming margin of defeat: 47,246 for repeal, to 10,005 against, a margin of nearly five-to-one! The campaign, which bred on the fears of the community(11) "caused tremors among gays from San Francisco to New York."(12)

Supporters of lesbian and gay rights probably wondered if the Wichita vote would embolden their enemies in the 30-plus jurisdictions that still had laws banning discrimination based on sexual orientation. They were still looking for light at the end of the long, dark tunnel, which had now become a nightmare.

Many felt relief would come as soon as a referendum was held in a favorable climate. With the scene shifting to a liberal, university town on the west coast, many lesbians and gays thought, "Now's our chance!"

The referendum in Eugene, Oregon differed from the others somewhat because its organizers did not cloak their position from a Christian fundamentalist viewpoint. They stuck to secular arguments alone. Nor did they invite Anita Bryant to town.

Anita or not, when the dust settled, voters in Eugene went for repeal two-to-one. Supporters of lesbian/gay rights were stunned again! Not only was Eugene the third defeat in one month, they began to wonder if they could ever reverse the tide that was sending many of their numbers back to the closet. Because Eugene was considered a progressive community, its loss was the most difficult to date, even though Dade County's referendum made the most news. As the *Nation* pointed out,

> Anita Bryant's victorious campaign to repeal anti-discrimination legislation in Dade County, Florida made the most headlines, but the defeat of homosexuals in Eugene, Oregon, a liberal, university community, was perhaps the contest most disheartening to the movement.(13)

But there was little time for proponents of lesbian/gay rights to rest. Two intense campaigns were gearing up for a November showdown: California's statewide Proposition Six and Seattle's Initiative Thirteen.

With the above victories under their belt, the foes of lesbian/gay rights understandably believed they could go as far as they wished. John Briggs, a homophobic state senator, seemed to feel he could capitalize on the anti-gay sentiment he believed was sweeping the nation. He initiated the famous anti-gay Briggs initiative. The California contest would be the first statewide arena for a referendum affecting lesbians and gay men. In this case a defeat would require public school teachers who engaged in "public homosexual activity" to be fired. There was, however, more to the referendums than allowing sexual minorities the right to keep their job. Once again, the ballot measures were in a very real way referendums over the appropriateness of lesbian/gay lifestyles.

Proposition 6 was not only a proposed law that would affect the public behavior of teachers, it was also a way whereby the meaning and place of homosexuality in American society could be defined and evaluated. Its functions as an instrument to achieve a goal are less significant than the fact of its acceptance or rejection by the voters.(14)

With the score Anita Bryant *four*, lesbians and gays *zero*, the sexual minority communities could have been pardoned for feeling defensive and frightened. They realized in Proposition Six they were not engaged in child's play, but up against a highly credible, well-financed opponent. The widespread feeling was that to lose in California would be a disaster. The *New Republic* said, "the impact [of losing Proposition Six] would be immediate and frightening."

What Proposition 6 supporters hope to accomplish is nothing less than a witch-hunt for homosexuals. The initiative authorizes the dismissal of any teacher who engages in "homosexual conduct," which includes "advocating, soliciting, imposing, encouraging, or promoting of public or private homosexual activity." In other words, anyone who opposes this initiative could be fired…

State polls give the amendment a good chance of passage. If it does, not just the rights of homosexuals are at stake. The quality of education, enhanced by teachers whose personal lives may cost them their jobs, would suffer. The influence of people like John Briggs and Anita Bryant, whose power has grown as the referendums proliferate, will spread as quickly as their deception.(15)

The supporters of lesbian/gay rights had their work cut out for them. All activists worthy of the name, in California and Seattle, rolled up their sleeves for an intense campaign. Rev. Troy D. Perry Jr., Founder of Metropolitan Community Church, played not a small role in the outcome of the Proposition Six campaign. He discussed the election in a speech in Seattle, four months following the vote.

If we didn't win in California it would've set us back a number of years. California is the largest state in population with a rich diversity. We just *had* to win! At first we were very discouraged. Our earliest poll showed that we were behind and that dried up a lot of money. But the polls showed us other things as well. We learned that people would believe in neither Anita Bryant nor myself, but that they would accept the explanation of who they felt were experts such as doctors and psychologists.

We also learned the most significant areas of concern or fear was in two areas: one, role models for children, and two, child molestation. So we went to the authorities and they came out in support for us. "The most significant age for influence for role models" they told the California public, "is from three to five years." As far as child molestation is concerned, "98 percent of all molestation is done by heterosexuals." It's just not a gay issue.(16)

What was unusual about this was that this may have been the first time since the anti-gay referendums began that proponents of lesbian/gay rights specifically addressed the fears of the person-in-the-street. When these fears were allayed, the average voter could then think about the measure in terms of fairness and civil rights. Rev. Perry continued:

> Then the tide turned. The polls began to show we had a chance and the money poured in. In the end we spent one million dollars in California. The day before the election, President Carter came to California. "Don't forget next Tuesday: vote *no* on Proposition six," [the President said]. At that moment...I knew we won.(16)

On election night, Rev. Perry found time through the excitement to call Seattle, trying to find out the results of the Initiative 13 vote. Reverend Perry said,

> It took forever to get someone to answer the phone at the [Seattle] Gay Community Center but they told me they were having a party!(16)

The vote in California was 58 percent against, and 42 for, Proposition Six, while voters in Seattle defeated Initiative Thirteen by a margin of nearly two-to-one. The results of both contests were featured prominently on national election night coverage by TV networks and newsprint media alike.

Clearly the tide had turned.

Following the California and Seattle votes, the tempo became more relaxed. To be sure, initiative and referendums would continue, and lesbians and gays would win some and lose some. But never again did anyone feel there was so much at stake, as in those early contests.

The intense national debate generated by the first round of anti-gay initiated referendums and initiatives left little room for anyone to be quiet about their position. The pressure to know just where every noteworthy person and organization stood on the issue of lesbian and gay rights finally was too much for even Christian Scientists to ignore, so even (or finally) The Mother Church felt the need to address the issue. In response to the unprecedented crescendo of public attention, the *Christian Science Monitor* stated its position in an editorial titled *"Homosexual Rights"* on November 8, 1977.

Elements of both progress and danger can be seen in the heightened public concern about the civil rights of homosexuals. Progress because there should be no room in society for discrimination and harassment against any group of individuals. Danger because implicit in the increasingly militant and open "gay liberation movement" is also a desire for social and moral acceptance of homosexuality....

There can be no justification for mistreatment of homosexuals who often suffer blatant discrimination in housing, employment and such areas as bank loans...But the law should also protect society's right to determine, on an individualized basis, whether certain rights ought to be withheld in cases where a person's sexual habits are relevant to performance of a job or could have adverse social consequences. In this regard, the same high standards ought to be applied not only to homosexuals but to all individuals with moral problems potentially harmful to society.(17)

While many lesbians and gays viewed the *Monitor* editorial as double-talk, there was also satisfaction that at last the newspaper saw the need for addressing sexual minority concerns. The *Monitor*, however, was only bowing to the intense publicity Anita Bryant's campaign had generated on a national scale. From the beginnings of gay pride at Stonewall, and for the next two decades, the *Monitor* downplayed the enormous struggle going on for lesbian/gay rights. No coverage was given to the first national March on Washington, D. C. in October 1979, where an estimated 100,000 marched down Pennsylvania Avenue. After the 1986 March on Washington, D. C., where an estimated 600,000 marched for lesbian/gay rights, only minimal mention was given to the event on a page two news summary. Early in 1980 when the *Monitor* was examining *"Activism in the Me Decade"* (the 1970s), its full-page feature had nothing to say about the unprecedented activism in the lesbian/gay communities. But the article did give substantial space to issues it favored such as non-smokers' rights on having more no-smoking areas.(18)

Homophobia within the Christian Science Church and society at-large fueled the desire by lesbian/gay Christian Scientists to organize. Another reason to come together, perhaps, was to tell the world that Mary Baker Eddy's Discovery includes within it neither a basis for prejudice, nor discrimination.

PART III
UNITING FOR A COMMON CAUSE

o o o o o o o o o o o o o o o o o o o o o o o o o o o o o o o o o o o o

For where two or three are gathered together in my name, there am I in the midst of them.

—Matthew 18:20 KJV

5

The Beginning of Lesbian/Gay Christian Science Groups

1978–1980

Trials are proofs of God's care.

—*S&H* page 66, lines 10–11

As the lesbian/gay movement grew more assertive in the late 1970's, the idea to "challenge the false teachings" in the Christian Science Church began to mature in Craig Rodwell's thought. What made the difference this time was that Craig was meeting other gay Christian Scientists. Some of those he met were as eager as he was, not only to form a support group, but to confront their denomination's homophobia in a very personal way.

Bob McCullough was raised in the Episcopal Church in Houston. He came into Christian Science as an adult, after he relocated to New York City in 1964. The homophobic policies of his new denomination instilled in him a desire to work creatively with others in endeavoring to educate his Church on same-gender sexuality.

Bob Mackenroth was equally concerned that his denomination had turned its back on sexual minorities. Bob was an unusually outspoken person for the rights of sexual minorities. This was at a time when almost all LGBT people hid in the anonymity of the proverbial closet. Bob was particularly upset over the anti-gay bias he found in the churches and periodicals. Perhaps the last straw for him was his excommunication from Ninth Church of Christ, Scientist, New York City. Bob had loyally served his branch church for two decades in a variety of capacities: reading room librarian, Coordinator of the usher staff, Chairman of the Board and most recently, Parliamentarian. One of Bob's "failings" was his inability to keep quiet on same-gender issues whenever the topic arose. Other gays in his Church suggested he should be quiet about such things. Bob reminded them that Christ Jesus and Mary Baker Eddy refused to be quiet in the face of adversity and they are our examples for living out our human experience. So he must address the situation.

As a result of an accident when he was six years old, Bob had a tumor in the center of the top of his head. By the time he became active in Ninth Church, the tumor was alarmingly large (about the size of a pigeon's egg) and becoming inconvenient for him. He decided to take the matter to a Christian Science practitioner. While he received some loving thoughts from the practitioner, he was also told he could not have a healing, "until you get over your homosexuality." The rebuke was not easy to take. He admits he didn't completely understand his sexuality at this point. Handling his same-gender attraction in the light of Christian Science was not the easiest thing in the world for him to reconcile. One day, he got to the point where he could no longer comb his hair and not have the tumor show through. The situation seemed almost unbearable. One day he broke down crying. He recalls standing in front of his mirror, tears rolling down his face and saying, "Dear God, I'm not trying to be a homosexual. I just tried to love with all my heart. What can I do?" He prayed then and there for God to tell him what to do. Three days later, he returned to the same mirror to comb his hair. The tumor had disappeared!

Bob gave the above healing in his branch church, also alluding to his homosexuality, but in closeted words. He said, "This didn't affect my bachelorhood."

The words were not lost on Bob McCullough who felt he understood what the testifier was saying. He approached Bob Mackenroth after the testimony meeting and the two Bobs became known to each other. The year was 1972. So began a friendship that would hold a wider importance many years later when they helped organize the first-ever support group for lesbian/gay Christian Scientists.

Years later, Bob Mackenroth gave this same testimony at The Mother Church's Annual Meeting. This time, however, he refused to mince his words. He related the practitioner's warning that his tumor could not be healed unless he first overcame his attraction for men. After describing his healing to the thousands of faithful gathered beneath The Mother Church's expansive dome, Bob revealed out loud, "And I'm still a homosexual."

While attending another Annual Meeting in 1978, Bob made another stir. He decided to attend a meeting promoted as being devoted to the special needs of single people. After listening to the talk, he felt slighted because the needs of gay people were not addressed. When the time for questions came, Bob's hand went up. He was the first to be recognized. "What about gay people like me?" he asked. This was a personal milestone for Bob. He said this was the first time he identified himself as gay in public and "I was both stunned and relieved [that I came out] with such ease." But he was instantly reminded this was not so easy for others to accept.

For a moment there was complete silence. Bob said, "You could hear a pin drop."

The silence was broken when another man, obviously shocked by Bob's words, thundered out, "You're what???"

Not to be intimidated, Bob replied loudly and emphatically, "I'm gay! And how does Christian Science apply to our need for companionship?"

Then the Speaker addressed the situation. Understandably ruffled by the query, she said, "That question cannot be dealt with here. Please see me after the meeting."

"While she was avoiding me after the meeting," Bob recalled, "a few gay people came up to me and whispered their support. But [the Speaker] and I finally got to exchange a few words (comprised of Bible quotes) then she quickly excused herself."

This event carried over to Bob's branch church, Ninth Church of Christ, Scientist, New York City. A young man stood up on Wednesday night meeting to say how grateful he was gay persons spoke up at the Annual Meeting.

The First Reader stopped him from going on. He said that word can't be mentioned here.

True to his audacious spirit, Bob Mackenroth immediately rose to his feet. He asked the First Reader to please rethink the situation.

> Maybe someone is at their first Christian Science service. Do we want them to go away with such an unloving feeling for what was said?

Bob's aggressiveness on gay issues was not taken well with other members at Ninth Church. He was told by them not to make such comments again. But his fellow congregants didn't really give him a chance. He was soon excommunicated.

Bob's outspokenness was not new. After serving with distinction in World War II(1), Bob enrolled at Principia College in 1946. Principia is the only school of higher-education in the world which confines its enrollment to children of Christian Scientists. Although racial segregation was then still entrenched in many areas of the United States, it bothered Bob that African-Americans were not then allowed to attend his school. He thought he might abet an awareness of the problem if he made a fuss about it. This he did constantly. He risked the ire of his roommate by placing a photograph of a male African-American friend on his dresser. These actions were not considered "correct" in post-war America. That didn't deter Bob. He didn't believe the school was living up to the high standards of Christian Science. Therefore, he brought up what he considered Principia's failing every time he had a chance. It appears his outspokenness helped him become elected president of the Inter-Racial Club on campus. In this new position Bob's ability was further helped to make others aware that Principia's policies were deeply rooted in racism. For Bob, consciousness-raising meant everything.

The College did not take Bob's aggressiveness on the race issue lightly. He was often countered with the then prevailing arguments that, "Negroes are inferior and unable to compete with whites." Eventually, the College came to feel Bob must be handled in a more direct way. He was called in to see Major Hubble, Dean of Men.

In trying to dissuade Bob from preaching that the College must change its position, Major Hubble told him bluntly and forcefully, "Negroes will never be accepted on this campus as students, faculty or administrators!"

The tone and the forcefulness of Major Hubble's words were discouraging to Bob. Bob believed "Jesus taught but one God, one Spirit, who makes man in the image and likeness of Himself,—of Spirit, not of matter." (S&H page 94, lines 1–3) This, believed Bob, does not allow room to entertain a sense of inferiority toward anyone or any race.

Believing that he could not help the College overcome its racism and knowing he could not tolerate living in a racist environment, he decided there was no other choice but to withdraw from Principia. In spite of his protests, however, the school wanted Bob to stay—so much that one of his professors offered him a scholarship if he would remain.

Bob withdrew.

Bob eventually wound up in Hollywood where he used the G.I. bill to get himself into drama school. The schooling he received augmented his natural talent in acting that would serve him well in later years.

Bob Mackenroth later took up a job with Revlon Cosmetics. This position required him to travel around the United States. Whenever he was on the road he visited Christian Science churches. At times he came across a church with a segregated policy. He would then confront the members by asking why they had such a policy. This Bob said, made the members uncomfortable. If the church had a segregated "colored" section, Bob would make a point of sitting there. Bob related that his activities "even made the Black people feel uncomfortable."

Years later Bob once more became involved in attempting to change his church's position. This time it was discrimination against members and potential members with a same-gender sexual orientation. He first recognized the "problem" following publication of an article in the *Christian Science Sentinel,* February 17, 1962 *"A Timely Warning"* by Helen Wood Bauman. This was one of the first times same-gender sexuality was mentioned in one of the Church's publications. The writer, Bauman, referred to it as a "vile, Scripturally condemned practice."

Eventually Bob settled down in New York City. There he joined Ninth Church of Christ, Scientist.

After he got to know Bob McCullough, the two men sometimes teamed up to discuss gay issues with other members of Ninth Church.

In the late 1960's when articles in the Christian Science periodicals strongly reflected the Church's anti-gay bias, Bob would not be quiet. The first article in the periodicals devoted entirely to the topic was *"Homosexuality Can Be Healed"* by Carl Welz (*Christian Science Sentinel* April 22, 1967). Sometime after the article came out, Bob, while attending an Annual Meeting, spotted Welz sitting only "a few pews away." Bob was never one to avoid confrontation if he felt it would do some good. "I recognized him and confronted him right there in the pews." The two men had a lively conversation there in the sanctuary which was followed up by correspondence. In one letter, Bob wrote:

> The boundaries of race, color, culture, nationality, creed, society, class, age, gender, sexual orientation are all crumbling, and it behooves Christian Scientists to be at the vanguard of human thought leading the way in *every* department! Not just medicine. The movement cannot afford to be caught napping like it was with the racial issue! We're still not up front with that.

Bob's persistence may have contributed to Carl Welz's eventual change of heart. Nearly eleven years later, Welz would be asked by lesbian/gay Christian Scientists to be the keynote speaker at their national conference. As part of the address he delivered to the then newly organized national group called Emergence, Welz said,

> Several articles and editorials have been written explaining why homosexuals cannot be admitted to membership. One of these I wrote myself…All I can say in defense of myself for writing it is that it was based on information I thought was authentic, but which later was disproved by further studies. If I

were to write another article on the subject now, I would probably entitle it, "We're All God's Children."

Bob also maintained considerable correspondence with other officials in the Church but he especially wrote to those who authored anti-gay articles in the religious periodicals.

From 1975 to 1978 the two Bobs endeavored to use their trips to Annual meetings to further their cause. In this period they met with two members of the Board of Directors, the Chairman of the Trustees, three editors of the religious periodicals, and the President of the Church (largely a figurative or ceremonial position).

◆   ◆   ◆

In the early 1970's, lesbian activist/writer, Kay Tobin Lahusen, felt the work by sexual minority activists and the gains of the movement needed to be documented. She decided to write a book of short biographies of selected lesbian and gay activists. Under the name, Kay Tobin, she wrote about contemporary lesbian/gay workers in the movement. Published in 1972, *Gay Crusaders* is one of the few books about lesbian/gay activism printed in those years. One of those she contacted to be included in her book was Craig Rodwell.

Perhaps being interviewed by a fellow activist who also had a Christian Science background helped Craig Rodwell think through his religion's influence on him. He was led to ponder the implications this had for him as a gay activist. *Gay Crusaders* records that Christian Science had a profound influence on Craig, to the point he wanted to be a Christian Science practitioner. Craig discussed his being raised in a boarding school for Christian Scientists.

> We had religion morning, noon, and night at school, but we were never ingrained with an anti-sexist attitude. I feel I had a non-sexist upbringing, in view of their teaching that God is a Father-Mother God.

Gay Crusaders goes on to describe Craig's work as an activist and his opening the Oscar Wilde Memorial Bookshop. It also emphasizes Craig's feelings about gay activism at The Mother Church.

> One day, Craig feels, he will go with other concerned gays to the Christian Science headquarters in Boston and confront that institution, protesting condemnations of homosexuality in the periodicals.(2)

The prediction Craig Rodwell revealed in *Gay Crusaders* was still eight years away. Meanwhile, he met other lesbian/gay Christian Scientists, almost all of them men. One Wednesday night in 1976 he was taken to Ninth Church of Christ, Scientist by a friend. This was when Craig Rodwell met Bob Mackenroth and Bob McCullough. Out of this evolved a small friendship group. The men would connect by having coffee after Sunday church services, and ride together each June to Boston to attend their denomination's annual meeting. Now and then Craig wondered how many others might be out there, but not yet in the context of organizing a support group. As to who first conceived the idea for a Christian Science support group for lesbians and gays, Craig said it was Kay Tobin Lahusen. He insisted she was the first to mention the idea. But it was left to the friendship group of men to eventually make it happen.

Craig had it in his mind to actively try to connect with as many lesbian and gay Christian Scientists as possible, but he let this slide for many years. He was more than occupied by the demands of the lesbian/gay movement, which he considered an "all consuming interest." He also had his book store to manage.

By the late seventies it dawned on Craig how he might learn of others who shared his same religious background *and* sexual orientation. The idea came to him one day to place a biography of Mary Baker Eddy in a conspicuous spot in his bookshop. Craig had never used his bookshop to promote his spiritual beliefs. But now he thought the very out-of-place aspect of a book about Mrs. Eddy might be enough to draw lesbian/gay students of her teachings to his attention.

Once he had decided that's the action he would take, he surveyed his sales area for the most appropriate spot. He settled on a place where he felt sure no one could miss it. Then and there he placed the Eddy biography. From that moment all he could do was wait. In this way the same book store that so well abetted the rise of the modern lesbian/gay movement would also play a role in establishing the world's first support group for LGBT Christian Scientists.

For many days after placing the Eddy biography in the book store, nothing happened. Then one afternoon a young man browsing the shelves was startled to see the Eddy tome in a shop clearly limited to lesbian/gay literature. Ray Spitale immediately picked up the biography. He took it to the counter. "What's the significance of this?" he asked the saleswoman.

The young woman behind the counter said, "Wait a minute, please." She went to the back room and came back a moment later with Craig Rodwell.

Then the two men who would become highly effective and tireless workers among lesbian/gay Christian Scientists became known to each other. They talked for some time. Ray explained he had an Episcopalian background and had just come into Christian Science. He did not know The Mother Church was homophobic when he joined. Most of all, he was grateful to know there were others like himself.

Craig, for his part, told Ray of his long-standing desire to make a pronounced stand against the homophobic policies of The Mother Church.

Soon Ray became active with the others. He joined the two Bob's when they visited Church officials at annual meetings.

In time, Craig met others who saw the Eddy biography on display in his book store. It wasn't long after that when Craig, Ray, the two Bobs, and others, came together to organize themselves on a formal basis.

The time period may have contributed to the sense of urgency the men felt. The Anita Bryant campaign had just scored victories in the south and Midwest and was planning important battles on the west coast. The men felt it would be important for The Mother Church to side with LGBT people. They wanted their Church to be an important ally in the forces opposing legalized discrimination. There was also a sense of stirring in other places. Reginald Kerry's letters were very much on the front burner of conversation, especially among disaffected Christian Scientists. Not quite a year had passed since his highly inflammatory letter number three had appeared, heavily-laden as it was with anti-gay rhetoric. Across the Hudson River a former branch church that had been excommunicated by The Mother Church was asserting in New Jersey's Supreme Court the right to use the words "Christian Science" in its name. It would declare itself an independent Church. This was an extreme rarity in the annals of Christian Science.

As sexual minorities awaited the tenth anniversary of the Stonewall uprising, their cause showed unquestionable signs of maturity. The loss of gay ordinances in four cities may have been a temporary backlash. But Anita Bryant's homophobic *blitzkrieg* across the nation also exposed the need for sexual minorities to be well organized. By 1979, many American cities had sophisticated political organizations for LGBT people. Equally well-established were lesbian/gay newspapers. In the wider media, lesbians and gays were gaining more respect. They were now treated as a credible movement, no longer an aberration. In 1975, Sergeant Leonard Matlovich's challenge of his dismissal from the Air Force earned him a cover story in *Time* magazine. *Time* gave yet another cover story to "Homosexuality in America" in 1979 which became one of its highest selling issues. The first National March for lesbians and gays brought an estimated 100,000 to Washington, D.C. in October, 1979. And there was no lack of stirring in traditional religious circles.

Some outspoken theologians were questioning centuries-old beliefs on sexuality. Calling for policies of nondiscrimination, Dr. Virginia Mollenkott and Letha Scanzoni in their 1979 book, *"Is the Homosexual My Neighbor?"* eloquently attacked the core of fundamentalist beliefs condemning same-gender sexuality. In 1980 John Boswell's well-researched *Christianity, Social Tolerance and Homosexuality* was gaining widespread attention and respect. And before Stonewall's tenth anniversary, LGBT support groups had become well established in almost all major religious denominations.

It was in the midst of these stirrings in both Church and sexual minority histories that the first-ever lesbian/gay Christian Science group was born.

It may be interesting to note that Christian Science itself appeared on the scene in the immediate aftermath of the nation's greatest domestic crisis. The Founder of the denomination wrote, "The voice of God in behalf of the African slave was still echoing in our land..." when the discovery of Christian Science took place.(3)

It was a century and twelve years following the discovery of Christian Science in 1866, and nine years after the Stonewall riots in 1969, when sexual minority believers of this uniquely American doctrine, first met to assert their freedom from ecclesiastical homophobia. Soon their formalized meetings began. Their organization would be named, "Gay People in Christian Science (GPICS)."

At first attention wasn't given to a name for the group. Bob Mackenroth contends the group's name came into existence when they needed a name to put on their banner to be carried in New York's Lesbian/Gay Pride March.

Bob McCullough said, "My memory is vivid of the session when we decided the name. We tossed around a lot of possibilities—e.g., should Lesbian be in the name? And my suggestion, 'Mother's Perfect Pansies,' [was] quickly rejected. Craig ruled that 'gay people' includes women as well—so that was it."

Proof, perhaps, that its time had come, almost as soon as GPICS was organized in New York, a group of lesbian/gay Christian Scientists was organized in Los Angeles. The West Coast group adopted the name "Emergence." For some time, neither organization knew the other existed. The goals of the two lesbian/gay Christian Science groups, nevertheless, appeared to be similar, not only with each other, but with nearly all lesbian/gay religious groups, regardless of denomination. Primarily, the groups sought to lend support to sexual minorities in a church or synagogue that may be indifferent or hostile to their sexual orientation. The second was to "educate" the larger church or synagogue to overcome whatever negative attitudes and beliefs it may have toward same-gender sexuality. A third goal was to testify to positive elements in their respective denomination throughout the lesbian/gay communities. If the New York and Los Angeles groups subscribed to these goals, this is where similarities ceased. For if goals were similar, emphasis and methods were as far apart as the coasts of the continent separating them.

Emergence in Los Angeles arose out of a suggestion to some gay Christian Scientists by a group of lesbian/gay Mormons called "Affirmation." The Mormons planted the idea of an organization with lesbian and gay Christian Scientists. These Latter Day Saints coached the Christian Scientists on the nuts and bolts of organizing and the group took off. The Los Angeles group found their purpose by holding discussion meetings about Christian Science within the lesbian/gay context. Their meetings often included speakers and potluck socials. One of their early speakers was Rev. Troy D. Perry Jr., Founder of Metropolitan Community Church.

GPICS (pronounced gay-pics by its members) in New York City, proved to be a different kind of group. It was committed to social action from the start, and in its brief history, triggered a number of head-on confrontations with The Mother Church, its authorities, its branches, practitioners, and members.

As we will see over and over, labeling GPICS/New York as an activist group might seem an understatement. As individuals, its members were willing to stand up for what they believed, regardless of the price. One of the reasons GPICS came together was because three of its members were excommunicated from their local branch church.(4) Those given the boot felt they had something to say to the Church-at-large. They therefore asked the Christian Science Board of Directors for a meeting, so they could plead their case.

Surprisingly, the Board told them "Yes." But they also said GPICS would have to wait until after Annual Meeting, as they were much too busy before the Meeting.

When Annual Meeting came and went, nothing was heard from the Board. The men asked again.

This time the Board said "No." It is too easy to be misunderstood, they said. The group was flatly turned down.

The men were frustrated. They wondered, "How can an organization stay alive if there is no dialogue?" "Is it beneficial for The Mother Church to adopt religious practices borrowed from the middle ages that stifled all dissent?" "Is tuning out minority opinions within the movement beneficial to the cause of Christian Science?" "Didn't Mary Baker Eddy have unusual patience with those in the Church with whom the rest of the movement had given up?" "Didn't she want her Church modeled after the teachings of Jesus to be a 'friend of the friend-less?'"(5)

The men did occasionally meet with various Church officials whenever they were in Boston for Annual Meeting. None of the meetings provided the desired breakthrough the men were working for. The following is an example of the treatment they received by one church official.

The men were granted a brief meeting with the President of the Church. The President is a largely an honorary position, appointed annually by the Board of Directors.

When they had all arrived, Bob Mackenroth spoke first. "I'd like to let you know who we are," he said.

""I know who you are!" the official answered sternly, and continuing said, "and you have exactly two minutes. I have to be on the platform tonight."

Bob Mackenroth said, "What can I say in two minutes? I wish to take issue with your article '*Homosexuality and the Bible*'."

Then a freewheeling discussion ensued.

As expected, the Official maintained the Church line and each side merely discussed the reasons for their position.

When the meeting came to an end, the men realized that, as in their meetings with other officials, little was accomplished. As they were putting their chairs back under the table, Bob McCullough asked the Official rather informally, "Do you think the Church might ever change its position on this issue?"

After a pause where she may have tried to choose her words carefully, the President said, "Not at this time!" And the meeting was over.

Now what? The various meetings with church officials over the years had produced only an accumulation of frustration. Still, the men were not about to give up. But perhaps the time had come to consider other ways if progress was to be made.

Those in GPICS/New York believed there was reason enough to pursue their goals, anyway they could. Although as individuals, Church officials would sometimes meet with the men out of a sense of courtesy, this alone, GPICS had learned, was not going to change a thing. So what else could the men do?

The men brainstormed. They may have prayed over the situation. They discovered the hard way it is not easy getting the attention of a Church hierarchy that doesn't provide a means for minority viewpoints to be shared with the membership. Unfortunately, the men's options were few. Still, they were determined to find a way to get the Board's attention. Eventually, they decided to take a second look at another individual who was also ignored by the Church.

The men watched from the sidelines when Reginald Kerry acted on his deep frustration. He too made endless but futile attempts to reason with the Board. Kerry solved his problem by going directly to the Church membership. The men who formed GPICS looked on with an understandable ambivalence as Reginald Kerry's letters made their sensational foray into the Christian Science world. But their awe and fascination turned to disgust when Kerry's acute homophobia and negative tactics repulsed their sensibilities. These were tactics that unscrupulously dragged lesbians and gays out of their closets before a hostile, homophobic, Church. Yet the men knew his letters had an effect on the movement. Then came a flash of inspiration. Why then, they reasoned, couldn't GPICS send a letter of its own to proclaim the opposite message, "Gay is good," before the Christian Science world?

After due consideration, the men came to embrace the idea. Taking their cue from Kerry, the men in GPICS/New York decided to do just that. They would write their own letter. They too would send it to all churches and practitioners listed in the *Christian Science Journal*. Beyond that, they would also mail it to all Christian Science college and university organizations. And they would take out ads in local newspapers inviting the public to send for a copy. This would prove to be a mammoth undertaking for such a small group with limited resources, but they made the decision to forge ahead.

Before it was possible to send a letter, the group had to write something sufficiently powerful, that if read by enough Church members, it could turn the organization around to where it would be more accommodating to sexual minorities. The men weren't kidding themselves. They knew from the outset the job of composing such a letter would be formidable. Therefore, they decided to split the responsibility among themselves. The assignment fell to the four men who from the beginning had been the core of their group: Bob Mackenroth, Bob McCullough, Craig Rodwell, and Ray Spitale. These men worked to come up with a reasonable, concise statement that would explain the errors of the Church organization, while simultaneously making a reasoned plea for the Church to renounce those errors and adopt a non-discriminatory policy.

The writing was divided between Bob McCullough, Craig Rodwell and Ray Spitale. Bob Mackenroth would play the role of organizer and see that all parts fit together. The project would prove a Herculean task for the men. The work of coming up with a readable statement took them approximately two months to complete.

What emerged from their efforts was not a letter. What their work became was a pamphlet—an eight-page pamphlet. They chose to have their text appear on light brown paper with dark brown lettering. The headline was of modest size, posing the provocative question of their organization's name: "*Gay People in Christian Science?*"

The purpose of their pamphlet as stated on its front page,

> is to appeal to all Christian Scientists and especially to The Christian Science Board of Directors to re-examine their thought on the subject of human sexuality in the light of Christian Science; and to take whatever loving and practical steps are necessary to rectify the present wrongs being done to Gay people in the name of Christian Science. [The full text of the Pamphlet appears in Appendix number one.]

The agreed upon final copy was sent to the printer. The men then began to prepare themselves mentally for the labor that lay before them. There was a mutual understanding that they would have to donate much time and energy if the project were to succeed. The men, however, had been committed from the beginning, and were more than willing to make the needed sacrifice. Their overall project would include mailing the pamphlet, "*Gay People in Christian Science?*" to all Christian Science churches, practitioners, and college organizations in the world. That meant over two thousand, five hundred churches and more than five thousand practitioners would be sent the pamphlet as well as approximately three hundred and fifty college and university organizations. They were all listed in the directory in the *Christian Science Journal,* a monthly publication. If that wasn't enough, in addition to the mailing, the men purchased newspaper ads. These would invite the public to write for a copy. Then, the most sensational feature of getting all 15,000 copies of the pamphlet out to the field would be a personal one-on-one distribution activity they would hold at The Mother Church itself. This was planned for the 1979 Annual Meeting when several thousand of the faithful would descend on the Church's Boston Headquarters to listen to reports about the movement. But as they were planning details of these endeavors, the unexpected happened. It would prove a major disappointment—the first of many in the intense work with the pamphlet project.

Their printer told GPICS unforeseen problems occurred. The problems were causing a delay in getting the pamphlets printed by the date requested. According to GPICS's timetable, they would be needed soon. Finally GPICS was flatly told their deadline could not be met.

What would the men do? The pamphlets would be needed soon. They studied the situation. They quickly discovered the impossibility of having everything in place for the 1979 Annual Meeting. The unavoidable decision was then made to postpone the demonstration. Now, the leafleting of Church members would not take place until the Annual Meeting in 1980—a delay of one year!

Eventually the pamphlets, all fifteen thousand of them, were delivered to Craig Rodwell's book store. In spite of the extra time they would have prior to the 1980 Annual Meeting, GPICS members went right to work.

The first step after receiving the pamphlets from the printer was to mail them out. They would be sent to every local church, practitioner, and college organization listed in the *Christian Science Journal*. This meant writing addresses and placing stamps on nearly 8000 pamphlets. The job was formidable. Perhaps those in GPICS came to see the extra time granted by the printer's delay as a blessing in disguise. The men were further kept busy by placing announcements in various newspapers. These would allow the public to write for a free copy. All requests would be answered. The return address on the pamphlet was Craig Rodwell's book store, the Oscar Wilde Memorial Bookshop, 15 Christopher St., New York City.

In due time the pamphlets were addressed and mailed. During the wait for responses, the men couldn't help but wonder, "What will happen now?" With every Christian Science Church and practitioner in the world about to receive a positive message re: same-gender sexual orientation, the men found themselves sailing in uncharted waters. The entire project was a ground-breaking achievement.

Having been frustrated in their attempts to convey a positive message to Church officials, they may have felt this to be their last and only remaining opportunity to turn the Church around. Their sacrifice of hard work and long hours gave them high hopes. But if the men had entertained thoughts the pamphlet might result in a stir anywhere comparable to that of Reginald Kerry's first letter to the Christian Science field, they would be greatly disappointed. Nothing approaching that magnitude occurred.

Within a week or so the first replies came in. Most responses came from practitioners or those who heard about it through advertisements in newspapers. The most memorable letter came from an African-American practitioner who wrote a letter that has become classic memorabilia within the lesbian/gay Christian Science world. (Text of the letter appears in Appendix number two.) There were practically no responses pro or con from college organizations. Only a tiny fraction of letters received were negative. GPICS/New York member Ray Spitale said,

There's a very small percentage, and I mean very small, that were really negative. The ones that were really negative are not only negative in the sense of being ignorant on the subject, but nasty.... We didn't take these seriously. One of them went as far as saying if we were in Iran we would be castrated.

Perhaps the kindest words spoken about the pamphlet came at the first national conference of lesbian/gay Christian Scientists meeting in Chicago, July 1983. Here, the late Madge Reinhardt in her role as Conference Keynote Speaker said:

> There is something especially warm about this pamphlet's approach, an approach to Christian Science different than we are accustomed to in the present-day church culture. But it is a warmth not unknown in the early writings of the Christian Science movement.
>
> It is interesting to me that this present-day expression of warmth—of recognizing and appreciating present humanhood and our best concept of ourselves, rather than escaping into an undemonstrated absolute—has appeared in a pamphlet written by Christian Scientists who are also gay. One wonders: Have gay Christian Scientists had to face their humanhood in ways others have not?

Those who worked on the pamphlet project will never know what conversations the pamphlet may have provoked in local church boardrooms around the world. The same was true for conversations between teachers, practitioners, committees on publication, association meetings, and especially among rank and file members. One thing, however, is certain. The pamphlet did not go unnoticed in the chamber room of the Christian Science Board of Directors. Those in charge of the denomination's business may have received significant amounts of mail, if not of a similar volume to that following Reginald Kerry's first letter to the Church field. Perhaps many members requested more detailed information on the Church's position on same-gender sexuality. But whatever the concerns were, the pamphlet definitely created a real or perceived need for the Church to react.

On September 17, 1979 a counter letter went out, "To each authorized Teacher of Christian Science, Practitioners and Committees on Publication in the United States and Canada."

> Dear Friends:
>
> Many of you have probably seen by now the flier entitled *"Gay People in Christian Science?"* which is being widely mailed to practitioners and others by a group of homosexuals who use this same title to describe themselves. It pre-

sents a fervent argument to accept homosexual activity as perfectly compatible with living the life of a Christian Scientist. Since you may be asked about the church's position on this question, the following reminder will be useful to you.

The letter then goes into two pages of rhetoric on the church's position. It starts with the "Judeo-Christian morality as summed up in the Ten Commandments and the Sermon on the Mount." Then the need for "all forms of sexual license as calling for progressive healing…" It points to "the present rush of social acceptance of homosexuality as a way of life…." and "Some predictions…we can expect before long to see 'gay marriages.'"

The few references in the Board letter to actual statements in the pamphlet are perhaps the closest the Board has ever come to a public dialogue with lesbian/gay Christian Scientists over theological specifics that gave the two camps such a different point of view. The Board letter continues:

> The writers of the manifesto…attempt to justify homosexuality metaphysically and even biblically, and resist the concept of it as something that needs to be healed. Referring to…testimonies of such healing in our periodicals, they write: "This, naturally prompts one to ask what exactly has been 'healed?" Has the person been "healed' of love, companionship or friendship?" The question is rhetorical and the answer is obvious…[Healing] replaces what the manifesto refers to euphemistically as the homosexual's "affectional orientation" with that wider, purer, truer affection which makes possible enriched and stable family, community and church relationships…."

In closing, the Board said:

> This letter is primarily for your own background. It should not be reproduced or given general circulation but may be shared in individual cases where you feel it will be helpful.
> (Signed)
> Harvey Wood, Chairman

At the top of the letter were the bold underlined words "**for your information only**."

Those in GPICS/New York found it interesting many practitioners forwarded copies of the letter to their address.

GPICS was not finished. They wanted to follow through with promoting their pamphlet in a manner beyond what Reginald Kerry was doing with his letters. They wanted to put it into the hands of as many individual Christian Scientists as they could.

As mentioned above, the most sensational feature of getting the pamphlet out to the field would be personal one-on-one distribution to individual Church members at Annual Meeting. This was mentioned in the pamphlet itself. Its first paragraph reads:

> The purpose of this pamphlet which is being distributed at the Annual Meeting of The First Church of Christ, Scientist…in June, 1980 is an appeal to all Christian Scientists…to re-examine their thought on…human sexuality….

This was considered the most important activity because it would place the pamphlet directly in the hands of individual Church members.

What was most difficult for the group was the anxiety the leafleting activity could give them on a personal basis. They knew a confrontation as personal as the one planned, on a subject as controversial as same-gender sexuality, could put them in sharp displeasure with the very members they sought to befriend. No matter how noble leafleting members of their own Church might be, those in GPICS/New York began to feel more and more uncomfortable as Annual Meeting approached. What the group simply had to deal with was fear. A lot of the fear was based on the unexpected. As this would be an unprecedented activity with their Church, there was no telling what might happen. When the time came for the greatest showdown the Christian Science Church has ever had from its own members on the position it should take with lesbians and gays, the main foe of GPICS/New York clearly was fear.

With the desire to have the leafleting activity go off as smoothly as possible, Craig Rodwell initiated correspondence with the head of security at The Mother Church. He wanted to assure him that the GPICS demonstration would be peaceful in all respects.

> I was assuring him and we had letters back and forth, that we were there peacefully expressing our American rights to dissent. We had no desire to disrupt Annual Meeting or to insult Christian Scientists because we *were* Christian Scientists.

The group wanted to do everything it could to show their peaceful intentions. They even decided to place geranium plants on their literature tables to symbolize their peaceful intent.

While the activists might've felt anxious knowing they would be approaching as many of the gathered thousands as they dared, they also had reason to feel uplifted. Foremost among their support was Christian Science itself. Weren't these daring men and women acting on their conviction that "the Lord upholdeth the righteous" (Psalms 37:37 KJV) and "God is our refuge and strength, a very present help in trouble?" (Psalms 46:1 KJV) Even in a human sense, it was being shown to them they were not alone. By now other lesbian/gay Christian Science groups had come into being. In addition to Emergence in Los Angeles, there were now GPICS/Chicago, Identity: gay and lesbian Christian Scientists in San Francisco, and Gay Christian Scientists in the Northwest in Portland/Seattle. Other communities were expressing interest including St. Louis, St. Paul, Cleveland, even Boston. A few members of Emergence/Los Angeles and GPICS/Chicago also came to the Annual Meeting to physically assist GPICS/New York by handing out leaflets at The Mother Church. The event also stirred interest in the wider lesbian/gay communities.(6)

Finally, the day for Annual Meeting had dawned.

Before going to The Mother Church to pass out their leaflets, the group held its own service by reading the Christian Science weekly Bible Lesson. Then the group headed out to The Mother Church, but they weren't feeling comfortable. Ray Spitale admitted very frankly, "We were scared to death. We didn't know what to expect."

The group learned that no matter how much planning they did and how much they tried to cover all bases, there would still be surprises. In spite of all their preparations, when the group arrived at their denomination's headquarters they were simply astonished.

The Boston Police Department, their patty-wagons, and Mother Church security people were present in highly visible force.

For their part, Mother Church officials also didn't know what to expect. No doubt they too had their own fear to contend with. They were, apparently, unaware how many persons from the lesbian/gay communities to expect. One member of a local gay Christian Science group had a parent who worked directly for the Christian Science Board of Directors. From that connection it was learned that large numbers of activists were expected by Church officialdom to descend on Church headquarters, perhaps as many as 500. When it turned out to be a small group, there must have been a sense of relief.

The lesbian/gay Christian Scientists arrived dressed as one would be expected to dress for Annual Meeting: skirts and blouses for the women; coats and ties for the men. After they registered for the three-day conclave, they pinned their identification card to their jacket lapel or blouse. This would entitle them to enter the Church and attend all the meetings. Craig Rodwell recalled, "We looked just like the expected image of Christian Scientists." Each one of the group also had an additional identification. This was a pink triangle.(7)

Tables were set up on the public sidewalks, not on Church property. The group knew how important it was to allay fears Church members might have toward a group of lesbian/gay activists, even though they were members of the same Church. For that reason, copies of the Christian Science textbook, *Science and Health with Key to the Scriptures* were conspicuously placed on the table next to the pamphlet, *"Gay People in Christian Science?"* all neatly laid out along with the potted geranium plants.

It was still early in the morning as Church members were gathering to register for the three-day meeting. Lines were forming outside the Publishing Society for registration when the leafleting of members began. GPICS members had fanned themselves out around the reflecting pool in the Church Plaza. They immediately proceeded to hand out their pamphlets to anyone passing by. The activity continued quietly and for awhile, without incident.

Before long, the inevitable happened.

Craig Rodwell recalled,

> Everything was going fine. [The leafleting activity] was very peaceful and quiet. Then the head of security came over to the table I was at. He looked at us and said, "Your tables are illegal."
>
> I immediately confronted him. I said, "Look. We've been corresponding about this for the last few months. We've assured you of our desire to observe all the laws, and what have you."
>
> He said, "Well, a law was passed last week."
>
> There was some major centennial in Boston or something [the 350th anniversary of the founding of Boston] and the City Council passed a special law to keep the harbor cleared. This was no-where near the harbor. The special law was that there would be no vendors on the public sidewalks. Of course the sidewalk near The Mother Church was a public sidewalk. They were using that law to govern the harbor area as a way of harassing us. I told the head of security "I'm not aware of that law. Why didn't you mention it to me?"
>
> Then he introduced his friend who was with him, from the Boston Police Department.
>
> This guy pulled his jacket aside and showed a gun and said, "Look! You take down your tables or we're taking you in." He was very cold.
>
> I said, "Well, I'll discuss it with the other people. I don't make decisions on my own here."

So we all got together and we took a vote whether or not to resist, which would have meant continuing our tables and being arrested or to take down the tables and continue to leaflet by ourselves.

It was a very close vote, but the group voted to take down the tables. I voted against that. So we did. The tables disappeared. So did the *Science and Healths*. So did the geranium plants.

But we continued to leaflet our pamphlet and talk to people. Still, the action was very successful. We got varying reactions from people. Some were just disgusted; others were very supportive. There was a broad range of reactions. It was a very exciting activity.

During the leafleting process, group members generally stayed in somewhat close proximity to each other. The area staked out for leafleting was near the end of the reflecting pool by the large fountain on the Church Center grounds. The usual method used by the pamphleteers was to approach an individual, nod, or smile, hand a member a leaflet, and say, "Have a nice day."

Most of the leaflets were passed out without incident. Bob McCullough recalls handing one to a gentleman he recognized as Mr. Otto Bertschi, a member of the Christian Science Board of Directors. When the Director saw what the pamphlet was, he pushed it back at him, "almost knocking me over," Bob recalled.

Most Annual Meeting attendees tried to ignore the pamphlet when they found out what it was. But there was enough positive reaction to satisfy the group for their work. Ray Spitale recalled,

> One mother came up to us and said, 'My son is gay. I would like him to read this pamphlet'…She asked for a copy for her and her son. "Don't worry," she said, "Someday this will all be taken care of. It will be healed in our Church. You're doing the right thing."

In spite of anxiety caused by the confrontation with the Church populace, Ray Spitale said,

> Some beautiful things happen when you do that type of work. During the third day we were giving out the pamphlet a plainclothes policeman came up to me. I thought, "uh oh! Here's more trouble." He came up to me, a rough-tough guy.
>
> He said, "Where did you get that pink triangle?"
>
> I said, "We brought them up from New York for this event." I proceeded to tell him what the pink triangle signified.
>
> He stopped me and said, "You don't have to tell me. I was in the liberation forces during the war. I know what it is. Where can I get one?"

I gave him one. He went to…the other police officers and asked one of them to pin it one his lapel, which he did, right in front of some Church officials and security people. They almost gasped.

When the group was not passing out leaflets they attended the Annual Meeting which as Church members they were entitled to be present. Craig Rodwell recalled,

> We went to The Mother Church services. They had security surrounding us all the time. They were just demonstrating to all of us the tremendous fear that mortal mind has of people of the same sex loving each other.

GPICS/New York had a provisional plan for a demonstration *inside* The Mother Church during the Annual Meeting. This would happen only in the event anti-lesbian/gay remarks were made from the podium. If so, the group would rise and remain standing for an indefinite time.

As it turned out, no reference to the lesbian/gay lifestyle was made. The pamphlet distribution remained the exclusive form of demonstrating at the 1980 Annual Meeting.

The pamphlet itself was the first positive significant expression of lesbian/gay identification within the ranks of Christian Scientists. It gave individual lesbian/gay Christian Scientists from coast-to-coast and around the world, a tangible expression of what their cause was about. For their part, the authors of the pamphlet thought their work would bring about positive change in the Church. Many years after the event, Craig Rodwell recalled,

> Those of us involved in writing the pamphlet *"Gay People in Christian Science?"* and distributing it really thought that the Board of Directors would, for the first time, think about human sexuality in the light of Christian Science and become the first denomination to joyously and wholeheartedly proclaim the rightness of same sex love to the world.

This of course did not happen. There were, however, a number of minor victories like those mentioned above. Possibly the group's biggest immediate coup was a formal branch church reaction to The Mother Church's behavior during the demonstration. Ray Spitale recalled,

> Eighth Church of Christ, Scientist [New York City] apologized for The Mother Church on their actions with the police on us. They told us point

blank that Eighth Church did not feel that The Mother Church had reacted with love toward us....

Distribution was not confined to The Mother Church. GPICS/New York also distributed their pamphlet at branch churches in their city before or after services and lectures. In Seattle, two members of Gay Christian Scientists in the Northwest gave out the same pamphlet before or after services at First, Third, and Twelfth churches of Christ, Scientist on the Sunday prior to the 1980 Annual Meeting.(8)

Strong reaction to the pamphlet came from an unwelcome source. Reginald Kerry's letter number six contained specific references to the GPICS pamphlet. Under the heading "*The Gay Situation*," Kerry told the Christian Science field,

> What about DeWitt John's comment at the 1976 Annual Meeting, "There are no known homosexuals employed at the Church Center?" In my Letters I have written of the homosexuality in our Church, especially at the Center. As you know a number of them have either quit or been fired. Since this question was first raised, a movement has begun to demand for gays equal recognition with heterosexuals. This movement in New York has published an 8-page pamphlet entitled "*Gay People in Christian Science?*" It states in part: "Today many Gay women and men are active in the Christian Science movement—serving as Readers, practitioners, branch members, employees at headquarters, and workers in the field...."
>
> ...It is noticeable that the C.O.P. [Committee on Publications]...who undoubtedly favor the Gays, did not answer the Gay people's stand, and that a letter dated September 17, 1979 [see above] was sent out *by the Board* and signed by Harvey Wood.... At last, the Church is taking a forthright stand on this controversial issue. We can express gratitude for the Board's action. My best sources inform me that due to my expose of the "Gay" situation in Boston, mostly "straight" people have been selected for roles of authority in Boston, and the situation there has improved with few exceptions, although the changes have not yet come to the branch churches, including my former branch.

No one knows the exact extent to which Reginald Kerry's letters influenced the Church to be more alert in identifying and removing lesbians and gays from employment in their Boston Headquarters. It appears certain, however, Kerry abetted the Church's anti-lesbian/gay attitudes and practices considerably. The Mother Church's discriminatory attitude was expressed by not allowing self-admitted sexual minorities to become Church members or employees. It was also expressed on the pages of its religious publications.

The Christian Science *Journal, Sentinel,* and *Herald* are the official religious publications of the Church. The three periodicals are considered the mouthpiece for the denomination. Articles and announcements appearing in these Church organs are never used for exchanges of ideas or differing interpretations of Christian Science or Church policies. There is no place in these magazines for viewpoints contrary to that held by Church officialdom. Church members, however, are always invited to submit articles and testimonies of healing for publication. These submissions are carefully scrutinized. Each article submitted must toe the line 100% as to Church doctrines and beliefs. The final interpretation of Church teaching has always been the Christian Science Board of Directors. In this context, several articles had been published over the years which lesbian/gay Christian Scientists found deeply homophobic and personally offensive. Numerous Christian Scientists, heterosexual and gay alike, did not believe they were in accordance with the teachings of Christ Jesus and Mary Baker Eddy. Neither Christ Jesus their Master and Way Shower, nor Mary Baker Eddy their denomination's Founder, was known to have mentioned human love expressed in the context of one-gender. For lesbian/gay Christian Scientists a new low for their Church came by way of a *Journal* article in November 1980.

"*Only One Kind of Man*," by Neil Bowles is considered by many to be the most negative and homophobic tirade against sexual minorities ever made by the Christian Science Church. It may, or may not be a coincidence that it appeared less than five months following the leafleting demonstration described above. In portraying lesbians and gays, Bowles used the words "aberration," "abnormal," "deviates," "outcasts from society," "perversion," and "unnatural." The article's contents produced much consternation among lesbian/gay Christian Scientists, and some wrote letters to Church officials and to Neil Bowles himself.(9) Such nonsense, graced as it was between the covers of "The official organ of the Church of Christ, Scientist" was disturbing. They knew members are conditioned to agree with writings in their periodicals as gospel truth. Gay and lesbian Christian Scientists knew this could only abet and increase the entrenched homophobia long-time present in their churches. There was little aside from prayer many felt they could do. Students of Christian Science are taught that every problem can be met and mastered by prayer alone. Some did just that. The article was discussed at length in some of the local lesbian/gay Christian Science groups. These groups were serving as forums where Church homophobia could be seen from a metaphysical perspective.

◆   ◆   ◆

Whenever a large-scale project involving hard work is concluded, its participants sometimes have a feeling of being in limbo. This was true with the members in GPICS/New York following the leafleting demonstration at The Mother
Church. When the project with the pamphlet was completed, much of the pur-
posefulness of GPICS evaporated. Ray Spitale said,

> What do we do now? We didn't know what to do. We laid low for awhile. We
> just had our meetings here in New York. We opened them up for any Chris-
> tian Scientist who wanted to come to them. We didn't do very much though
> on the Church scene. It was just a local meeting…we would choose a topic
> like…"Christian Science and racism." We announced the topic and asked
> people to look up readings from Mary Baker Eddy and the Bible, etc. and
> bring it in to share…. It was a very successful thing. One month we had
> Christian Science and gay relationships. We were doing that but we had noth-
> ing major to work on.

Meanwhile lesbian/gay Christian Science groups in other cities also found it
increasingly difficult to maintain interest and a purpose for continuing. Poor
attendance and lack of purpose were cited as reasons for the decline. In some
groups, regular meetings had come to a standstill by mid-1982.

It was possible at this juncture the lesbian/gay Christian Science groups
might've died out altogether.(10) But there were in some cases, a small cadre,
most often two or three in a city with a group, who had a desire that their activities continue. There were also other forces at work.

In 1981 a conservative government came into power at the national level in
the United States government. The feeling was that the effort for legal rights for
lesbians and gay men would, at best, be put on hold for some time. When one
feels threatened, there is a yearning for a supportive climate. The idea for a support group took on new importance.

In 1982, a new disease, acquired immune deficiency syndrome (AIDS), was
making its way into the headlines. It was referred to as a gay men's disease that
ultimately would take the patient's life. Prospects for a medical solution were
beyond reach. Again, the need for a support group, especially one emphasizing
healing, took on a new, added importance.

In the Christian Science world, there was a sense of stirring going on. This
was, for the most part, outside lesbian/gay circles. A disaffected church in New

Jersey that was excommunicated in 1977 was making progress in the courts. It was showing signs that it had a chance to win its lengthy and expensive court battle against The Mother Church over its right to call itself an independent Christian Science Church. No branch had left the fold since Fourth Church in Rochester, New York withdrew in 1950. As far as is known, all previous churches that left the Boston organization, whether voluntarily or excommunicated, faded into history.(11) The Plainfield, New Jersey congregation, however, did not seem to fit that mold.(12)

A man named David Nolan, leader of United Christian Scientists, was making noise about copyrights to Mrs. Eddy's books. He believed the extended copyright for the Christian Science textbook, granted by the U. S. Congress during the Nixon administration, was illegal. He further contended the copyright served as a stranglehold, preventing significant publication and distribution of *Science and Health*.

A number of Christian Scientists were setting up their own publishing and book selling firms. These publishing houses were audacious affronts to Church policy regarding "unauthorized literature." The policy prohibited members from reading any work related to the denomination and/or its Founder not deemed suitable by the Church.

In 1980, independent Christian Scientist Ann Beals founded The Bookmark. She amassed a large collection of writings pertaining to Christian Science, its Leader, and her students. For the most part, her collection included works not available through regular Church channels. She offered to share her resources with open-minded, free-thinking students of Mrs. Eddy's writings. A similar service was being done by the Rare Book Company in Freehold, New Jersey, Aequus Foundation in Claremont, California, Emma Publishing Society in Cuyahoga Falls, Ohio, Gethsemane Foundation in St. Maries, Idaho, and others. In this way the Church was losing its grip on what its own members were reading as pertains to Christian Science and its Founder, Mary Baker Eddy.

Keeping tabs on these activities were, of course, Reginald Kerry's letters, which continued to the mid-1980's. The polarizing letters, themselves a focal point for unrest, were becoming more widely recognized as an effort to cry "foul" that was being heard.(13)

This stirring, both in and out of the Church, contributed to a sense of purpose for lesbian/gay Christian Scientists and a wondering of where it all might lead.

Meanwhile, low key activity turned out to be only a breather for GPICS/New York and other activists among lesbian and gay Christian Scientists around the country. They were about to embark on yet another adventure. Up in Boston, a

PART IV

"SPIRITUAL WICKEDNESS IN HIGH PLACES"

o o o o o o o o o o o o o o o o o o o o o o o o o o o o o o

Conflict and persecution are the truest signs that can be given of the greatness of a cause...provided this warfare is honest and a world-imposed struggle. Such conflict never ends till unconquerable right is begun anew, and hath gained fresh energy and final victory.

—**Message for 1900**, *by Mary Baker Eddy, page 10, lines 5 to 8.*

6

The Chris Madsen Affair

1981–1985

…[T]he spiritual recompense of the persecuted is assured in the elevation of existence above mortal discord and in the gift of divine Love.

—*S&H*, page 98, lines 1–3

Toward the end of 1981, a rumor was circulating at the Church's Publishing Society about the lesbian activities of a young reporter for the *Christian Science Monitor*.(1) Word was out that the reporter attempted to seduce the wife of a Church manager. The situation was considered serious. So serious that authorities could no longer ignore the rumors. It was decided the young reporter must be confronted with the allegations.

Chris Madsen was a newcomer to the religion. She was raised a Roman Catholic but felt a yearning toward "a spiritual basis, and I found Christian Science." This was shortly after her coming out as a lesbian.

> It appealed to me because it was such an individual religion. I thought it must be full of the most liberal thinking people around.

Chris took her religion seriously. During these years she was healed through Christian Science of a knee injury, allergies and other ailments.

Chris was employed by a small daily newspaper in Maine in 1974 when she accepted a position at the *Monitor*. This was when she was only 22. She started out as "nearly every young writer starts out at the Monitor: sharpening pencils, answering phones, and performing other small duties." Slowly she began writing and editing.

Due to her position with the *Monitor*, Chris was not active in local lesbian/gay organizations. That didn't prevent her from keeping abreast of news in the sexual minority communities. She regularly read newspapers and magazines written by and for lesbians and gay men. She couldn't have imagined the effect her perusal of one such paper would have in her life.

> One day I saw a tiny ad in *Gay Community News (GCN)* advertising a book by Madge Reinhardt. It piqued my curiosity. I wondered if it was going to tell me what a bad person I am. So I called *GCN*. I asked if they could tell me something about the person who placed the ad, and what kind of a book it is.
> They said they didn't have that information, but I might call the group in New York.
> "What group?" I asked.
> "The gay Christian Science group," was the answer.
> "A *gay* Christian Science group?!" I asked.

This was big news to Chris. She took the group's phone number from *GCN* and decided to call and ask them about the book.

Nervously, she dialed their number, not sure what to expect. A few rings and someone answered.

"Hello," said Chris. "I'm calling about the Gay Christian Science group."

The voice on the other end said, "Wait a minute." Then someone else got on the phone and asked for my number. After I gave it to him, he said, "We'll call you right back."

It was a long five minutes before the phone rang. The caller turned out to be Ray Spitale, a member of Gay People in Christian Science (GPICS) in New York City. Ray gave her basic information about the role of the organization as a support group.

Then Chris told him who she was and where she worked.

The two of them instantly hit it off and continued talking "about an hour."

In time, Chris said,

> I became very close to the guys at GPICS/New York, even going so far as to travel to New York on occasion, to march with them in gay pride demonstrations.

Although GPICS/New York was pretty much a men's group, it became very important to Chris. The group lived the type of brotherhood and sisterhood she felt was missing from the Church. She felt in her heart, the object of one's love and affection is totally an individual demonstration. This, she believed, was consistent with the teachings of Christ Jesus and Mary Baker Eddy. There comes a time in many relationships when the partners need to express themselves to each other, as did Ruth of old to another woman:

> Intreat me not to leave thee, or return from following after thee for whither thou goest, I will go, and where thou lodgest, I will lodge: thy people shall be my people, and thy God my God…The Lord do so to me, and more, also if ought but death part thee and me. (Ruth 1:16–17 KJV)

No individual, no government jurisdiction, no organization, no, not even a Church, Chris believed, has the right to obstruct or hinder that demonstration in any way. She knew it was important that GPICS existed to heal homophobia in the Church. Therefore, she supported the group every way she could.

From the first moment they met, GPICS/New York was very supportive of Chris and she said she felt it.

After spending seven years with the *Monitor*, Chris had become a feature writer as well as an assistant editor for the *Monitor*'s Special Sections department. At that time the department produced a weekly magazine supplement in the Special Sections department for domestic and foreign distribution. She had also been responsible for designing *The Home Forum* page. Chris was well on her way to a successful career in journalism, until one day her job came crashing down. In the process she found herself confronted with her greatest test of inner strength.

She had become aware of the rumors circulating about her private life, and felt that was probably why she was asked to see an official of the Publishing Society. The job of confronting Chris about the rumors of her being a lesbian fell to J. Anthony Peritin, Manager of the Church's Publishing Society. Chris was sent notification to meet with Peritin exactly one week before Christmas Day, 1981.

Having a good idea why she was called gave her time to think through the situation. Therefore, her decisions on how to conduct herself were made well before their meeting.

At the appointed hour, she went to Peritin's office. The following discussion is from Chris's notes, which she wrote immediately after their meeting:

> Tony and I had an appointment for 1:30 p.m.
>
> I start by saying that I am concerned that the bylaws are not being adhered to.
>
> He explains that is his interpretation of them (I guess he is the one who comes to me in private…)
>
> Then I ask what the accusations are.

He says that [1] I tried to entice [a manager's wife] into a relationship, [2] that I am gay, [3] that I go to gay meetings.

I flatly deny the first. He asks if I go to meetings.

I tell him I will not discuss my private life.

He says something about people interested in women's issues might go to meetings one thinks are gay.

(I refuse to take the cheap way out or fall into the trap)

He says something about avoiding the appearance of evil. (I can see he is getting frustrated.) He says, "Well, you answered one of my questions."

I said, "Yes. You have asked me two and I have answered one, but you haven't asked me the third question."

(A long pause)

"All right then, I will. Are you gay?"

"Yes."

"Thank you," he says. "Thank you for your honesty."

(The mood changes.)

(I think now he can see that I wasn't trying to duck the issue. I was just stating clearly my boundaries. We had quite a discussion on how thought was so important to Christian Scientists. In my private life this was significant.)

He said, "There are some on the Board of Directors who don't find the two incompatible." (Confirmation of what GPICS/New York has said.)(2)

He asked, "Are you trying to heal this?"

I said, "No. I understand that in cases like this it was policy to let the employee go. I stayed this far because of my love for the *Monitor* and Christian Science."

He said "Yes, that is usually the case, but I'd like some time to think about it."

Several times during the conversation I asked him who it was who had accused me. He steadfastly refused to tell me. He didn't have permission to do so. So now I will hear from him.

The firing which dragged out "for more than two weeks over the holidays (I spent Christmas and New Year's frantic)" "devastated" Chris. "But" Chris added,

the occurrence was not totally unexpected. The folklore at the *Monitor* includes stories of firings. So you become pretty careful—quickly. In fact, I spent a lot of time being careful at work.

Her termination became official on January 4, 1982, but it was not without some consternation within the *Monitor*. Chris's supervisor, Curtis Sitomer, tried unsuccessfully to persuade the newspaper from firing her. He reportedly said, "She's a competent writer. She researched things well and she's intelligent."(3) Other employees also tried to intervene to no avail.

What transpired after Chris was officially notified of her termination is momentous in the history of lesbian/gay Christian Scientists. Chris Madsen hired a lawyer to begin legal action against the *Christian Science Monitor*. There appears to have never been any doubt in Chris's thought about suing the *Monitor*. She felt she was wronged and that was that. Fighting her termination was more than a simple act of bravery. In the past, untold numbers of persons had been fired from the Church and the Publishing Society for their sexual orientation. The difference was that until Chris came along no one had ever demonstrated the slightest inclination to fight the injustice. One reason is that some could not overcome what lesbians and gays refer to as internalized homophobia. This means they could not help feeling ashamed in terms of who they were and the "disgrace" they had given themselves. Others, who may not have been concerned about themselves, did not want to bring "shame" on their families.

Chris Madsen, on the other hand, represented a new generation of lesbians and gay men. This new generation was being molded by such lesbian/gay pioneers as: Ernest Barnum, Rev. Troy D. Perry Jr., the members of GPICS, and other like-minded activists including Chris Madsen. They were no more ashamed of their God-given identity than were first century Christian martyrs who died for their beliefs.

The next thing Chris did was to telephone her friends at GPICS/New York. She told them she had just been fired from the *Monitor* and she was going to sue the paper.

In contacting GPICS/New York, Chris went to the right people, for no group among the followers of Mary Baker Eddy were more disposed to do everything they could to help. Their efforts would go far beyond Chris's immediate needs. They would go all-out to help her capitalize on her termination from the *Monitor*. These efforts would become a weapon in the "good fight" against Mother Church homophobia. The injustice served to such an outstanding *Monitor* reporter as well as a devout Christian Scientist was repugnant to their senses.

What may have shocked GPICS even more than learning about her termination was that the *Monitor* did not make provision for Chris to receive unemployment compensation. This meant she suddenly found herself with no income whatsoever.

The shock may have helped GPICS/New York set priorities. Ray Spitale said,

> Immediately after she was fired and we found out Chris wasn't collecting unemployment [insurance], we started a fund in New York for her.

But this was only the first step in many months of intense work to seek justice in the Christian Science organization.

Of this action, Chris recalled,

> When I was fired, I called them. They were so supportive! They actually gave me sustenance money so I didn't have to give up my apartment and I could go on living life. Their support was so strong! It was so affirming! This is where more than anywhere else in my experience, I felt Christian Science.

Once Chris's personal needs were met, GPICS set out to use her termination as a means to re-focus attention on the discriminatory practices of The Mother Church. They were determined to do everything they could to bring about an end to unfair treatment of sexual minorities in the name of Christian Science. They would accept assistance from anyone or any group who would help, but primarily they went after support from the wider lesbian/gay communities, other lesbian/gay Christian Science groups and individual lesbian/gay Christian Scientists around the country.

In order to generate much needed support, it would first be necessary to let the world know what happened to Chris. So they went to the media beginning with the gay press in Boston.

At this point, the crisis deepened.

It was on March 8, 1982 that Jil Clark, reporter for Boston's *Gay Community News (GCN)* went to the Christian Science Publishing Society to interview Personnel Director Karen Gould and other Church officials about Chris Madsen's termination.

Coincidentally, the same day, Gould confronted Jim Ogan, a 36-year-old business and cost analysis supervisor for the Buildings and Grounds Division with a written complaint about his job performance. Ogan was fired three days later, but he maintained it was not because of his job performance, but his sexual orientation. He maintained he was fired because Church officials suspected he was gay and because they had received two letters, one unsigned, assailing the Church for employing "this overt homosexual in such an important position" and threatening to spread the rumor about Ogan among Church members.

Shortly thereafter, *GCN* broke Jil Clark's story of Chris's firing to the local lesbian/gay communities with a page-one headline and feature story. In the story, Chris said,

> I didn't become aware of the homophobia in the Church until I started working at the Center [Church Headquarters]. I've spent years thinking about the

two and can't find any way that the two can't go together…. Over the years I'd imagine someone taking it into his or her head and saying something [about my sexual orientation], so I thought I was prepared, but it was awful.

The *GCN* story didn't go unnoticed by Jim Ogan. He soon contacted Chris Madsen. Then he went to *GCN* himself which in turn published a front-page story about his job termination.

An important decision that came out of the meeting between Chris and Jim was a decision to work together to sue the Church of Christ, Scientist. Ogan told *CGN* he would sue the Church for a year's salary. "I gave them nine years of my life; it's the least they can do."

While there was a lot of determination by Chris, Jim, and their supporters, to fight the Church's ruling, their position was not legally strong. Boston's only ordinance banning discrimination on the basis of sexual orientation at that time was confined to city employees. Several years were to pass before the City of Boston and the State of Massachusetts would pass legislation prohibiting employment discrimination based on sexual orientation. But even if those were already in place they might not be enough. The strongest ordinances banning discrimination against sexual minorities, where they already existed, had broad exemptions for religious institutions.

Because Chris and Jim's legal options were few, GPICS/New York hoped to score heavily with publicity to possibly intimidate the Church into taking what they felt would be a more reasonable position. Unfortunately, Jim Ogan, for personal reasons, did not continue. He soon dropped out, leaving Chris Madsen to confront the Church organization by herself. Chris, however, was getting new support all the time, especially within the wider lesbian/gay communities.

Lesbian/gay newspapers from other parts of the country soon picked up on the *GCN* stories about Chris and Jim. Between that and the lesbian/gay Christian Science groups, word got around in sexual minority communities coast-to-coast about the firings. As Chris's protracted suit against The Mother Church continued in the courts, that, together with lesbian/gay demonstrations at the Christian Science Church Center yielded intense negative publicity in lesbian/gay media against the denomination. The result is that sexual minorities came to view the Christian Science Church as one of the more homophobic institutions in America, perhaps on a par with their perceptions of extreme Christian fundamentalists, Latter Day Saints, and orthodox Jews.

Another job the GPICS/New York steering committee took on to support Chris Madsen was to prepare yet another visible demonstration at The Mother

Church. Plans were made to participate as Christian Scientists in Boston's lesbian/gay Pride March while having a separate demonstration at the headquarters of the Christian Science Church. This proved to be no small undertaking. GPICS/New York endeavored to garner all the support they could for this demonstration and/or any other related activity that would help Chris Madsen and/or deal with the problem of homophobia in The Mother Church. There was only one problem.

The New York group was very enamored with Chris Madsen. They had known her for years. In the rest of the country, however, her name held no special meaning. So GPICS worked hard to promote Chris Madsen's name among other lesbian/gay Christian Science groups and individuals throughout the country.

As the act of blatant Church discrimination became more widely known among lesbian/gay Christian Scientists, its impact sank in.

For the first time lesbian/gay Christian Scientists had their own *cause celebré,* their own Rosa Parks. Chris Madsen, an individual of unquestioned integrity, had been unfairly subjected to blatant discrimination. As a result, she became the personification of all that GPICS/New York stood for. Her very name became synonymous with Mother Church homophobia and discrimination. "Chris Madsen" became a rallying cry for concerned lesbian/gay Christian Scientists around the country as well as others beyond the denomination.

GPICS/New York evoked Madsen's name to gain needed support. They wrote to the other lesbian/gay Christian Science groups in the country. They urged them to support the demonstrations that lay ahead and encouraged everyone, everywhere, to write letters to the *Christian Science Monitor.* The group used their newsletters to exhort, not only their own members, but other groups of lesbian/gay Christian Scientists in Chicago, Los Angeles, San Francisco, and Seattle.

> Won't you join us in lifting the Christian Science Movement out of the morass of homophobia, racism, sexism, and heterosexism? Your efforts, both metaphysical and physical, are needed *now.* Get involved: write letters to the Church Center; organize in your area, join the march, send a donation.(4)

As a result of the groundwork by GPICS/New York, hundreds of letters poured into the offices of the *Christian Science Monitor* protesting its treatment of Chris Madsen.(5)

In a much more significant move, GPICS/New York sent Ray Spitale to the West Coast to meet and talk with lesbian/gay Christian Science groups about the planned demonstrations in Boston. Meeting face-to-face with groups in San Francisco and Seattle, Ray was able to discuss Chris Madsen's firing in great detail. He also explained how her firing led to their planned demonstrations and other responses. The New York group sent with Ray a proposal for a national ad-hoc coalition. The proposed coalition would consist of two members from each lesbian/gay Christian Science group in the country. GPICS/New York was also open for suggestions on action and other ways of organizing they hoped would come from other groups.

Although lesbian and gay Christian Scientists in other cities shared an intense interest in what GPICS/New York was doing, little initiative came from them. A few members from other groups did go to Boston to assist the New York group but they went as individuals, not as representatives from their local groups. An immediate result from the urgings by GPICS/New York was the development of sharp differences among lesbian/gay Christian Scientists around the country as to the appropriateness of what was sometimes called "militancy." But it wasn't only a sense of militant behavior that caused the division. Some sexual minorities held The Mother Church in such high esteem that regardless of what was happening with the human side of church they could not bring themselves to openly oppose the headquarters of their denomination.

Then there were those lesbians and gays who were closeted to their branch churches while serving as active members. They felt unable to do anything that might draw attention to their sexual orientation. Some of them felt the only activities of the lesbian/gay Christian Science groups should be spiritual in nature.

Ray's meetings on the West Coast may not have resulted in significant joining of forces but they are important in this history as the first efforts to combine energy and talent on a broader scale than groups had heretofore practiced. His talks with Identity in San Francisco and Gay Christian Scientists of the Northwest in Seattle helped develop a greater sense of bonding among these isolated groups. When the second major confrontation took place at The Mother Church by GPICS/New York, those far from the scene felt more connected.

As Ray revealed his group's plan on the West Coast, GPICS/New York would first make a protest at the opening day of The Mother Church's Annual Meeting, Monday, June 7, 1982. About two weeks later they would march in Boston's Lesbian/Gay Pride parade. The next day, they would attend the Sunday morning service at The Mother Church. For the second time in two weeks they would hold a peaceful demonstration at the Church Center again passing out leaflets and displaying their banners and signs. These types of demonstrations at The

Mother Church would be a first. Besides bringing attention of Chris and Jim's firings to the attention of Church members, the protests kept Mother Church discrimination focused in lesbian/gay media throughout the country.

Although there had been a lesbian/gay demonstration at the Church two years earlier, it was confined to leafleting and was very low key. By comparison, this would be a flamboyant, in-your-face demonstration. Marchers would yell chants, while holding banners and signs with their messages. The centerpiece of the demonstration was a large professionally made banner with the printed words "*GAY PEOPLE IN CHRISTIAN SCIENCE*" and signs carried by members of GPICS/ New York and others. The group would also be chanting the slogans so often heard in lesbian/gay marches. These would be tailored to the Church. As before, leaflets were printed for this event to be handed out at the Church Center. This would indeed be another "ground-breaking" event. And, as in 1980, no one could predict what might happen. Even those who did not go to Boston were filled with suspense waiting to learn how it would all work out.

As it was, the protestors on the first day of Annual Meeting, 1982, were confronted with a chilly, rainy day. This was unfortunate as most Church members scurried inside, instead of lingering in the Church plaza, as is their custom at these events.

Nevertheless, when the lesbian and gay Christian Science contingent entered the grounds of the Church Center, they literally caught some old guard members unprepared. Seeing lesbian and gay Christian Scientists brazenly parading across the Church Center plaza chanting slogans and waving conspicuous banners, jolted their sensibilities. Could it be that some of them felt the 1960's had finally reached The Mother Church?

As the protesters marched, onlookers could read their signs:

STOP THE WITCH-HUNTS!

BIG MOTHER IS WATCHING.

FATHER, FORGIVE THE BOARD,
THEY KNOW NOT WHAT THEY DO

THEY GOT CHRIS & JIM.
ARE YOU NEXT?

Many who could not make the event, would read about the demonstration in Boston's *GCN* or in lesbian/gay papers from other cities that picked up *GCN's* story.(6)

Eager to learn how the Church saw this activity, the author phoned The Mother Church to talk with an official directly. He called the Committee on Publication the day following the demonstration. He did this in his capacity as reporter for *Seattle Gay News*. The conversation revealed a downplaying of the event. Robert Nelson, speaking for the Church, witnessed the demonstration, which, he said, was "completely peaceful."

> As to numbers I counted about 15 in the line of people carrying placards. One of the newspapers reported 50, but I counted 15 people. I really don't think there were 50. But we had a couple of days of terrible, constant rain, so it was a bad day. They were there in the rain and they were marching around the Church itself and had complete and easy access to wherever they wanted to march and they were distributing some printed material stating their position and in about a half-hour they dispersed.

So went the Annual Meeting in 1982.

The next event to take place was Boston's annual lesbian/gay Pride March about two weeks later. It was here that other lesbian and gay Christian Scientists from around the country would join GPICS/New York.

The group met at Arlington Street Church, Boston at 9:30 a.m., Saturday morning to plan the day over coffee and donuts. They first held a prayer meeting at 11:00 a.m. Then they collected themselves in front of the Christian Science Reading Room on Coply Square with their signs and organizational banners. The March began at noon. Here, GPICS/New York joined thousands of other marchers in Boston's annual Lesbian/Gay Pride March. The route of the marchers wound around the Back Bay area leading to Boston Commons, site of the Lesbian/Gay Pride Rally where Chris Madsen was a scheduled speaker.

The March as described by those present went well. The GPICS/New York contingent was conspicuous. Quite a few people on the sidelines joined the procession when they discovered the Christian Scientists as they marched, including a former employee of the Church's Publishing Society. At the rally immediately following the March, Chris Madsen, a scheduled speaker, told of her ordeal with the Christian Science Church. Ray Spitale said, "She got quite a response."

The next day the group attended the Sunday morning service at The Mother Church. Following the service, they again leafleted Church attendees as they filed out of the edifice. The event was followed with a photo session and a luncheon before dispersing back to New York and other hometowns.

A colorful description of the demonstration was given about a week after the protest by Ray Spitale.

> Our response last week…the publicity was so great on Chris, we were practically cheered on every corner…. There were 50 people or so [in the Christian Scientists contingent of Boston's Lesbian/Gay Pride March]. We walked right across Church property…. We walked through the Church Center shouting:
>
> *"Two-four-six-eight.*
> *How do you know the Board is straight?"*
>
> *"Stop the witch-hunts!"*
>
> People were stunned by our presence. These women especially weren't looking where they were going. They were tripping and falling all over the place…Two of them were picked up by two lesbians…It was wonderful to see because it was the first time I ever saw them at the Church Center lose their complacency and deal with the real world out there. They were shocked! They were horrified! The expressions on their faces were priceless…
>
> On Sunday, we [attended services at] The Mother Church. There were about 20 of us and we all sat in the same section of the Church with our pink triangles on…First, we assembled outside the Church in front of the portico. One of the security people came up to us…[H]e was the head of security. He wanted to feel his way out—to see what we were up to. We recognized him from two years ago. He was the one who called the police on us.
>
> He said to Craig Rodwell, "Hi. I remember you from two years ago."
>
> And Craig said, "Yes. I remember you from two years ago. I remember the police and the guns. In fact, I remember you too well."
>
> He said, "Well, I just want to remind you about the rules about not giving out literature on Church property."
>
> Craig said, "Well do you mind if we go to Church.?"
>
> He said, "No, no. Of course not! Everyone's welcome."
>
> Craig said, "Well thank you. That will be enough from you."
>
> So we dismissed him. Of course that left him without knowing what we intended to do. We went inside the Church and went to the service. We were all wearing pink triangles and sitting together. Everybody was whispering and talking and looking at us. They knew what was going on. We stood up during the postlude and just stood our places as people were leaving. There were some security people around us. When we walked out of the Church to unfurl our banner, there were police and a paddy wagon. Needless to say, the police didn't do anything. They were just there in case anything happened. The Mother Church must have called them immediately. We unfurled our ban-

ners and took pictures. We even took pictures with police paddy wagons in the background. It was a beautiful day for it. There were people looking from the Church standing at the portico and staring at us, some of them in disbelief.

Then one of the COP [Committee on Publication] came out. He gave each of us a sheet. It was about the Church's position on homosexuality. It was a prepared statement they must have done a few days before we arrived. They knew we were coming up. We talked to him awhile. He [Robert Nelson] was a friendly guy. He was not bitter or anything.

As expected, the Church's position statement was not acceptable to the protesters.

According to Unitarian-Universalist minister, Bob Wheatley, one of the leafleters, COP Manager A. W. Phinny's statement(7) "betrays his ignorance of homosexuality, a misunderstanding which," says Rev. Wheatley,

is the root of the problem that many [Christian] sects are having about gays. This is not a fad that is going to change. Homosexuals have been present in Eastern and Western cultures in all times.

Rev. Wheatley also criticized those responsible for the firings, which include top officials of The Mother Church, for acting in a manner

antiethical to Christianity. To cut off a person's livelihood…flies in the face of the religious teaching to be helpful to people in their needs. Even if they do misunderstand homosexuality, there is no excuse for this cruelty.…

The event produced some local media coverage. Chris Madsen was interviewed by three Boston TV stations. The Boston *Globe* and Boston *Herald* also printed stories on the demonstration.

◆   ◆   ◆

When the group arrived back in New York and other hometowns, they settled down for another tranquil and reflective period. It became apparent the Church had tried to minimize the effect from the protests. Other than the COP's press release, there was no reaction from the Church. And there was certainly no change in blatant discrimination policies toward lesbians and gays.

As brought out above during Chris Madsen's meeting with Anthony Peritin, Manager of the Publishing Society, two of the five members of the Christian Science Board of Directors favored a change in the Church's policy toward lesbians and gays. That being the case, it is highly probable the Board has had lengthy discussions over its policies vis-à-vis the Church's position toward lesbian and gay sexuality. Accounts of those meetings, were they available, would have made interesting reading. These deliberations, like all deliberations of the Board of Directors, are highly confidential. It is surprising, therefore, that Peritin acknowledged to Chris Madsen that two of its members were sympathetic to the lesbian/gay cause. Partly due to their awareness of the Board's division, GPICS/New York sent the Directors a copy of everything they mailed to their members: newsletters, announcements, whatever went out.

It is important to note that all action taken by lesbian/gay groups was only to raise the social consciousness of the Church. There was no significant movement to hurt the Church or the *Monitor* with a boycott or other economic action. One attempt did occur, but it was not sponsored by a lesbian/gay Christian Science group. In this case the National Gay Task Force (NGTF—later renamed National Lesbian Gay Task Force) urged a boycott of the *Monitor* by Broadway Theater organizations. NGTF Executive Director Virginia Apuzzo wrote to twenty New York theatrical companies and individuals asking them to boycott the Boston paper. In the letter Apuzzo noted the *Monitor* has fired several employees due to their sexual orientation.

According to Boston's *Gay Community News*:

> ...[T]he real impetus for the *Monitor* boycott...was the paper's response to an inquiry from George Furth, an award-winning playwright, and a longtime member of the Church. The paper's manager told Furth: "For a Church member to work in the headquarters of the organization that was founded 'to reinstate primitive Christianity,' as the Church *Manual* states, is to represent them uncompromisingly to the world. It just doesn't make sense for anyone who is unalterably committed to the gay lifestyle (and believes that the healing of homosexuality is neither possible nor desirable) to seek or expect employment in our Church organization...."

George Furth resigned his membership in The Mother Church on March 21, 1984.

The only other known action came from the American Friends Service Committee in Boston, which discontinued its advertising in the *Monitor* around this time due to the paper's discriminatory practices towards sexual minorities.

Within the lesbian/gay Christian Science world, the actions taken by GPICS/New York had a stirring effect. Many group members pondered this type of action and wondered if confrontation politics toward one's Church is the best recourse for a Christian Scientist, gay or non-gay. Some believed prayer alone to be the only standard for a Christian Scientist. Prayer, they conclude, is the only sure remedy for healing any ailment including chronic homophobia. Others contend it was their prayers that led them to take a position of confrontation.

Such was the meat of many discussions in the various lesbian/gay Christian Science groups. The controversy also spilled out onto the pages of the groups' newsletters.(8)

The debate is one that will no doubt go on as long as the standoff between gays and the Boston-centered Church of Christ, Scientist continues. Since the inception of the national organization for lesbian/gay Christian Scientists, however, the tendency has been to become much less emotionally involved with The Mother Church and its policies. In this way it has been possible for lesbian/gay Christian Scientists to understand more objectively what has happened in Boston since Mrs. Eddy's time while at the same time enriching their own spirituality.

Lesbian/gay Christian Scientists have begun to realize that the conditions in The Mother Church that have allowed officials to be so uncompromising against them are, in part, the same reasons that Christian Science itself may be lost in the near future. These include members idolizing the Board of Directors as, if not completely infallible, as having a better intuition of God's will than do rank and file Church members, Mrs. Eddy's teaching to the contrary notwithstanding.(9)

By mid-1983 few meetings were being held for lesbian/gay Christian Scientists among the five original groups. GPICS/Chicago appeared to be the most active group in the period, most likely due to its work on the National Conference for lesbian/gay Christian Scientists which it sponsored in July, 1983. When the various groups first began holding meetings, just the idea of having an organization for lesbian/gay Christian Scientists caused enough euphoria to sustain momentum. After a while it would take more than that to keep the groups alive. Internal problems also jeopardized the work of the local groups. This was particularly true for the three west coast groups.

When the organizers of the Seattle group first advertised their group's meetings, they placed ads in both local newspapers serving sexual minorities. Perhaps they didn't think through the fact that one of these papers was also distributed in Portland, Oregon. Soon, inquiries came from both Oregon and Washington states. This led to meetings being held weekly in each city. In addition, they arranged a monthly meeting for LGBT Christian Scientists from both states, with the host state going back and forth. This venue worked for awhile but soon proved too cumbersome to continue. Adding to the difficulties of meeting, dissention arose when GPICS/New York began asking all local groups for help in their efforts supporting the demonstrations at The Mother Church. Some in the Seattle group believed the activities New York proposed were too "militant" for their tastes. Much discussion came from the proposed demonstrations. In the end, Gay Christian Scientists in the Northwest did not get involved. But the dissention did hurt the group and its attendance.

Identity in San Francisco had "irreconcilable" differences between its women and men attendees. Eventually, the women left and set up a separate group.

The most disruptive dissentions took place in Los Angeles. For half a century, roughly 1900 to 1950, southern California was the site of the fastest growing area for Christian Science. Nowhere else in the world did the denomination take hold like it did there. At one time forty-five churches were listed in the Los Angeles area alone. Some of these branch churches could boast large, magnificent edifices. After the lesbian/gay group Emergence was born, it surprised no one that they had by far the largest attendance of any local group. Unfortunately, disagreements over confidentiality concerns caused an irreparable rift. When new officers were elected, they could not access membership and financial records. The result was that a majority of members left to form a new organization. While the new Emergence continued for awhile, it never attained the strength of the original group.

An important activity of the earliest groups was their newsletters. Responding to the example set by GPICS/New York, from 1979 to 1982 all five groups produced regular newsletters, usually on a monthly basis. These were exchanged not only with members within each group, but among the different groups as well. The newsletters included discussions of past meetings and plans for future get-togethers. They also included metaphysical articles and testimonies and well as information on local events. They were sometimes used as a sounding-board for responding to Church homophobia. The newsletters contributed to a sense of cohesion between groups as well as helping members maintain an interest in local activities.

Soon after Chris Madsen's court settlement with The Mother Church, in October 1985, GPICS/New York stopped holding meetings. About a year later, a lesbian/gay Christian Science study group was begun in New York City by Bob McCullough. As the name suggests, this group has been study only and has not involved itself in activism of any sort. This has become one of the most successful local groups in the country continuing to this day.

Groups would later form in other cities. The first city outside the original five where an in-depth organization developed in this period was Houston, Texas which began in 1983.(10) Other local groups that followed included, Atlanta, Phoenix, Washington, D.C., London, U.K.(11), and Toronto, Canada. Groups in Atlanta, Houston, Phoenix, and Washington D.C. also served as host for one of Emergence International's yearly conferences.

Local group meetings were almost always conducted informally. Readings were included from the Bible and the writings of Mary Baker Eddy. The main difference between these meetings and Church services in most groups was the discussion period. These often included testimonies of healing, but in most groups these were part of a greater discussion. Sometimes these centered around a chosen topic and sometimes not.

One of the events that caused momentary excitement in the groups was when one of the members was going through the process of excommunication from a branch Church. GPICS/New York had three members excommunicated early in its history and others elsewhere would be given the boot.

One of the tangible results of the lesbian/gay Christian Science movement was that it gave new resolve to group members. When one's sexual orientation was discovered by a branch church, the lesbian or gay member was more likely than ever to stand up to her/his accusers. While they were always turned out of the Church, the stereotype of the sad, effeminate, shame-ridden homosexual was shattered. Many opted to drag out the excommunication process to achieve maximum dialogue with branch church members. This must have caused some difficulty for them, as branch church members were not accustomed to dealing with this new breed of lesbians and gay men. The branch church congregations had to come to terms with their reasons for excommunicating a lesbian or gay member. Their response generally was to continue as before, taking Biblical quotes out of context. The mainstay verses usually came from the Biblical book of Leviticus. They did this in spite of Mrs. Eddy's aspersion on that antiquated book of Hebrew law.(12) Beyond this, many felt that it was not only wrong to invoke Leviticus because it was not inspired writing; they believed it was against their Leader's teaching to quote any Scripture in order to bar individual freedoms.

The Leader of Christian Scientists went on record in the final month of the 19th century to oppose use of the Bible as a means to curb individual freedom. She told the *New York World* that among "the most imminent dangers confronting the coming century are: the robbing of people of life and liberty under the warrant of the Scriptures...." This quotation was later included within her published writings.(13)

When the dust settled on the efforts GPICS/New York and others made in attempting to change discrimination policies in The Mother Church, it had become obvious their actions had little or no effect. Church officials knew the activists would not change many minds. They knew attendees at Annual Meeting were not likely to be swayed by a small group marching, shouting, and carrying signs. Although officials felt it proper to answer every letter in the orchestrated campaign protesting Chris Madsen's termination, its authorities gave no evidence of changing their opinions. If the activists among lesbian and gay Christian Scientists expected Mother Church officials to react as if they were publicly elected politicians, they were sorely mistaken. It would take a larger and more formalized effort to create a climate of justice in the Church of Christ, Scientist.

One who had a sense of how difficult it would be to create such a climate of justice in the Christian Science Church was Chris Madsen. She was also determined to do just that.

7

Chris Madsen's Trial

1982–1985

When the smoke of battle clears away, you will discern the good you have done, and receive according to your deserving.

—*S&H* page 22, lines 18–20

Throughout much of this history the Christian Science Church appeared immune from whatever actions sexual minorities contrived to affect its policies. Major letter writing campaigns, leafleting demonstrations, individual meetings with officials and the formation of support groups were having no significant effect. *What a let down!* GPICS/New York and its friends were saddened that the endless hours they worked to change Church policy seemed in vain. Worst of all, for them, there seemed no apparent way they could ever have a reasoned dialogue with their Church. In trying many ways to get that institution's attention they had run out of ideas. They could only foresee a continuation of the same homophobic policies continuing indefinitely.

Sometimes in mortal history it is the unexpected which causes eventual change. In this context no one was expecting Chris Madsen to be fired, though it always seemed a possibility. Beyond that, who would have imagined the young lesbian would play the role of David by taking on the mighty Goliath, the Christian Science Church, to court? In this time period this may have been the one thing and the only thing relating to lesbians and gays that had the potential to threaten the status-quo. This was a very real threat. One could almost hear the consternation it must have created in the chamber room of the Christian Science Board of Directors that a relatively young lesbian was taking on the Christian Science establishment. After all, Chris Madsen was asking not only for reinstatement with back pay, but for one million dollars in damages. To be sure, the Church was not unaccustomed to litigation. It had lived with courtroom drama since its inception. Many lawsuits were filed in Mrs. Eddy's time involving both her and her Church. The Church had developed a wealth of legal experience in confrontations over an individual's right to seek healing through spiritual means offered by Christian Science, as opposed to medical means. Chris Madsen's suit, on the other hand, opened a whole new legal arena.

Church authorities knew they must react. Because Chris Madsen was the first to challenge the Church for discrimination, they knew her case could set a precedent for or against the Church. What they needed was a plan that would protect them for the present as well as mitigate the possibility of future litigation by sexual minorities. How long they studied the situation is unknown. What is known is that they eventually came up with a counter-offensive. Their plan appeared to consist of three parts.

First, they had to confront Chris and her attorney in the courtroom by providing the strongest defense possible. *Second*, they sought to prevent lesbians and gays from being admitted as Church members and employees. If sexual minorities didn't get in the Church in the first place, they likely reasoned, there would be no one to protest in the future. *Third*, they would use whatever influence they had to stem the rights of lesbians and gays in the greater society wherever they thought they might affect The Mother Church and its employees and their right to terminate and not hire on the basis of sexual orientation.

The Directors probably began considering ways right away that would stem the numbers of lesbians and gays from gaining admittance to the Church. There was one problem. The *Manual* of The Mother Church governed the organization in all areas. The *Manual* had no provision that would allow the Church to discriminate on the basis of sexual orientation. There was no way for the Manual to be amended. The Bylaws in the governing *Manual* were written by Mrs. Eddy herself. She wrote them to govern the Church and its operations for all time. She had even gone as far as designing the membership applications. There was no legal way Church officials could modify or add to the applications. It is possible then, that significant time and energy were expended in finding a way to get around the *Manual*. But eventually, a way was found to codify discrimination against sexual minorities in Church law.

Twenty-two months following Chris Madsen's termination, a revised membership application packet was introduced to the Christian Science field. In October 1983, the packet was sent to all churches and reading rooms around the world, as well as those asking to join The Mother Church. The revised application packet contained a new provision. This was listed under a section titled, "*Information for Applicants and Approvers.*" The new phrasing read:

The standard in Christian Science includes freedom from promiscuity, adultery, and homosexuality.

By inserting this statement on a separate sheet of their own, "Information For Applicants and Approvers" the Church was sidestepping actual tampering with the application and the *Manual* itself.

Word of the new statement in the Church membership packet to applicants spread fast throughout the lesbian/gay Christian Science communities and their supporters. While adding "freedom from…homosexuality" to the application procedure wasn't a change in the Church's position, it did reflect a hardening of its resolve. Sexual minorities in the Church also found it sad that their sexual orientation was equated with promiscuity and adultery. Due to The Mother Church's proclivity not to dialogue or reason with anyone on this matter, the new application packet served primarily to widen the rift between GLBT Christian Scientists and their Church hierarchy. This was taken as one more sign of the Board's intransigence. Again, this drew attention to the Board itself and lesbian/gay Christian Scientists were asked through one of their newsletters to ponder the legality of the Directors' actions:

> The problem is not homophobia. The problem, much larger, is the Directors' usurpation of Mary Baker Eddy's role as Leader of the Christian Science movement….
>
> Their newest statement…is yet another flagrant arrogation of Mrs. Eddy's leadership. Under the Church *Manual* who besides Mrs. Eddy is empowered to set a "standard" for Christian Scientists? And not a word from her pen can ever remotely be construed to deny that homosexuality is a facet of our God-given nature….(1)

Another decision, as a reaction Church authorities made from being taken to court by Chris Madsen, was to work against political inroads lesbians and gays were making, especially as they might affect The Mother Church. The state of Massachusetts and the City of Boston would be the governing arenas for present and future legal matters re: GLBT persons. Fortunately, from the Church's point of view, these jurisdictions did not have protections for sexual minorities written into their laws. And the Church of Christ, Scientist appeared to want to keep it that way.

It has to be considered, therefore, as no small coincidence that efforts to extend legal redress to lesbians and gays against discrimination were then taking place in both the City of Boston and the State of Massachusetts. Church officials had to decide how to react.

What they decided to do was to put their Church's no small influence on the line. They would do whatever they could to either defeat any pro-gay rights legislation that they believed might affect the Church adversely. If they could not defeat a gay rights bill, then they would then work to water-down the measure by making churches exempt from them.

This stirring between gays and Church authorities, of course, was not at all limited to Christian Scientists. Victories and losses for lesbian/gay communities were occurring in many religious denominations as well as in countless secular political jurisdictions.

Lesbians, gays, and their supporters had a bill in the United States Congress since 1977 that, if passed into law, would amend the Civil Rights Act of 1964 to include "sexual orientation" alongside "race, color, creed, or national origin." The bill was making little headway in Congress. Lesbian/gay activists believed the bill would not have a chance until there were a number of states with a similar law. Getting a lesbian/gay rights law passed in a reasonable number of states appeared to be a Herculean feat, but activists saw no other way and pressed on toward that goal. The goal seemed only slightly more feasible in the early days of 1982 when Wisconsin Governor Lee Dreyfus, a Republican, signed the first-ever statewide gay rights bill into law. Then in 1984 a near miss in the nation's largest state, California, caused no small heartache for supporters of lesbian/gay rights. After intense work by activists, both houses of the Golden State's legislature passed the lesbian/gay rights bill, only to see it vetoed by Governor George Deukmejian, also a Republican.

Another state where a gay rights bill had a clear chance of passage was Massachusetts. Efforts to obtain such a law in the Commonwealth's legislature began in 1975 and continued every year since. On the tenth anniversary of its first introduction, lesbian/gay activists sensed a real possibility of passage. A full-time lobbyist, Peg Lorenz was hired to work for the bill. The legislature's Joint Committee on Commerce became a major battle ground for the bill as hearings were being arranged to air the issues it presented. Lorenz set up four hours of testimony in favor of the bill. This included one and a half hours of testimony from legislators who wanted to speak in its favor. Other speakers included: an aide to Massachusetts Governor Michael Dukakis, labor groups, women's groups and officials from the Unitarian-Universalist Church.

Testimony against the bill lasted only one hour. The hour was divided up between leaders from the Baptist and Christian Science churches. The Christian

Science Church worked to kill the bill, but failing that, they would seek to add an amendment which would exempt religious organizations. The vigor with which The Mother Church was pursuing this is reflected by Peg Lorenz who told Washington, D.C.'s gay newspaper, the *Blade* (April 5, 1985) "They [The Mother Church] have a full-time lobbyist who seems to dog my heels—every [legislator] I visit, he comes right behind."

The bill did not pass the Massachusetts State House in 1985. It would take another four years before the Bay State would become the nation's second state to free sexual minorities from legal discrimination.(2)

The City of Boston, however, was a different story. Support to ban discrimination based on sexual orientation was a given fact. So strong was its perceived strength that most opponents did not bother to show up at public hearings. That, however, did not deter the Church of Christ, Scientist. In that regard Boston's *Gay Community News* (*GCN*) reported on June 30, 1984:

> More than 40 people, representing political, social service, civil liberties and religious organizations...[spoke] in favor of a comprehensive human rights ordinance.
>
> A representative from the Christian Science Church was the only person to speak against the ordinance. "The Christian Science Church," he said, "recommended an amendment providing an outright exemption of churches from the requirements of the ordinance."

Of more immediate concern to the Christian Science Board of Directors, however, was Chris Madsen's lawsuit.

To represent her in court, Chris chose Katherine Triantafillou to be her Attorney. Although Triantafillou brought with her a significant background in having "worked on a number of cases dealing with gay rights," the most important feature may have been the deep respect the two women developed for each other. In describing Chris, her Attorney used words such as "ethical" and "dedicated." She was impressed with the extent and depth of "Chris's knowledge of Bible teachings." Ms Triantafillou said, "I was always impressed with her. Chris is a very special person." Chris was, of course, unique in being the only person known to have sued the Christian Science Church for discrimination based on sexual orientation. Triantafillou said her suit "was not a selfish gesture by any stretch of the imagination. She wanted most of all to create change."

In this regard Chris said of her decision to sue the Church,

I was not fighting for the money after all. I wanted to set in place my bricks that would make up the wall protecting the rights of lesbians and gay men.

Her Attorney, Katherine Triantafillou was all the while immersing herself in Christian Science. She and Chris had extensive talks about Bible teachings.

As mentioned above, Chris asked the Court for reinstatement with back pay and one million dollars in damages. The Mother Church attempted to thwart the suit in the Massachusetts Superior Court. The attempt failed. The Church then decided to appeal the ruling. The case was then put under the jurisdiction of the Massachusetts Supreme Judicial Court (SJC) for review. It wasn't until October 4, 1984 that oral arguments for both sides were aired.

Whenever it was necessary to provide a defense for its actions over the years, the Christian Science Church had relied on the First Amendment to the Constitution. This seemed to be what they perceived was their greatest strength. In this context it was no surprise that would be their course of action in upholding their discriminatory policies. When it came time to give oral argument for its position, Ted Dinsmore, attorney for The Mother Church told the Court:

> The Christian Science Church asserts its first Amendment right to make and implement employment policies on the basis of its religious beliefs. The Church requires employees to make a spiritual commitment to Christian Science.... Christian Science doctrine provides that homosexuality is immoral...."
>
> ...[T]he Church dismissed Madsen because of her immorality, or more specifically because of her refusal to seek healing.

Dinsmore pleaded with the SJC to put religious freedom above the right to freedom from discrimination in employment. "To rule otherwise would undermine the First Amendment right to institutional autonomy."

Apparently there was no attempt by Chris Madsen or her Attorney to show that Mrs. Eddy's teaching does not include a discriminatory disposition in relation to sexual orientation. Mrs. Eddy wrote, "The Sermon on the Mount is the essence of this Science..." (*S&H* page 271, lines 23–24). Yet nowhere is a same-gender orientation mentioned in this Sermon. Nor is it mentioned anywhere else in the recorded sayings of the Master, Christ Jesus. The same is true for all the published and (as far as is known), the non-published, writings of Mary Baker Eddy. The only proscriptions against same-gender sexuality in the Christian Science Church came from Church officials decades after Mrs. Eddy's passing. But this was not a position taken by Chris Madsen or her Attorney in their Court appearances.

Attorney, Katherine Triantafillou's reaction to The Mother Church's defense is that "they were beyond reproach, like, '*How dare we*' [try to sue the Church]?" She said they gave an "almost sarcastic response." And the parties remained cool to each other throughout the proceedings. Asked if any contact or conversation took place between her and The Mother Church Attorney or other Church officials outside the courtroom, she said, "Absolutely not!"

In the presentation of its case against Chris Madsen the Church may have reached its all-time low in presenting its active opposition to fairness and equality for those with a same-gender sexual orientation. The Founder of their Faith revealed how the Biblical book of Revelation allegorizes such behavior in God's name. In the Apocalypse the serpent is the term or symbol used to signify the devil.

> The serpentine form stands for subtlety, winding its way amidst all evil, but doing this in the name of good. Its sting is spoken of by Paul, when he refers to "spiritual wickedness in high places."(3)

Chris Madsen spoke of what may have been the proceedings lowest moment with "spiritual wickedness in high places,"

> I will never forget sitting in a courtroom while my lawsuit against the *Christian Science Monitor* was being heard. The Monitor's lawyer stood not ten feet from me, wagging his finger at me and trumpeting, *"She is a lesbian!"* [This] meant to signal the judge that I had no standing in the court. I have never felt so dirty. The dozen or so friends who were there with me had the same reaction.(4)

It appeared the Church was not only relying on the First Amendment to see them through the case. They were also counting on what they perceived was society's revulsion of same-gender attraction and sexuality to buttress their case. Nevertheless, the main hurdle for Chris's lawyer would be to prove why the First Amendment does not allow the Church to fire employees of the *Monitor* on the basis of sexual orientation. The only way, perhaps, would be to show that the *Monitor* is a secular publication. It would not be easy. When her time came, Triantafillou told the court,

I think Chris Madsen should not have been fired, and I think a secular court can examine the reasons and the manner in which she was discharged without offending either the Free Exercise clause or the Establishment clause of the First Amendment.

Our job today is to strike a proper balance between the types of interests that may or may not collide…[The Church's legal arguments were so] cloaked in liturgy that I am beginning to think that buying a copy of the *Monitor* is tantamount to accepting a communion wafer.

Chris Madsen is an exemplary employee whose only transgression in seven and a half years is to say the words "I am a lesbian."

The Church is involved in secular commercial activity by publishing an international daily newspaper….

Triantafillou went on to let the court know that the Church has other business enterprises, and these are in no way related to religious expression.

What if they undertake to evict the tenants of the many apartments they own in the Back Bay [neighborhood where The Mother Church is located], for immorality?(5)

Speaking of this approach, Triantafillou said, "We spent a lot of time separating the Church's activities and its religious teachings." What also made it difficult for Chris and her Attorney was that discrimination based on sexual orientation was not illegal at that time.

According to Boston's *GCN* (October 13, 1984) Triantafillou was working to overcome the fact that Massachusetts had no statewide employment protections based on sexual orientation. She was trying to establish that a "public policy" had existed in the state against such discrimination.

So the battle lines between freedom of religion and the right to employment without discrimination were drawn. It was not a clear-cut case. It would take the Supreme Judicial Court of Massachusetts another ten months to reach a verdict. At that time, on August 21, 1985, the Court ruled in favor of the Christian Science Church.

Justice Joseph Nolan, writing for the majority, found that the constitutional right of the Church to exercise its freedom of religion took precedence over Madsen's right to employment without discrimination.

However, the Court also made it clear to Chris and her Attorney she had alternative ways in which to sue the Church. This could be based on defamation of character, invasion of privacy, and/or intentional infliction of emotional distress.

This was not lost on Chris and her Attorney, as they again filed suit against The Mother Church. The charge they chose was invasion of privacy. Unfortunately, there is no publicly accessible information on these proceedings. They were all determined behind closed doors. As these deliberations were declared confidential, neither party has been allowed to discuss them. All that is known is that a settlement was reached, but its outcome cannot be made public. One of the conditions imposed on the settlement was that its conditions never be divulged.

In summing up their suit against The Mother Church, Attorney Katherine Triantafillou believed that the time period had much to do with prevailing attitudes. The year "1983 was very early in terms of activism, at least in the Boston area. [Our suit] was very cutting-edge at the time."

Several years after her trial, Chris reflected on her standing up to the Christian Science Church.

> As to whether I would do this [confront The Mother Church] again: Yes I would! They may have done it [terminated employment on the basis of sexual orientation] before me and may do it after me, but I wasn't going to let them get away with it.

Chris said she relied very heavily on her understanding of Christian Science during the trial and is convinced, "I did the right thing."

PART V

PERSEVERANCE AND VICTORY

○ ○

Love is the liberator.

—S&H page 225, line 21

8

The Christian Science Board of Directors

For this Principle [God] there is no dynasty, no ecclesiastical monopoly. Its only crowned head is immortal sovereignty. Its only priest is the spiritualized man. The Bible declares [Rev. 1:6] that all believers are made "kings and priests unto God."

—*S&H* page 141, lines 17–21

It is neither the purpose of this chapter, nor this book, to bash the Christian Science Board of Directors (Board). The temptation, of course, is strong. The Board is the highest authority in the non-democratic Mother Church. There are no checks and balances.

Would it be too simplistic to lay the blame for all Church ills with that five-member, self-perpetuating body?

No doubt it would. Perhaps there is a culprit more encompassing than the Board. It is suggested here that it might be the ages-old human proclivity to circumscribe spiritual authority in the trappings of human organization as well as human prerogative.

Mary Baker Eddy made her views well known about human authority in ecclesiastical areas, as well as human church organization in general. Her writings show a deep ambivalence in this area, as for example, in her autobiographical work, *Retrospection and Introspection*, page 45, she wrote:

Despite the prosperity of my church, it was learned that material organization has its value and peril, and that organization is requisite only in the earliest periods in Christian history.(1)

Whenever an idea is born, the temptation to give it human form, by building an organization around it, is so strong that the form often takes precedence over the idea itself. History provides countless examples. An obvious one is Christianity itself.

In an appendix to his book, *The Cross and The Crown*, Norman Beasley chronicles a "Brief History of the Early Christian Church." Beasley equates the desire and attainment of power among Church officials in its first 300 years as the main reason for the loss of spiritual healing.

> The Church had grown rich. Bishops were competing with each other in the splendor of their edifices…. With a zeal for converts that was only equaled by their avarice for authority, they reconciled all the vices of politics, and introduced them into the management of their churches. The spiritual was subordinated to the material, and healing was lost.(2)

Is it an oversimplification to say that history has repeated itself, comparing the Christian Science Church with the early Christian Church?

Perhaps it is. Certainly circumstances are such that Christian Science Church leaders did not get involved with temporal political authority as did early Christian Church leaders. Nor are there parallels that can be likened to the building of huge cathedrals, save The Mother Church itself and some ornate branch churches in large cities. But there may be some pertinent likenesses worth noting.

Setting forth her teaching in the denominational textbook, Mrs. Eddy boldly asserts, "For this Principle [God] there is no dynasty, no ecclesiastical monopoly…."(3) Perhaps unfortunately, most Christian Scientists seem to feel otherwise. The authority over its members that took the Christian bishops three hundred years to gain, the Christian Science Board of Directors (Board) attained in no more than two decades following Mrs. Eddy's passing. Again, the fault may lie more with the members' adulation for human organization. Over the last several decades Christian Scientists have looked to the Board as the final arbitrator for the meaning of sacred writings, organizational procedures in every facet of Church activity, and in defining members' conduct in highly personal areas.

Once allowed to serve as spokespersons, both the bishops in the early Christian Church and the Board began as leaders in administrative affairs only. Bishops and Board alike began as spiritual equals to the congregants they served. Beasley says the office of bishop in the first century was "the servant of the congregation. It held him accountable for all his acts and reposed in him no spiritual authority."(4)

Once the precedent to serve as arbiters for Mrs. Eddy's writings was established as a Board function, it was but a small step toward deciding appropriate behavior for Church members that was not included in the Church *Manual*. Instead of exhorting Church members to look away from personality as Mrs. Eddy had done by urging her followers to put on the Christ consciousness, the Board defined an array of "correct" behaviors. Therefore, the Board conducted its affairs believing that they, along with Mrs. Eddy, were empowered to set standards for Christian Scientists.

The feelings of lesbian/gay Christian Scientists toward The Mother Church and the Board in particular have been ambivalent. Lesbian/gay Christian Scientists in general seemed to agree to disagree on how The Mother Church and the Board should be dealt with, if at all.

Many felt it made no difference. As the Church did not show a desire for change, then why bother with it? Some believed the Church was a dying institution. They contended the only salvation for their religion was among independent Christian Scientists and their organizations.(5) This is where they believed their energy would be best served. Others averred that organization itself is the culprit. Putting Christian Science teachings in the trappings of human organization, they believed, has a suffocating and debilitating effect. Still others took a directly opposite view. They held the conviction that no matter what happened in the past, their Church *could* heal itself of homophobia and other sins and move on. Some of these sexual minorities were active in both The Mother Church and a local branch church. Some cited progress by the Church in overcoming racial divisions. They recalled the days when African-American practitioners and branch churches composed of the same minority had no choice but to accept the stigmatizing label "Colored" beside their listing in the *Christian Science Journal*. Practitioners had the further stigmatization of having had to live with the word "Colored" on their office doors. In that period African-Americans were not given jobs at The Mother Church higher than janitor, regardless of their education. Nor were they allowed in the sanatoriums owned and operated by The Mother Church.(6) In time, it is averred, the Church "healed" itself of racism.

Critics of that reasoning say the Church never really had a healing. Societal pressure from the outside forced the Boston-based Church to change policies when the nation-as-a-whole made progress in race relations. They pointed to South Africa where even Christian Scientists were segregation-minded until fairly recently, implying that changes in policies have nothing to do with Church enlightenment.

In another area, Church policy made a substantial change, once again bowing to societal pressure. Fluoridation of the public drinking water became an issue for the Church in the early 1950's when the scientific community said adding fluoride to the public drinking water would reduce tooth decay. The Christian Science Church saw this as a means by their government of forcing individuals to take medicine without their consent. Christian Scientists, therefore, led the fight against having fluoride introduced in the public water supply. In some communities they proved able to prevent that from happening.(7)

In time, however, the Church became a pariah on the issue. The Christian Science position was widely criticized. By the middle to late 1960's, little was heard from the Church on this issue.

While I never saw or heard a general announcement, there was a definite shift in policy. One evening at a branch (local) church meeting in the early 1970's, a state Committee on Publication Manager said substantially,

> We don't concern ourselves with opposing fluoridation anymore. The Church does not feel it right to prevent those who want it in their water supply from having it.

There was no known organized opposition to the Church's position on fluoridation within The Mother Church organization, but it is possible that individual Church members told their officials the havoc their position was creating in their communities.

These situations may give us clues as to how the Board works. The fluoridation issue didn't bring about any significant known divisions within the Church membership. All criticism appeared to be outside the Church. The same is largely true for racial issues. No doubt there were murmurings within the denomination before racist practices were eliminated. But these were isolated and unorganized. It was society as-a-whole in both cases that created the change. It may have followed then that if the Church were to renounce its anti-lesbian/gay policies, society must first lead the way. This was in spite of Allison Phinney's pronouncement, "The Church simply believes that society doesn't make the rules for Christians."(8) This would seem to imply that lesbian/gay Christian Scientists and their supporters were wasting their time trying to have the Church change at a time when society was not yet ready to give them carte blanche rights.

Another parallel within the history of The Mother Church might serve to confirm this. As far as is known, only one minority group, apart from lesbians and gays, organized themselves to support their interests within the larger denomination. These were conscientious objectors. Like lesbian/gay groups, pacifist organizations came about because they perceived themselves as a persecuted minority among Church members. Church historian Charles S. Braden tells us that

> Christian churches in general moved in the direction of pacifism during the interval between world wars one and two. As war clouds became darker prior to the second world conflict, churches made provisions for their young male adherents to classify themselves as conscientious objectors. Churches also successfully lobbied the government to provide non-military alternative service resulting in the Civilian Public Service Camps.(9)

The Church of Christ, Scientist was not one of the denominations supporting conscientious objectors. Quite the contrary. The Mother Church went out of its way to deny its pacifist adherents the right to claim their religion as reason for their unwillingness to participate in war. In spite of this, some draft age Christian Scientists defiantly declared their pacifism was in line with Mrs. Eddy's teachings. They quoted statements from her that would lend support to a pacifist position.(10)

With the emerging clouds of World War II on the horizon, pacifist Christian Scientists banded together creating local groups that would further their ideas and support the pacifist adherent of Mrs. Eddy's writings. They did this by lobbying The Mother Church with their views, publishing newsletters and holding meetings. Charles Braden describes these efforts as small and "definitely opposed by the Board of Directors." As far as is known, these pacifist organizations were the only groups created within the larger Christian Science movement to advocate a minority position until lesbian/gay support groups were formed nearly four decades later.

As firm as the Board of Directors' position was in opposition to the pacifist viewpoint, it is noteworthy that society could even here affect attitudes on the "correct" position for Christian Scientists. The Board's position was modified when the citizenry of the USA turned more and more against our country's involvement in the Vietnam war.

By January of 1970, with violent opposition to America's Vietnam adventure tearing our populace apart, the Board softened its public position by declaring in the *Christian Science Sentinel* (Vol. 72, page 24) that

> the Christian Science Church does not enjoin on its members either support of, or opposition to, military action as an instrument of national policy.

The crux of any discussion on policy-making by the Christian Science Board of Directors is whether or not that Body has the right to make such regulations. Was it Mary Baker Eddy's decision to give the Board all the power that she herself had in deciding policy for her Church? The answer to this question is critical. It would determine whether the Board has a right to legislate in matters of sexual orientation, Church membership, and other issues. With Mrs. Eddy not here to answer for herself, getting a feel for her design for her Church is difficult. Some are working to prove that she meant for The Mother Church to dissolve following her passing. This view is based on her *Manual* directive that the Directors "shall fill a vacancy occurring on the Board *after* the candidate is approved by the Pastor Emeritus [Mrs. Eddy]" [emphasis added]. This and other estoppel clauses would, according to this reasoning, prevent Mother Church business from taking place after Mrs. Eddy's demise.(11)

Another way to look for Mrs. Eddy's intentions is to learn what those who knew her well thought about those matters. At this point none of those who lived with the denomination's Founder are with us. The only place to extrapolate such information from them would be to search their writings. Perhaps there is much to be found on this, and perhaps too, this is one reason the Board of Directors did not permit even members from having access to the archives of their own Church. These archives contain a wealth of unpublished writings by Mary Baker Eddy. They also contain intimate glimpses about her from writings of those who lived with her and knew her best. Some revealing insights, however, of the Board's attitudes in the early years of the Church can also be gleaned from so-called authorized sources. A speech given by Adam Dickey in The Mother Church to the Committee on Publication, October 1921 is a good example. Dickey was Mrs. Eddy's chief administrative officer from 1908 to 1910. He was also her last appointment to the Church's Board of Directors, a position he held for fourteen years.

Actions of the Board even as recent as 1921, the same year the Directors won a major power struggle against the Board of Trustees, are believed by Dickey to have little concern for the personal life of Church members. Its conduct is more in line with Mrs. Eddy's teaching, "For this Principle [God] there is...no ecclesiastical monopoly...Its only priest is the spiritualized man." (*S&H* 141:17–19) Dickey told the Committees on Publication:

> The Board of Directors has been charged with certain responsibilities, which they must carry out. For instance, one of the By-laws in the *Manual* [Article I, Section 6] states, "The business of The Mother Church shall be transacted by

its Christian Science Board of Directors." This does not mean that the Directors are at liberty to inflict their will or their desire upon the Christian Science movement. Indeed, the very opposite is true. The movement could not endure if the Directors should arbitrarily undertake to tell the members of The Mother Church how to conduct themselves. This must needs be a question of individual demonstration with which the members of the Board of Directors have no personal responsibility.(12)

There are other areas where some feel the Board has gradually assumed too much control. One of these is dictating to Church members what is appropriate and inappropriate reading matter. During Mrs. Eddy's lifetime an attempt was made to let Christian Scientists know what literature dealing with their denomination originated from their Church, and what did not. Apparently a great deal of literature was being circulated about Christian Science that did not originate in the Church. This may have led to confusion particularly with new members, and in 1891, just about every member was new. To resolve the "problem" a Church committee was organized. It was called "The General Association for Dispensing Christian Science Literature" (GADCSL). It would let members know which literature was Church originated and which was not. The new committee's purpose, nevertheless, was not to tell members what they could or could not read. An official of The Mother Church, William G. Nixon, announced the new committee in the *Christian Science Journal,* May 1891. Official Eddy biographer, Robert Peel wrote that the Christian Science Leader strongly opposed the activities of the new committee from the start.

> When [Mrs. Eddy] finally realized that the organization was set up to prevent the circulation of unauthorized literature among Christian Scientists quite as much as to distribute authorized literature to non-Scientists, she was *greatly distressed.* To Nixon, who had supported the scheme and wrote the announcement for the *Journal,* Mrs. Eddy wrote:
> "Can it be that one who has written to me as you have on oppressive measures used in our Cause could have done this?
> I will rip up my business relations and take all into my hands before this *most wicked, proscriptive, unchristlike* measure shall be carried.
> I never read the May *Journal* and never knew till now the *curse* in this platform of Stetson's."(13) [All emphasis added.]

According to Church historian Norman Beasley, "News of the indiscretion came to Mrs. Eddy's ears in June, and in the July issue of the *Journal* she published this 'card':

Since my attention has been called to the article in the May Journal, I think it would have been wiser not to have organized the "General Association for Dispensing Christian Science Literature....

I consider my students as capable, individually, of selecting their own reading matter, as a committee would be chosen for this purpose. [Emphasis added.]

I shall have nothing further to say on this subject, but hope my students' conclusion will be wisely drawn, and tend to promote the welfare of those outside, as well as inside this organization.(14)

There is no known record that Mrs. Eddy brought this subject up again. There was no further attempt by Mother Church officials to control members' choice of reading material as long as Mrs. Eddy was here. After her demise however, The Mother Church instituted what is called "Authorized Literature of The First Church of Christ, Scientist." While the activities of GADCSL were limited to letting members know the origin of works about Christian Science, the policy on "authorized literature" was more encompassing. It actually told members what they could and could not read pertaining to Christian Science. In essence it censored reading material for Church members. This took on its most negative form when church officials in some communities tried to remove "unauthorized" books and literature from public libraries. The over-riding difference this time was that Mrs. Eddy was not here to intervene.(15)

In governing various activities of the Church there has been a gradual increase of control over the activities of the branch churches and other activities. Christian Science college and university organizations provide us with a good example. In regard to college organizations, the Church *Manual* provides for the activity, but says nothing about its "precise form and content." In the early years of the Church, it was felt that the "precise form and content" of meetings should be left to the individual college or university organization to be worked out.(16) In time, The Mother Church assumed responsibility of deciding for these groups the exact order of their meetings and a vast array of rules governing their activities. Today there are periodic field trips from the College Organization Division of the Department of Branches and Practitioners to the campus of every *Journal*-listed organization. There are also biennial conferences in Boston for those who attend colleges and universities, the "precise form and content" of which, is planned by Church officials.

Negative treatment towards lesbian/gay Christian Scientists by the Board made it easier for many sexual minorities to concede malfeasance in other areas of ecclesiastical affairs such as the ones described above as well as the more recent revelations brought out in the letters by Reginald Kerry.

The lesbian/gay Christian Science groups that came into being in the late 1970's were probably no more than a minor irritation to the Board. This did not prevent the groups from being a powerful force in the lives of individual lesbian/gay Christian Scientists. For one thing the groups helped a number of LGBT Christian Scientists maintain an interest in the writings of Mary Baker Eddy regardless of how they were treated by their Church. With their self-identification as a Christian Scientist intact, many were able to find spiritual solutions free from ecclesiastical controls. Many were able for the first time to discuss denominational controversies in a free and open atmosphere with like-minded Christian Scientists. In all groups, individuals were not only free, but encouraged, to form their own opinions regarding controversies in the Church of Christ, Scientist as well as to determine what Christian Science meant to them. Many felt this to be so liberating they could maintain their allegiance to Mary Baker Eddy without worrying what another individual or organization felt about their progress as a Christian Scientist. In this regard they could take no small comfort from their Leader's opening words in her published sermon, *The People's Idea of God*.

> The great element of reform is not born of human wisdom; it draws not its life from human organization; rather it is the crumbling away of material elements from reason, the translation of law back to its original language Mind, and the final unity between man and God.(17)

Through all this, lesbian/gay Christian Scientists began to see that ecclesiastical discrimination against them was only symptomatic of a larger evil in the Church. Some were led to believe that the Board had usurped far more power than it was ever intended for them to have.

Nevertheless, it was not the purpose of lesbian/gay Christian Science groups to take a position on any controversial subject, except those dealing specifically with lesbian/gay issues. The groups occasionally saw themselves as forums where controversial issues in the Church could be researched and openly discussed. Again, members were not only free, but encouraged to reach their own conclusions through study and prayer.

While many lesbian/gay Christian Scientists relished the freedom to chart their own spiritual journey, they found it difficult, if not impossible, for them to influence Church direction in any way. This seemed to show that those sexual minorities and their supporters, who still wished to work through the existing Church structure, had enormous challenges before them. Perhaps the best advice to them would be to follow the example of their Leader. In a human sense, she had monumental challenges of her own to face.

> To-day, though rejoicing in some progress, she still finds herself a willing disciple at the heavenly gate, waiting for the Mind of Christ.(18)

9

"That City of Ceaseless Enterprise"

1979–1985

Chicago is the wonder of the western hemisphere.

—*Misc.* page 275: line 26

Jim Huer, a Chicago native, was enjoying his stay in New York City. He especially wanted to learn more about Greenwich Village's famed lesbian/gay neighborhood. When he came to the Oscar Wilde Memorial Book Shop, he decided to go in and have a look around. In time, his eyes fell on the novel, *You Can't Ride the Subway*, by Madge Reinhardt. Leafing through the book, he was surprised by its contents. As a Christian Scientist he was not accustomed to seeing dilemmas in The Mother Church discussed in situational settings that a novel provides. As he glanced through the pages, he learned of a woman censored by The Mother Church and prevented from continuing to write for the Christian Science periodicals due to her playwriting with homoerotic content. Jim bought the book.

He continued reading on his return trip to Chicago. As he read, he became deeply impressed. Once home, he penned a letter to Madge Reinhardt telling her "how much your book meant to me."

A grateful Madge Reinhardt put Jim Huer in touch with Craig Rodwell and other members of GPICS/New York. From this connection, Jim learned about the activities of GPICS/New York and their planned confrontations against The Mother Church's homophobia and other projects.

Jim was inspired by the New York group of LGBT Christian Scientists. He soon began to wonder if he could form a similar group in Chicago. He decided to put an ad in Chicago's *Gay Life* newspaper. Due to Jim's ad, it wasn't long before he came to know other Christian Scientists in his city with a same-gender orientation. Gay People in Christian Science/Chicago (GPICS/Chicago) was organized in the fall of 1979. It was instantly a success. In time GPICS/Chicago became as important to the early movement of lesbian/gay Christian Scientists as did the Windy City to the early history of Christian Science itself. With the advent of the lesbian/gay movement and especially the establishment of lesbian/gay Christian Science groups on each coast, it was only a matter of time until the process began in the city that meant so much to the early history of the denomination.(1)

Due to Jim Heuer's groundwork and the work of others, GPICS/Chicago soon became one of the most active and influential groups for lesbian/gay Christian Scientists in the country.

After the excitement of the demonstrations in New York, and little else to spark interest, the lesbian/gay Christian Science groups were at an impasse. They were clearly on their way out. By 1983 only GPICS/Chicago and Emergence/Houston were holding regular meetings. Something to generate interest was needed. Yet as far as can be determined, it was not the state of the lesbian/gay Christian Science groups that prompted those in the Windy City to come up with the idea for a national conference. It came about after one of its members lamented, "As gays, most of us are unable to go to our association meetings."(2) Out of this discussion came the idea for developing an "association type experience."

What the "association type experience" ultimately became was the First National Lesbian/Gay Christian Science Conference. GPICS/Chicago made the decision to organize and host it. With purposeful duty, the group got busy. One of the first arrangements was to find a keynote speaker. This was followed by a general announcement of the Conference to other lesbian/gay Christian Science groups.

The idea of a Conference began to take on a sense of reality when the first letter of its announcement went to lesbian/gay Christian Scientists throughout the country on March 21, 1983.(3) Just as the earliest adherents of the denomination held their first national gathering in Chicago (June 13, 1888), so did its lesbian/gay component 95 years later. For all who attended the Conference, it would be a novel experience, even for elderly life-long Christian Scientists.

On balance, the First National Conference of Lesbian/Gay Christian Scientists was a success. Though attendance was disappointingly low, participants came from many regions of the country. Seen in retrospect, the opportunity for networking over a four-day period, may have been the very key to keeping the movement alive. While there was no known mention of an attempt to create a national organization, the face-to-face encounters may have planted the seeds. It was beginning to be evident that few groups could maintain their own local organization with regular meetings and newsletters. Also folks attended from communities too small to even think of supporting a group of lesbian/gay Christian Scientists.

The Conference began on Friday night when attendees were welcomed at an outdoor roof-top party. The Conference hosts had invited a number of guests from the local lesbian/gay communities especially members in the local Good Shepherd Metropolitan Community Church (MCC). One attendee recalled, while it was a nice party, there were so many MCC members present, it was difficult finding other Christian Scientists, which was the purpose of the affair.

Saturday morning the Conference began in earnest. The meetings were held at Wellington Avenue United Church of Christ which is also used by Good Shepherd MCC.

The first-ever National Conference of lesbian/gay Christian Scientists was opened by James Barr. He warmly welcomed everyone on behalf on GPICS/Chicago. He then introduced Richard Whittiker to the podium. Richard told the gathering that the primary purpose of the Conference was to share love and ideas with Christian Science as the common binder. Then he introduced the Conference Keynote Speaker, Madge Reinhardt.

The Keynote Address by Madge Reinhardt was the heart of the Conference. Reinhardt was somewhat known by lesbian/gay Christian Scientists around the country. She had written a series of novels exposing, in her own way, some of the problems of the Christian Science Church. Her books include a discussion of the Church's ostracism of sexual minorities, and she found a delighted readership among many lesbian/gay Christian Scientists. In her keynote speech, "Open the Gates of the Temple," Madge Reinhardt addressed one of the main concerns lesbians and gays had with their Church.

> Are the gates of the temple closed? And if so, is there a special service gay people who are Christian Scientists can offer in opening them? Certainly we know that gay people understand gay people—a persecuted people in most churches and in much of society today—and can help open the gates of the temple to the gay community. That is live your understanding in the gay community....

In closing she said:

Your special mental and spiritual gifts are doing much to shock a church culture into the sensitivity and wholeness it needs if its gates to mankind are to be reopened. We cannot know precisely how changes will come, but your very being and gifts are important in the present ferment of a great religious movement. In Clara Shannon's memoirs, Mrs. Eddy is quoted as having said, "If we are misjudged, persecuted, it is a sure sign we are ascending the Mount." This must inspire you to go forward, up a steep and rugged hill.(4)

Other conferees addressed what was considered in 1983 as the most significant issues of the time. In addition to Ms. Reinhardt's talk, five attendees addressed the Conference. The talks gave a metaphysical response to major concerns in the larger sexual minority communities. These included aging and a new disease that was decimating the gay community. The Conference closed following a panel discussion and general rap session on activism.(5)

It was hoped that lesbian/gay Christian Scientists in a different city would continue the work Chicago had begun by sponsoring a national conference in 1984.

Apparently, no other group of lesbian/gay Christian Scientists was stable enough at this point to take the ball and host a such a meeting. No conference was held in 1984.

With the lesbian/gay movement going nowhere in the mid-1980s, the members of Chicago/GPICS saw themselves once more as the only group capable of getting something going. It was decided by the Windy City group to sponsor a second conference in their city. After all, Chicago is somewhat geographically central to the rest of the country. A new announcement went out early in 1985 that a conference would be held in Chicago over Columbus Day weekend.

The second conference saw the beginning of a marked change in attitude by many lesbians and gays toward an older institution: the Christian Science Church. The first conference in 1983 was centered on the idea of activism, so strong in the hearts of many who attended. Its central focus was the theme of its keynote speaker: "Open the Gates of the Temple." Lesbian/gay Christian Scientists, along with other members of their denomination, had been ingrained with the idea that The Mother Church and Christian Science are nearly one in the same. All were taught that the Church was the mouthpiece for everything Christian Science stood for. There were, of course, dissidents since Mrs. Eddy's day and offshoots that tried to rival The Mother Church, but these were ineffective. Their very failure to survive was offered as "proof" of the correctness of the Boston-based Church in all matters relating to Christian Science. It was only natural, therefore, for lesbian/gay Christian Scientists to want to work through the existing Church organization. But that was only true for most of the members in the earliest days of the lesbian/gay Christian Science groups. Group members soon learned to cherish the freedom and open discussion that had been denied them in their churches. Now they were introduced to concepts such as the independence movement in their denomination. They also became aware of the vast amount of writings on Christian Science their Church had tried to hide from them. These included memoirs of Mrs. Eddy written by those who had lived in her household. They began to see how a small number of people in Boston could determine all Church policy without taking account of how rank and file members felt. By the 1980's there were several groups of individuals and organizations teaching Christian Science apart from the movement centered in Boston. The second national conference abetted this awareness. Instead of focusing on how to "Open the Gates of the Temple," the second conference dramatized the belief that as a spiritual entity, church is not a place where one person gives another person permission.

> The cornerstone of church is self-determination and self-government—in a word, democracy. Christian Science provides the freedom to think and act from the standpoint of the individual's highest sense of right, unfettered by external authority. In that bond of love which is real church, there is no totalitarianism, no ecclesiastical despotism, no vaticanization of Christian Science. "...[M]an's individual right of self-government" [*S&H* page 447, line 2] is both the foundation and superstructure of real church thinking.

So spoke Kentner Scott(6) in his conference address: *"Mary Baker Eddy's Vision of Church."*

The work to establish a national organization was not part of the planned agenda. The formal part of the conference was held Friday and Saturday. The agenda provided for open-ended discussions Sunday afternoon for those who might remain in town. Several stayed. The conference organizers, however, rented a hall for Friday and Saturday only. With no place to go for the Sunday afternoon meetings, one member of GPICS/Chicago, said, "Well, you can use my hairdressing salon."

Once the Sunday meeting got underway, a discussion ensued about forming a national organization. When the time came to vote, representatives from around the country sitting on barber chairs voted "aye." The second decision made was that its name would be "Emergence: Gay People in Christian Science."(7) And so lesbian/gay Christian Scientists then and there founded their national organization. If its birthplace wasn't exactly "cradled obscurity"(8), it was, at least, an out-of-the-ordinary and unexpected setting. The historic locale is 4702 North Damen Avenue, Chicago.

One of the first activities of the new organization was to develop a publication. Its newsletter *Emerge!* (originally called *Emergence*) evolved from a few stapled pages to a serious magazine with a professional format.(9) Its editor was Kentner Scott.

Apart from resources offered by Emergence, the attitudes of lesbian/gay Christian Scientists were also being formed by many other organizations. A number of independent groups and individuals were writing newsletters and selling books about Christian Science that were banned by the Boston Church. Most Christian Scientists were growing up being told it is wrong to read books and other reading material that are labeled "unauthorized" by the Church. Emergence helped bring these ostracized writings to the attention of individual members at annual conferences and through the organization's publications. This was particularly true of the works of early writers in the Christian Science movement. These early writers included Mary Baker Eddy herself, and her students. By focusing on the spiritual needs of the members as to promoting their individual growth, Emergence became a highly valuable resource for many in their study of Christian Science. It especially became highly supportive for members on issues relating to sexual orientation. The newly created national organization, "Emergence: Gay People in Christian Science" (later changed to "Emergence Inc." and still later "Emergence International") stayed clear of confrontation with the Boston Church. The attitude reflected a growing feeling among some members that the human expression of Church was not essential for them to live and practice Christian Science. The Boston organization was becoming irrelevant in the experience of more and more lesbian/gay Christian Scientists. Emergence also saw itself as apolitical. This attitude was reflected in the organization's guidelines for maintaining a local chapter.

> POLITICAL ACTIVITY: Collective attempts to influence The Mother Church or the political process are not part of the mission of EMERGENCE or its chapters. (See *No and Yes* [by Mrs. Eddy] page 9: lines 8–13) Members are free to take individual action they feel to be right.

The third National Conference of lesbian/gay Christian Scientists (Houston, October 10–12, 1986) was the first held under the auspices of the national organization, Emergence. The theme of the Conference was "Emerge gently" (*S&H* page 485, line 14 and *Message for 1901*, page 10, line 27).

Emergence International (EI) did not dictate to its members how they should, or should not, relate to The Mother Church. What EI did see itself as being was a support organization and a forum for the exchange of ideas and information. *Emerge!* magazine published links to other independent Christian Science groups and resources in every issue. While EI members were not only free, but encouraged to explore other independent groups, EI itself developed neither formal nor loose ties with any of them.

Meanwhile, EI kept growing(10) Its conferences became more sophisticated sometimes with big name attractions.(11) For awhile, local chapters would be added to the fold, including two outside the United States: Toronto, Canada and London, U.K. In time, however, EI's Coordinating Council (Board) would disavow responsibility for local chapters. Local groups might be encouraged by the international organization, but they would be legally separate entities, even though some of them would use the name Emergence/(local city) to identify themselves.

With lesbian/gay Christian Scientists no longer lobbying and clamoring on an organized basis to change discriminatory practices in the Church, it would appear that the possibility of finding acceptance in the Boston organization would become even more tenuous.

From the Church's point of view the attitude of lesbian/gay Christian Scientists always seemed irrelevant. If a potentially successful dialogue were to come about with the Church, such a pro-lesbian/gay advocate would require significant clout just to be credible. Clout or not, The Mother Church's position on same-gender sexuality appeared to be chiseled in stone. If it proved impossible for lesbian/gay Christian Scientists to effect a credible challenge to the Church's position, it may have appeared even more unlikely for its Board to heed serious attention to any person(s) or organization(s) that were not Christian Scientists. But as improbable as that may have seemed, that is exactly what happened.

10

The Healing Begins

1985–1990

Justice waits,…and right wins the everlasting victory.

—*Misc.* page 277, lines 10 to 12

Charles Linebarger was concerned. The reporter for San Francisco's gay newspaper, *Bay Area Reporter* (*BAR*) just learned the local public radio station, KQED, had recently added Monitor Radio to its broadcasting lineup. This was a daily program of national, world news and commentary produced by the *Christian Science Monitor*. Like many gay activists, Linebarger saw the *Monitor* as an anti-lesbian/gay publication. He recalled that it discriminated in its employment policies against sexual minorities.

KQED already was on the defensive with the lesbian/gay communities. Activists had leveled charges at it for neither having an openly lesbian or a gay man on its Board of Directors nor on its 26-member advisory panel.

Believing he must act, Linebarger telephoned KQED. His call was directed to Program Manager Carol Pierson. Linebarger reminded Pierson about the *Monitor*'s blatant discrimination policy as evidenced by Chris Madsen's firing, only a few years before. Therefore, he insinuated, KQED should not air Monitor Radio. Carol Pierson told him she was sympathetic to his concerns. On the other hand, she said she was unable to remove Monitor Radio from her station's programming. This left Charles Linebarger(1) to consider other options if he wanted Monitor Radio out of KQED's airtime.

Carol Pierson knew about the *Christian Science Monitor*'s personnel policies. She was living in the Boston area and working for Boston's Public Radio station WGBH in 1982. This was the very time Chris Madsen was terminated from the *Monitor*. Pierson knew the newspaper was well known on its home turf and was highly regarded by New Englanders in general. No doubt it was her familiarity

138

with the *Monitor's* high level of journalistic endeavor, that made her receptive to including the program at KQED.

This was not a clear-cut case for Carol Pierson. Although she is openly lesbian, her main concern stemmed from the *Monitor's* being backed by a church. KQED was uncomfortable broadcasting a program that was influenced by a church. She had only come to KQED a few months before she decided to put Monitor Radio on the air in October 1985. Now she had to battle not only her own misgivings, but also she had to face whatever strategies Linebarger would employ against KQED.

What Charles Linebarger decided to do was alert San Francisco's sexual minority communities with a series of articles in *BAR* about KQED's newest broadcast venture. He reminded them of the homophobic policies of the *Christian Science Monitor*. So strong were his feelings that it became an issue on which his newspaper would not let up. Furthermore, *BAR* urged the lesbian/gay communities, as well as straight supporters of sexual minority rights, to write letters directly to the *Monitor* to protest its discriminatory position. Finally, Linebarger himself sought to contact authorities at the *Christian Science Monitor* and he did so directly by telephone. In this way he learned for himself just how intractable they were.

When he phoned the *Monitor's* offices in Boston, he was connected with Paul Daugherty, the Public Broadcasting Activities Manager for Monitor Radio. In their conversation Daugherty told him hundreds of letters have been received complaining about Monitor Radio's refusal to hire lesbians and gays. Daugherty added that because same-gender relations are based on "animal gratification" sexual minorities could never work for Monitor Radio.

If Charles Linebarger's purpose was to get an unambiguous statement of homophobia from a policy-making Church official responsible for Monitor Radio, Daugherty gave him exactly what he needed. While Linebarger listened, Daugherty told him why sex between persons of the same-gender is more sensual than that between a husband and wife. Gays, according to Daugherty, can never experience love at a higher spiritual level.

These unyielding statements from a spokesperson at Monitor Radio, led Charles Linebarger, and soon San Francisco's lesbian/gay communities, to adopt a totally uncompromising position toward Monitor Radio and equally important, its Bay Area outlet: KQED.

Faced with the threat of retaliatory action from the Bay Area's lesbian/gay communities, officials at KQED would not stop carrying Monitor Radio. They understood this would cause an almost certain exacerbation of their existing difficulties with the sexual minority communities. This they did in spite of their own pronouncements that discrimination based on sexual orientation is morally wrong. To back this up, however, the station made another decision. They decided they would do all they could to change Monitor Radio's discriminatory policy. This would not be a meaningless gesture. KQED would follow through on its decision. The highest officials at the radio station sought to work directly with appropriate officials at the Christian Science headquarters in Boston. Fortunately for KQED, officials at the Church were receptive to the radio station's request for a dialogue.

It wasn't long, therefore, before correspondence began to flow between KQED and officials at Monitor Radio. To further augment their decision, the public radio station asked for face-to-face meetings. It is significant that Monitor Radio agreed. Given the many years of futile confrontations between gays and the Christian Science Church over the issue of discrimination, these efforts by KQED may have seemed useless. Nevertheless, the Bay Area's public radio station felt it had no choice but to pursue a dialogue.

Face-to-face meetings were held at the Christian Science headquarters in Boston, as well as at KQED's studios in San Francisco.

Finding the right place for its broadcasting to fit the over-all objectives of the greater Church organization may have caused some difficulty for Christian Science officials. If so, concerns raised by KQED over the Church's posture could only have added to their challenge.

Historical Perspective

Radio was not in use in Mrs. Eddy's lifetime. Therefore, she left no guidelines for her Church about its use. With the advent of radio broadcasting, however, her Church eventually reached out through the new medium. From the mid-1940's to the mid-1970's, the Church was involved with some type of radio broadcasting. This included religious programming(2) as well as secular news broadcasting.(3)

Starting in the mid-seventies, the Christian Science Church no longer engaged in on-going broadcasting. But in 1983 the decision was made once again to carry a news program in the *Monitor's* name.

The decision by the Church to re-implement broadcasts for news analysis appears to have been part of a larger plan to mitigate the dwindling number of readers for its newspaper, the *Christian Science Monitor*. The *Monitor's* high water mark in circulation was 240,000 in the early 1970's. Within ten years, its subscribers plummeted to 150,000.(4) The overall plan to improve circulation in the early 1980's included changes in key personnel. Chief among the changes was a new manager, John H. Hoagland, Jr. and Editor, Katherine W. Fanning. Other changes included merging the *Monitor's* four regional editions into one copy for the entire country, including advertising. In 1983, when the decision was made to produce Monitor Radio, the median age of its readers was 60. The paper had a deficit of $10 million the previous year on revenue of $30 million. This would be enough to kill many papers. But as part of a much larger organization, the Christian Science Church, the newspaper was seen as a mission that must continue at all costs.

Since 1978 the Church had an endowment fund as a means for members to contribute to the newspaper's stability. The endowment fund reached $20 million by 1983. Nevertheless, it was the intention of the Church to make the *Monitor* pay for itself. Its then new manager, John H. Hoagland, Jr. told the *Wall Street Journal* (*WSJ*) "Over most of its life, the *Monitor* has operated as a break-even proposition. We want to return to that." "To return to that," the *Monitor* would have to significantly increase both readership and advertising. In some 1983 issues, advertising space was down as low as 25% according to *WSJ*, "well below the 62% average for U. S. newspapers."(5) As a result, the *Monitor* was opening advertising bureaus for the first time in New York, Chicago, Los Angeles, *and* San Francisco.

The *Monitor* also looked to its new editor, Katherine W. Fanning, to help its revitalization. Fanning had previously served as publisher and editor of the *Anchorage Daily News.* Under her leadership the Alaska paper won a Pulitzer Prize in 1976 while circulation quadrupled to 50,000 in four years.

"But all these changes will be wasted," Hoagland said, "unless more people know about, and then presumably buy, the paper."(6)

One of the ways under consideration to let the public know about the paper was the broadcast media. So in 1983 the decision was made to launch Monitor Radio and have it carried over as many National Public Radio stations as possible.

Monitor Radio was launched as an offering by American Public Radio based in St. Paul, Minnesota. The program blended in well with Public Radio's format of objective in-depth news analysis. Local National Public Radio (NPR) stations were free to air it at their discretion. The program endeavored to attract skilled personnel to run the program, but Monitor Radio admitted to a bias in hiring Christian Scientists.

Continuation of Monitor Radio on KQED

Officials at KQED soon realized they had their work cut out for them. The hiring practices at Monitor Radio, they soon discovered, went beyond discrimination against sexual minorities. The program was also in violation of the FCC's Federal Equal Opportunity Employment (EOE) guidelines as the Church admitted to giving preferential hiring treatment to Christian Scientists. It then became the position of KQED to attempt to change Monitor Radio's hiring practices, not just with sexual orientation, but discrimination on the basis of religion as well.

A valuable card in KQED's hand was the fact that the San Francisco Bay area was an important link for Monitor Radio in its national network. Monitor Radio apparently wanted to keep San Francisco and the Bay Area in its lineup at almost any cost. As noted above, San Francisco was one of four cities, the first outside Boston, to have its own *Monitor* advertising bureau. Perhaps the Publishing Society saw the new advertising bureaus as complimenting Monitor Radio with each of them advancing the newspaper's support and eventual success.

Controversy is nothing new to officials of the Christian Science Church. For much of their history they have had to fight political battles on every level of government just to allow adherents of their faith the right to rely on its teachings for their health as opposed to forced medical intervention. The Church has found that its most successful legal defense has been the First Amendment. No doubt their right to maintain a course of action consonant with their conscience and religious beliefs were highlighted in conversations with KQED. Representing Monitor Radio early in the negotiations was John Parrot who was in charge of the broadcast organization and then subsequently became responsible for public relations.

Lobbying for KQED, Inc. was station President Anthony S. Tiano and KQED station manager Valena Williams. The main argument they put forth was that while

> the employment practices of a church are protected by the Constitution.... KQED program policy...does not provide a place for religious material...thus, the standards applied to employment practices at Monitor Radio must be secular standards.

Meetings continued, but nobody was giving in. Then, on March 25, 1986, an event occurred that outraged lesbians and gays coast-to-coast and significantly intensified local community animosity towards KQED.

KQED Television, along with other public TV stations broadcast the controversial Frontline documentary *"AIDS—A National Inquiry."* Lesbians and gays across the United States may have roared their disapproval, but in San Francisco it was seen by many as one more display of wholesale insensitivity by KQED against sexual minorities. The story was that of Fabian Bridges—an African-American gay hustler who claimed he had sex with six partners every night. He refused to stop having sex even though he knew he had AIDS. The program was widely criticized as inflammatory and racist. Then when it became known in the lesbian/gay communities that the news team admitted paying Fabian Bridges to stay on the street, the methods were denounced as "ugly, inflammatory, shady, journalism."

In San Francisco, the Fabian Bridges story brought the already strained relations between the lesbian/gay communities and KQED to the breaking point. Whereas the documentary may have incited pickets and protests against PBS elsewhere, it resulted in nothing less than a well organized community-wide boycott in San Francisco. Yet, that was hardly the beginning. As an extension of their boycott, lesbian and gay activists sought to convince corporate sponsors to withhold financial support from KQED. Here they had some success. But instead of getting from this the results they wanted, the lesbian/gay communities could find nothing correct about KQED's posture.

Early in 1986 gay activist and comedian, Tom Ammiano, brought charges against KQED over the station's failure to include gay comics in its locally produced and nationally syndicated series "Comedy Tonight."

Sexual minorities also saw their community slighted through KQED's viewer magazine *Focus* which featured *"The New San Francisco"* a story about Asians becoming the new majority in San Francisco. According to *BAR*,

> Leaders in the gay community point out that the article ignores the city's huge gay minority and the fact that 65,000 to 75,000 gays and lesbians have migrated to San Francisco over the past 15 years.(7)

Still, most potentially damaging to the station was the original boycott that might dry up support in lesbian/gay communities during fund-raising telethons. Yet it is difficult to determine the extent to which the boycott played a role in getting station management to the bargaining table. The lesbian/gay communities found they also had other weapons.

Soon after the airing of the controversial Fabian Bridges documentary, leading activists in the lesbian/gay communities met with San Francisco City supervisors.

Their object was to see if their city's hotel tax used to support public broadcasting could be withheld from KQED until the demands from the sexual minority communities were met. This would not be easy. Such a step would require a majority vote from the Bay City's Board of Supervisors, which in turn must be preceded by public hearings to determine if KQED was, in reality, guilty of discrimination. The supervisors most agreeable to working with the activists were John Molinari and Harry Britt. Supervisor Molinari tried to put himself in the role of mediator going back and forth between KQED and the sexual minority communities. Molinari told *BAR*,

> I want to talk to them first, before we haul them into a public forum. I want to see if we could possibly reason with them and show them what our concerns are.(8)

He tried to set up a meeting with KQED officials as early as September 1986. KQED showed a willingness to hold meetings, but may have been reluctant to actually go through with them. The station abruptly canceled the first meeting. A second meeting wasn't held either; the station claimed a misunderstanding over the dates. For awhile, it looked as if the radio station wasn't going to budge. Then without warning, KQED General Manager Anthony Tiano took two steps towards reconciliation with the lesbian/gay communities. First, he wrote a letter to the Christian Science Publishing Society criticizing their discriminatory policy. Second he asked for a meeting with representatives of the sexual minority communities. This was held February 23rd with representatives of the boycott committee together with San Francisco supervisors Harry Britt and John Molinari. *BAR* speculated Tiano called the meeting only after he was convinced the lesbian/gay communities were making major inroads on influencing individual supervisors. No city supervisor, it appeared, sided outright with KQED.

Supervisor Willie Kennedy was reported to want more time to consider the issue.

Supervisor Bill Maher said,

> …in view of the concerns of the public, we're not going to fund them…Government funding and a free press don't go together. And as for church and state, the more separate they are, the better off we are…This is probably not a wise expenditure of public funds. It raised a lot of issues: free press, discrimination, etc., especially when a significant section of our community feels it's inappropriate.

Supervisor James Gonzales said,

> I think that as a board we can use our influence on KQED to persuade them
> to take corrective action. We have a lot of ordinances in this city whereas
> we...agree not to do business with organizations that discriminate. But we do
> give them a chance to change their course of action.

The entire situation put KQED in a bind. The station did not feel any segment of the community should dictate its programming. It also felt Monitor
Radio was wrong in its hiring bias against both sexual minorities and non-Christian Scientists. At the same time KQED felt Monitor Radio's programming was
of high quality and the station wanted the broadcasts to continue. All the while,
KQED was looking for a way to accommodate both the lesbian/gay communities
and Monitor Radio. The heat was on. KQED had to prove to the sexual minority
communities where it stood.

Anthony Tiano was put in the position where he had to do something to
improve his image in San Francisco's lesbian/gay communities.

Prior to the meeting with representatives of the lesbian/gay communities,
Tiano wrote a letter to the *Christian Science Monitor*. In it he severely chastened
the paper for its discriminatory practices.

> Most of the country's best journalists would not be considered qualified for
> Monitor Radio. The narrow breadth of ethnicity and lifestyle dictated by such
> a hiring policy does not encompass the world on which your radio programs
> report. Nor does it define the world to which you promise sound news cover-
> age.
>   The make-up of KQED's staff reflects the community. We cannot accept
> less from the organizations which supply our programs. If Monitor Radio
> reports only through the experience of Christian Scientists, its scope narrows
> to reporting from a religious viewpoint rather than news: KQED has interest
> in the program because it is a news program.(9)

In spite of Tiano's efforts, community activists maintained a strong desire for
KQED to remove Monitor Radio from its lineup. Rick Pacurar, out-going president of the Harvey Milk Democratic Club said:

> We are setting a national precedent if we can force Monitor Radio off public
> radio. We are saying that you can't discriminate against gays and lesbians and
> get away with it.

And openly gay city Supervisor Harry Britt said:

> There is a strong commitment on everybody's part that Monitor Radio has to be dealt with.

The long-awaited meeting between representatives of the lesbian/gay communities and KQED general manager Anthony Tiano finally took place. The meeting was organized by supervisors John Molinari and Harry Britt. The basis of the get-together was a list of ten demands given KQED by sexual minority community leaders. According to *BAR*:

> The demands ranged from items as specific as condemning Monitor Radio, ending the station's boycott of gay comics on Comedy Tonight, and regularly scheduling gay programming on television and radio, to items such as that of presenting a positive image of gay people…[P]articipants called the gathering "polite" and respectful.(10)

The willingness of Anthony Tiano to meet with representatives from the lesbian/gay communities was also seen as a sure sign by sexual minorities that their boycott was working. Tiano's move was seen as succulently sweet to community activists. They openly reveled in the thought they might be winning. Sexual minority newspapers reflected this feeling. Writing satirically and derisively in *BAR*'s column, "*Don't Touch That Dial,*" Brian Jones said:

> The boycott of KQED is succeeding. Oh, you can still see wombats copulating or tarantulas eating their young, in stop action, almost any evening on channel 9. But clearly the folks at KQED are worried, and clearly they have reason to be.
>
> One indication of heightened anxiety at KQED TV and radio is that Tony Tiano, the general manager who started this whole mess, has emerged from his bunker deep beneath the blinking monitors at Eighth and Harrison. Tiano, who may or may not eat his young, in stop action, crawled forth last week and made it all the way to City Hall.
>
> Big bucks are on the line. KQED is in peril of losing $150,000 in city money from the Hotel Tax Fund. This is because the boycott has demonstrated that KQED discriminates against gay people, both in staffing and programming…(11)

It could be argued that the lesbian/gay press was going out of its way to portray the management of KQED as insensitive to the sexual minority communities. It appears little effort was given to show KQED's position or the work being done by KQED to attempt a healing on the confrontation issues it had with both the lesbian/gay communities and Monitor Radio.

Throughout the standoff between KQED and the lesbian/gay communities, the radio station had been working to get concessions from Monitor Radio. Throughout 1986 and 1987, KQED continually corresponded with Monitor Radio to try to mitigate its discriminatory positions on the basis of both religion and sexual orientation. The lesbian/gay communities didn't seem to care about, or even notice the *Monitor's* preference for hiring Christian Scientists. It was, nevertheless, an important issue to KQED. One of the many letters sent to Robert H. MacLachlan, General Manager of Radio Broadcasting at the *Monitor* said:

> We do not question the worth of news stories broadcast on Monitor Radio…We have, however, had occasion to question the selection and assignment process which rest entirely with editors defined as practicing Christian Scientists. We are concerned, Mr. MacLachlan, with the error of incomplete journalism, the error of omission, not the error of commission or doing poorly what is broadcast.(12)

Throughout this time, KQED's Board of Directors backed their radio station's position that "programming should be selected solely on the basis on the talents of the producer and the quality of programs."(13) The Board also maintained that Monitor Radio's quality was worthy of KQED's high standards and should be continued.

To underscore the concern in their letters, KQED President Anthony Tiano and Program Director Carol Pierson again traveled to Boston to meet with Monitor Radio officials. The positions Monitor Radio was taking revealed major differences still remained. The hiring policy statement given by Monitor Radio to KQED in 1987 was that "we will hire the most qualified individual with preference given to members of the Church of Christ, Scientist."

Meanwhile, the pressure to resolve the Monitor Radio dispute from the lesbian/gay communities was growing in intensity. In April 1987 came the most tangible evidence the boycott was having an effect. It was reported(14) that KQED's telethon ended with $30,000 less than the station's projected goal with 500 fewer members signed up than were hoped for. This was only the beginning. Pressure had been building in the sexual minority communities for political action that might force KQED's hand, once and for all.

Ever since sexual minority leaders first met with city supervisors, City Hall had been deeply involved in trying to negotiate a settlement with all parties. The bottom line remained, however, that Monitor Radio would not end discrimination practices and KQED-FM would not stop airing the program. After attempts to settle the matter between the parties did not produce results, City Supervisor Richard Hongiso introduced on August 10, 1987 a resolution to terminate city funding for contractors or sub-contractors that discriminate. Ignoring a last minute plea from KQED, he asked the city to accept the following resolution:

> Resolved, That it is the policy of the City and County of San Francisco not to tolerate any form of discrimination, and in so doing, urge the Chief Administrative Officer to discontinue, not fund, or participate in supporting any organization or program that is directly or indirectly discriminatory.(15)

The action was a slap in KQED's face. The resolution would be sent to the Human Services Committee of the Board of Supervisors. It would be the Committee's job to hold public hearings on the resolution and send it back to the full Board with its recommendations.

The ante in the standoff had been raised. The radio station's annual income of $150,000 from the city's hotel tax revenues was at stake. To make things worse for KQED, the first line of offense confronting KQED had been transferred from the Bay Area's lesbian and gay leaders to the City of San Francisco. Lesbian/gay activists were nearly salivating in anticipation of hearings and the vote by city supervisors.

Regrettably, a number of frustrating delays required postponing the hearings again and again, but not all were requested by KQED. One postponement, that of October 15, was requested by the sexual minority communities because it coincided with their national March on Washington. It was not until February 4, 1988 that hearings on City Supervisor Hongisto's resolution were finally held.

The highlight of the hearings was the resolution made by a representative for Supervisor Hongisto. The resolution "called on the city to cease funding any station or city contractor which did business with organizations that discriminate on the basis of sexual orientation."(16) The resolution was a clear embarrassment for KQED. But there were more to come.

State assembly candidate and directing attorney of the Lesbian Rights Project, Roberta Achtenberg, led off the speakers calling for a cutoff of city funds to KQED. She believed the Monitor's position on discrimination to be particularly offensive.

Christine Madsen worked her way up from copy girl to reporter, but when they found out that she was a lesbian they fired her. The fact that they fired her because of her sexual orientation was never in dispute.

In all, a half dozen sexual minority activists and KQED supporters gave testimony.

Following the hearings, Supervisor Hongisto's office requested the City Attorney to draft a secondary discrimination amendment to San Francisco's existing anti-discrimination law. This was a major blow for KQED.

All during this time negotiations between KQED and Monitor Radio were on-going. In the spring of 1988, the San Francisco station was helped along by the request of the Christian Science Church to obtain a broadcast license for broadcasting in Boston. A requirement for obtaining the license was the applicant must be an "open employer." This meant the Christian Science broadcast operations had to abide by hiring standards which covered all types of discrimination covered by Federal guidelines which did not include sexual orientation. The requirement for full equality in hiring on the basis of race, color, and *religion*, resulted in the formation of a syndicate within the Church as a broadcasting organization in full agreement with federal guidelines. Anyone with inside knowledge of the workings of the Church, and its operations, might appreciate the enormity of this event. KQED's Program Director, Carol Pierson, while not a Christian Scientist, was one who understood the significance. Pierson, who had met with Church officials countless times over this issue, believed, "It was a big, big step for the Christian Scientists, but it did not satisfy the people who had been our main critics," namely, the lesbian/gay communities.

Public Broadcasting agencies outside San Francisco also understood. On May 9, 1988 a detailed FAX memo was sent to all member stations by American Public Radio.

There has been on-going, candid and constructive dialogue between The Christian Science Publishing Society, American Public Radio and several stations, including KQED, San Francisco, about the hiring policies of The Christian Science Publishing Society.

The memo then quotes a statement from John H. Hoagland Jr., Manager of the Christian Science Publishing Society. The statement included the following:

It will be our policy to provide employment opportunity to all qualified individuals without regard to their race, color, religion, national origin, or sex in all personnel actions including recruitment, evaluation, selection, promotion, compensation, training, and termination.

It will also be our policy to promote the realization of equal opportunity through a positive, continuing program of specific practices designed to ensure the full realization of equal employment opportunity without regard to race, color, religion, national origin or sex.

If Public Radio officials outside San Francisco were pleased with the decision by Monitor Radio, those at KQED were jubilant. The action appeared to whet their appetite for a resolution of the biggest obstacle of all: discrimination based on sexual orientation. KQED officials would not let up. Carol Pierson, who was close to the negotiations, sensed what might be the biggest stumbling block for progress. She understood the Church was in a pinch as it stood to lose face with its membership if it did anything appearing to condone same-gender sexuality. With this in mind, KQED worked with Christian Science officials to help them find a face-saving way to change their policy. Carol Pierson said,

After they changed their policy to abide by the Federal standards we had continued to meet with them and to write to them suggesting different kinds of ways they could change their discriminatory policy toward gays. They were concerned about openly stating that they would not discriminate on the basis of sexual orientation causing a furor within the Church because it would be counter to the policies of the Church.(17)

In some ways the situation was highly frustrating for KQED, because the lesbian/gay communities did not see Monitor Radio's compliance with Federal hiring practices as a breakthrough. Carol Pierson said,

It actually made a lot of people who had been working on this issue for a long time, even madder that they were willing to change their hiring policy, and not discriminate on the basis of other factors, but continued to discriminate on the basis of sexual orientation.(17)

The meetings were frustrating for both sides. The Christian Science officials, according to Carol Pierson, were exceedingly afraid to upset the members of the Church. This didn't mean they didn't want to be as accommodating to KQED as possible. One can only wonder at the intensity of discussions this must have caused Church officials to have amongst themselves. Unfortunately, such conversations are never made public. What is known is the deliberations resulted with a curious effect. It became obvious the Church officials wanted to please both their members, and KQED. This resulted in a most unusual decision by Monitor Radio officials. They told KQED they were actually willing to agree *not* to discriminate on the basis of sexual orientation. But this was providing and *only* providing, they didn't have to make it known publicly. Monitor Radio appeared to be bending over backwards. The radio program apparently wanted to appease everyone. But some observers may have wondered whether Monitor Radio's decision was based on practicality or on fear. They might also have wondered if Church authorities felt they were following their denomination's Leader at this point. She wrote,

> The author [Mrs. Eddy] has not compromised conscience to suit the general drift of thought but has bluntly and honestly given the text of Truth.(18)

But KQED officials were not Christian Scientists. They could not negotiate on those terms. Their recommendations had to be more earthly. Carol Pierson said the station suggested the Church

> could at least phrase it [to their members] that they abide by the hiring policies of the City of Boston which forbids discrimination based on sexual orientation.(17)

The lesbian/gay communities in the Bay area appeared to give no importance to KQED's negotiations with Monitor Radio. Their position was that the Monitor program should be dropped from the public radio station's line up once and for all. For this reason, the many lesbian and gay employees at KQED felt caught in the middle. They held a strong loyalty to the lesbian/gay communities. On the other hand, they also understood why the radio station didn't want their programming dictated by any segment of the community. They were definitely caught between two loyalties. Searching for a way out of the dilemma, openly gay KQED staffer, Tom Yeager, drafted a letter politely venting their frustration to John H. Hoagland, Jr., Manager of the Christian Science Publishing Society. In it he told Hoagland:

> We [KQED's lesbian/gay employees] joined together six months ago to counteract the distortions about KQED in articles in the gay press. These included allegations of job discrimination by KQED. As both members of the gay community and employees of the station, we presented a different point surrounding [City Supervisor] Hongisto's resolution to deny KQED city funds as long as we aired Monitor Radio.

> The *Christian Science Monitor* has taken the commendable position of editorially supporting civil rights for Gays and Lesbians. We ask that you take this opportunity to display moral leadership consistent with your editorial position and expand on the FCC's definition of non-discrimination.
>
> It is our understanding that private assurances were given to KQED station management that you would not discriminate based on sexual orientation. We appreciate this statement and your FCC broadened hiring policy but feel that without publicly stating your position, this response is not acceptable. It leaves the gay community, which has been at the forefront of this effort, still waiting for justice. We are disappointed that you are unwilling to take a more humanistic and courageous position.

Added to Tom Yeager's signature, were those of thirty-nine other lesbian/gay employees at KQED.

Hoagland responded to Tom Yeager's letter on September 1st. He thanked Tom Yeager "and your colleagues who have supported Monitor Radio's right to be heard." The letter did not mention sexual orientation issues, only reaffirming their adherence to federal EOE guidelines, which the Church's broadcasting departments have "voluntarily adopted." Only in closing, did Hoagland hint at the differences separating their organizations.

> Even if we do not agree on every issue, the simple fact is that we greatly respect all the individual workers at KQED and appreciate very much the discussions we've had.

What a contrast between John Hoagland's letter to Tom Yeager and those sent to other sexual minorities from the Church over many years! Hoagland did not scold Tom Yeager and his associates. They were not chastised, for "moral blindness," "laxity" or "an evil with which you have identified yourself" as Ernest Barnum was once told by Church officials. Nor were their lives described as "animal gratification" as Paul Daugherty more recently defined same-gender sexuality to Charles Linebarger. Still, the bottom line was that the Church remained unwilling to publicly acknowledge that it will not discriminate against sexual minorities.

Neither Monitor Radio nor San Francisco's lesbian/gay communities were willing to back down. KQED was faced with losing city funding on the one hand, or the sacred privilege of determining its own programming on the other. KQED desperately wanted to seek a resolution to these issues. Therefore it was important for the station to continue the dialogue with both parties. Unfortunately, everything that could be brought up had already been said. There appeared nothing else the station could say to either side. This meant KQED was faced with the decision of giving in to the lesbian/gay communities by taking Monitor Radio off the air. Their other option was to continue indefinitely their confrontation with the sexual minority communities and absorb all the problems stemming from this conflict. Neither option seemed viable. Despite all the intense efforts by KQED, removing the impasse seemed beyond its reach.

As so often happens when the situation looks the bleakest, outside events have a way of saving the day. In this context, two events made a difference.

New hope was heralded when Governor Michael Dukakis signed the Massachusetts lesbian/gay rights bill into law in November 1989.(19) The new law bans discrimination on the basis of sexual orientation in employment, housing, and credit. Coupled with Boston's ordinance protecting sexual minorities from discrimination, which had been law since 1987, the legal ramifications became very strong against organizations based in the Hub City that might discriminate on the basis of sexual orientation. It is interesting to note that unlike other years, the Christian Science Church made no apparent move either to defeat or to modify the Massachusetts lesbian/gay rights bill in 1989. Is it possible Church officials foresaw the humiliating handwriting on the wall? Did they believe that someday they might have to accommodate KQED and others like them, by abandoning their time-honored refusal to hire sexual minorities? Could they have seen the Massachusetts lesbian/gay rights law as a way to save face with their own constituencies? This would include many with deeply homophobic feelings. As it was, 1989 marked the first time since Chris Madsen's termination from the *Monitor*, the Church did nothing to thwart, or amend, the statewide lesbian/gay rights bill in Massachusetts.

Still, this was not enough. Monitor Radio remained adamantly opposed to changing its discrimination policy, at least publicly. A more concerted effort was needed.

The second event was KQED's request to the City of San Francisco to float tax-free bonds. For some time, KQED had felt the need to expand its physical plant with the purchase of a new building. To make the purchase, the station needed to float $15 million in bonds. To have the bonds tax exempt, would save the Public Broadcasting station between $4 to $5 million. The only thing needed to obtain the tax exemption would be San Francisco Mayor Art Agnos signature. At first, it wasn't thought this would have anything to do with KQED's conflict with Monitor Radio.

When the time came to act, however, Mayor Agnos informed KQED it could *not* have tax exemption on the bonds unless Monitor Radio set an acceptable date for changing its hiring policies. Otherwise the radio station would have to drop the program.

What a shock! Could KQED do anything without controversy? To make matters worse, this time the public radio station could lose over $4 million dollars, an incredible sum for any radio station and especially for one seriously beleaguered with community relations problems.

So the ball went back to KQED. This put the station in an incredible bind. Its final decision would rest with its Board of Directors. Of course, they could decide to drop Monitor Radio once and for all. That decision would not be easy. It would be a capitulation for all of what KQED felt it stood for. On the other hand, the station would be forced to pay additional millions for essential non-tax-exempt bonds. The decision no doubt caused deep anxiety with KQED's Board and staff and a wondering of how far their standoff with San Francisco and the Bay Area would take them. But they could only ponder this so long. Soon it was crunch time. The moment had come for KQED's Board of Directors to make what would be, for them, a most fateful decision.

As individual members of KQED's Board of Directors filed themselves into their station's chamber room they may not have yet decided which road to take. The dilemma must have almost certainly seemed a lose/lose situation for them.

As the station's Board of Directors met, they gave a full airing of the issue. It was not an easy time. In spite of the nature of their difficulties, however, they appeared to approach the situation with cool heads. They voted for principle.

Despite the enormity of the sums at stake, not to mention the depth of community abhorrence for their position, the Board of Directors at KQED voted to *continue* airing Monitor Radio. The station clearly took a risk that might have meant financial ruin for them. But they did find some support in the larger community. Their action was praised by the *San Francisco Chronicle*, which chastised the Mayor for intimidating the public broadcasting station.

> Given the choice between letting Mayor Art Agnos dictate its programming and spending an extra $4 million to $5 million to preserve its independence, KQED did the right thing. It voted to spend the money...
>
> Agnos should realize that if public radio stations succumb to economic pressure, it won't be conservative views that are apt to be suppressed in the long run. Positions held by people like Agnos are much more likely to go unheard.
>
> Agnos has moved into dangerous territory.(20)

KQED knew well that its historic decision could also be its downfall. The station, therefore, desperately wanted to find a way to make amends with its nemesis: the Bay area's lesbian/gay communities. The only way out, it appeared, was via Monitor Radio.

Trying to save the day for KQED, Station Manager David Hosely and President Anthony Tiano, felt they had nothing to lose by resuming their negotiations, now in their fifth year, with the Christian Scientists. So David Hosely and Anthony Tiano packed their bags for yet one more trip across the continent. Once they were gathered with Monitor Radio personnel, KQED officials wasted no time. They came right to the point. They centered their argument on the critical position in which KQED found itself. They told Monitor Radio officials point blank,

> Look here! You're being picky on this one point is going to cost us over four million dollars!(21)

What followed provided what may be the most historic moments in the ongoing saga between sexual minorities and the Christian Science Church.

For the first time in the many years of justifying their discriminatory posture, there was no retort from Church officials. Only silence. What *could* they say? How could discrimination be justified in such circumstances? Did reality finally catch up with the Christian Science Church? One wonders. Still, KQED officials who had come once again from San Francisco waited patiently for an answer.

Church officials were in a bind. They were forced to go off and contemplate this new landscape. They had to decide what to say to KQED's directors. Perhaps, just perhaps, these events caused Church officials to partake in what may have been intense introspection. They almost certainly knew many business, medical, educational, political, religious, and social organizations were taking a fresh look at their response to sexual orientation issues. They may have known these organizations realized it is not the clear-cut issue it was once thought to be. Church officials also knew the governments of their City of Boston and their State of Massachusetts outlawed discrimination against sexual minorities in employment, as did many political jurisdictions across the country.(22) Perhaps more importantly, they may have recalled previous Church officials were mistaken in such matters as abetting racial segregation in their churches and opposing fluoridation of the public water supply. In their deepest introspective moments, might it be that they dared ask themselves, *"Could we be wrong again?"*

But whatever thoughts they had, whatever feelings the situation engendered upon them, Church officials were caught in a bind of gargantuan proportions.

After what must have been intense discussions, the substance of which is known only to themselves, a major shift was made. Whatever they personally felt, whatever they perceived their denomination's spiritual teachings to be, the pressure to end a discriminatory policy was way too much for them. This, then, became a very clearly defined moment for sexual minorities in the Church of Christ, Scientist. This was when the Church caved in. Monitor Radio and the Church which supports it, made the most difficult decision to agree *publicly* to abide by the State of Massachusetts' anti-discrimination law, not yet three months old, in its broadcasting activities.

One wonders if Church officials finally saw what supporters of lesbian-gay rights had been telling them all along: that a same-gender orientation is no more an aberration than is being left-handed. Is it possible they finally saw what the real onus is: discrimination. Worst of all for the Church, radio station KQED, the City of San Francisco, and many others laid the onus directly at the Church of Christ, Scientist.

The exact thoughts of Church officials in this period may never be known. But might the situation have brought to mind the well-known lines from Walt Kelly's *Pogo* comic strip of years ago?

We have seen the enemy and he is us!

The historic date was February 5, 1990 that KQED President Anthony Tiano received the word he was looking for. KQED was told the Christian Science organization would no longer bar lesbians and gays from employment in its broadcasting activities.

Needless to say, this change in position by Monitor Radio caused no small amount of euphoria and relief among KQED personnel. It also caused a positive stirring among lesbian/gay activists and their supporters throughout the San Francisco Bay Area.

When word of the shift in Monitor Radio's policy reached Mayor Art Agnos, he was elated. Mayor Angos' aide Scott Schafer, explained to the media, the mayor was "extremely satisfied" about Monitor Radio's announcement. He went on to say how pleased the Mayor was that both the City of San Francisco and KQED could influence an organization thousands of miles away by maintaining a firm stance on principle and human rights.

Word soon got out by the lesbian/gay press to sexual minority communities around the country.

One organization some might feel should've been one of the first to know of the Church's new position, was actually one of the last. When members of Emergence International did learn of the change in policy by The Mother Church, they were taken completely by surprise. Some found it bewildering. Recalling how inflexible the Church had been, some questioned the very validity of the reports.

The author was one of the doubting Thomas's. He resolved his dilemma by telephoning the Christian Science Publishing Society directly. He called in his capacity as a reporter for *Seattle Gay News*.

As it turned out the Personnel Manager for the Christian Science Publishing Society was very open about discussing the change in policy. He said,

> In our broadcasting activities, sexual orientation is not a job criterion. It is not something that is the basis for hiring, or not hiring, or promoting, or not promoting, etc.

In our conversation he went on to praise KQED for playing

> a very influential role in helping us come to some decisions in terms of what our posture should be in that area, but that's something they've been working on over a period of time. It actually received the results they desired.

The author could not help but wonder if the Church was going to yield in other areas as well.

As positive as the Personnel Manager was on employment in the Broadcasting department, he politely refused to speculate whether or not the Christian Science Church might someday admit openly lesbians and gays as Church members.

Another call that was made upon hearing the announcement was to a former reporter for the *Christian Science Monitor*.

Chris Madsen said, she too, was "really surprised." Her first reaction was "It's going to be wonderful for the many gays and lesbians who work there." After reflecting about it, however, she called back. In our second conversation Chris wondered out loud how it will be put to use. "Have they put it in writing?" she wanted to know.

> Is it in the personnel handbook? Will they do anything to inform the gay and lesbian people who work there now, of the change in policy? That is when it

> becomes real. I find it very interesting that they have now changed their policy when it became economically necessary, almost. They took a stand on principle, on morals, on separation of church and state, in all those years during my lawsuit, and now economic pressure is what finally makes them crumble…This is not at all to slight all of the wonderful work that the gay and lesbian groups in the San Francisco area did to bring it about.

As we have seen the change in policy was not easily obtained. In summing up their lengthy discussions with Monitor Radio, KQED Station Manager David Hosely, who was close to the negotiations, said the change in position to hire lesbians and gays, "was very, very difficult" for the Christian Scientists.(21)

While changing the discrimination policy at Monitor Radio might have been "very, very difficult" for the Church, it remained a small step. The Church still did not allow lesbians and gays into membership and all other forms of discrimination remained intact.

For many sexual minorities, Church membership was the number one issue. It seemed to them basic to everything else. If one could not become or remain a member in the Church they were raised in, the separation seemed large indeed. Therefore, every nuance in Mother Church statements regarding membership were intensely scrutinized by many sexual minority Christian Scientists. A small, but noteworthy, change in the membership packet in 1990, therefore, stirred unusual interest in the lesbian/gay Christian Science community.

Information in the packet to accompany membership applications that read, "*The standard in Christian Science includes freedom from…homosexuality*" was replaced with one that did not specifically mention same-gender sexuality. Finding this development most interesting, the author wrote The Mother Church asking if this meant open lesbians and gays could now become members. The answer was frustrating. The response did not bring a precise answer.

What William E. Moody, Clerk of The Mother Church said in response was, "members must lead an upright and moral life." Perhaps it was wishful thinking, but the ambiguous tenor of his letter and the absence of specific wording on same-gender sexuality may have indicated sharp differences at the Church's highest levels regarding sexual orientation and membership. At the very least, some internal dialogue had almost certainly taken place, perhaps to an intense degree.

While The Mother Church may have been painstakingly studying the issues as to the place of LGBT people in their midst, they apparently did not share these proceedings with their branch churches. Lesbians and gays were still being thrown out of their local churches.

Almost always the removal of a lesbian or gay member was handled quietly. Few people outside the Church knew what happened, unless the expelled member shared the information.

There was no doubt that a long way remained before a non-homophobic posture would be reflected in every activity in Church affairs. Gays were acutely aware of the intense amount of work that remained ahead. They knew first hand how hard it was to achieve even the smallest signs of progress.

But in spite of the difficulties, sexual minorities everywhere had reason to rejoice. The simple fact is, cracks had begun to appear in what has been seen to be as obdurate a position in an organization as can be imagined.

Clearly, the long awaited healing in the Christian Science Church had finally begun.

PART VI
EPILOGUE

o o o o o o o o o o o o o o o o o o o o o o o o o o o o o o o o o o
Let us hear the conclusion of the whole matter:

—Ecclesiastes 12:13

Epilogue

1990–2004

*Every great scientific truth goes through three stages. First, people say it con-
flicts with the Bible. Next, they say it has been discovered before. Lastly, they
say they had always believed it.*

—Professor Louis Agassiz, quoted in *Message for 1901*, page 27 lines
27–30.

As world citizens were awaiting the arrival of the third millennium, momentous changes had already come to the Christian Science Church favoring sexual
minorities.

Perhaps the most significant change was the opening of doors to membership
by The Mother Church to those who are openly lesbian or gay. This was another
big move for the Church. As during past changes in controversial policies, this
was accomplished without fanfare or even a general announcement. Apart from
Church officials, no one knew exactly when the policy change took place. Nor
was it explained anywhere what it was that triggered the Board of Directors to
change their position.

The media discussed battles going on elsewhere. News items circulated widely
about sexual minorities successes and setbacks among the Episcopalians, Methodists, Presbyterians. and others. These were discussed on TV, radio, newspapers
and the Internet. The *Christian Science Monitor* participated in covering the
struggle going on in many denominations. But there were limits to the *Monitor's*
normally comprehensive coverage. While the Boston newspaper would seem the
most logical place to learn of changes in the Church that sponsors it, there was
only silence. The *Christian Science Monitor* never mentioned the changes relating
to gay issues occurring in the Christian Science Church. Yet the changes were
among the most momentous in the Church's 125 year history.

There are no public records of how the reforms came about. The identity of
officials supporting or resisting inclusion of GLBT persons in Church affairs may
never be known, much less the arguments they used to buttress their positions.

Very few even knew when these decisions were made. There were no press conferences or press releases. Not even members were directly informed. But in time, members and outsiders gradually learned new decisions had been made.

It was in 1999, when word began to filter through the Christian Science lesbian/gay communities that The Mother Church would accept sexual minorities as members, if all other requirements were met. This became known through the Mother Church's Internet web-site. This may have been seen as the best way to handle a most controversial subject at the lowest key possible. On the web-site, the public in general could ask questions by e-mail about Christian Science.(1) Sometimes questions involving sexual orientation and membership were asked. The Church responded directly and to the point. Part of one official response, via e-mail, was:

> The question really isn't whether membership is open to anyone who considers himself or herself either gay or lesbian. The real questions for anyone considering membership in the Church of Christ, Scientist are whether the individual loves and believes in the doctrines of Christian Science.

Most Christian Scientists who affiliated with the Church organization had dual memberships. They belonged to The Mother Church as well as their local branch church. Referring to the branch churches, the Mother Church communiqué told inquirers, in the same e-mail:

> Each branch of The Mother Church is democratically governed, and we cannot speak definitely about the exact criteria each may have for membership.

These responses reflect the great care that seems to have gone into their preparation. It appears that the Church was trying very hard not to alienate members who held opposite beliefs with respect to the place of gays in their Church. It is as if Church officials were only too aware of the deep divisions and consternation sexual orientation issues had aroused in other denominations. Apparently they wished to avoid similar battles at all costs. The Church, therefore, backed out of the fray. They decided this was not to be a Church decision, but an individual one. The official response continued:

> When it comes to homosexuality, there are several points to be made. One is that The Church of Christ, Scientist, does not dictate what its members are to think about such societal and personal issues as homosexuality, gun control, the death penalty, and so on. Instead, it turns everyone to prayer, to the Bible,

and to *Science and Health with Key to the Scriptures* and other writings by Mary Baker Eddy (the Discoverer and Founder of Christian Science) for individual insight and guidance. When this guidance is sincerely sought and then faithfully followed, blessings for all flow from it.(2)

Church officials may have felt that including same-gender sexuality within an array of social issues served to lessen the impact of an emotionally divisive issue. But while the Church itself never put its handling of controversial social issues in the spotlight, these would sometimes arise in forums outside the Church.

The Mother Church's new position on homosexuality was broached on CNN's internationally televised program, "*Larry King Live*" on May 4, 2001. This was King's second interview in less than two years with Virginia S. Harris, Chair of the Christian Science Board of Directors. Following a commercial break, King asked Harris about the Church's position as to homosexuality and abortion.

Harris replied these are individual decisions. They are not decisions for the Church to decide.

In 2001, Christian Science teachers were told by their Church, via the Board of Education, that sexual orientation could no longer be a reason to deny Class instruction to prospective students. Some saw this as a watershed event. This was felt by many to be another defining moment when attitudes throughout the field became more friendly and relaxed to LGBT people.

Sexual minorities in the Christian Science Church were, in general, pleased with the progress being made by their denomination. But they also learned their Church would only go so far.

While openly lesbian/gay students were now allowed to take class instruction, there were limits as to the private conduct of teachers.

As this book went to press, there has been no known statement by Church authorities regarding a position opposing or condoning same-gender marriage. This apparently was also left for members to make their own decision. For those higher in the ranks, however, the situation was different. One who tested the limits of the Church's new posture was to suffer the consequences.

On May 17, 2004, Massachusetts became the first state to allow same-gender marriage. Three days later an authorized *Journal*-listed Christian Science teacher, married her long-time partner. The couple were married while wading their feet in the water at a public beach. The idyllic scene was captured by an Associated Press photographer resulting in a picture that made its way around the world. When this came to the attention of The Mother Church, the teacher lost her teaching credentials. She was told she needed to "repent" and would be placed on a three year probation. Her response was to leave the Church of Christ, Scientist. "I don't feel I have anything to repent for more than anyone else," she said in an interview with the Fort Myers, Florida *News-Press*. The action by The Mother Church and the former teacher's reaction were also carried widely by the Associated Press.

This action by The Mother Church was, of course, painful to lesbian/gay Christian Scientists. For several years they had seen nothing but progress. Now homophobia once again reared its ugly head. Such treatment to a respected teacher brought confusion to sexual minority Christian Scientists. For some, it was a slap in the face. The action did cloud the picture. Many wondered, "Where does The Mother Church really stand on our issues?" "Was this action a backpedaling?" "Were homophobic members threatening to withhold financial support if the Church went too far with lesbians and gays?" There was a feeling among sexual minorities that The Mother Church was receiving much negative mail re: the lesbian wedding. Was the action a means for the Church to tell those in higher positions, "Conduct your private life quietly. And never, but never, flaunt it?" In other words, had The Mother Church adopted an ecclesiastical version of "Don't ask, don't tell?" Or was this just a blip on the road to eventual total equality for all members? The bottom line was no one really knew. Also The Mother Church was mum on its action with the former teacher. They had no comments for the media. This led many sexual minorities to think perhaps the Church is reviewing its position with lesbians and gays. Unlike times past, however, sexual minorities were not about to engage in collective activism to challenge the Church's stance.

The Christian Science denomination is unique in that it does not allow marriage ceremonies in its churches. Neither is there an official ceremony, nor one suggested by Church officialdom, for Christian Scientists. No one in the denomination is legally sanctioned to perform marriage ceremonies in the name of the Church. According to the Church *Manual*, (Article IX, section 1, page 49):

> If a Christian Scientist is to be married, the ceremony shall be performed by a clergyman who is legally authorized.

This is the only mention of marriage in the *Manual*. Therefore, one might argue, The Mother Church has no basis for opposing or not recognizing same-gender marriage. In the Christian Science textbook, *Science and Health with Key to the Scriptures*, however, the thrice-married Leader of Christian Scientists devotes an entire chapter of 14 pages to marriage. Here she clearly depicts marriage as between a husband and wife. It should be added though, that the concept of a formalized marriage between members of the same gender was not at all in vogue in Mrs. Eddy's day. At any rate, the denomination's Leader did see an eventual coming together of male and female qualities in one person. In her Chapter on "Marriage" as in other chapters of *Science and Health* and her other writings, she brings androgyny to the forefront.

> ...[T]he time cometh of which Jesus spake, when he declared that in the resurrection there should be no more marrying nor giving in marriage, but man would be as the angels. Then shall Soul rejoice in its own, in which passion has no part. Then white/robed purity will unite in one person masculine wisdom and feminine love, spiritual understanding and perpetual peace. (*S&H* page 64, lines 18–25)(3)

Another area of considerable importance to sexual minorities is the way they have been described in the Church periodicals. From the 1960's to the 1980's, articles about homosexuality in the denomination's religious publications had always condemned the gay lifestyle. They stressed healing as the only adequate response to a same-gender orientation. But even here there were signs of change. In 1997, an article with a different perspective appeared in the *Christian Science Sentinel*. The article, *"Homosexuality—how do I respond?"* turned the subject around. For the first time a Church-sanctioned article broached "the need to free ourselves from judging and condemning individuals" who happen to be lesbian or gay. The article was heartily welcomed by lesbian/gay Christian Scientists.(4)

One reason for disagreement over the years between lesbian/gay Christian Scientists and officials of their Church is the absence of any statement by the Founder of their denomination regarding sexual orientation. Until very recently, all of Mrs. Eddy's biographers stayed clear of the topic. By century's end, however, lesbian and gay sexuality had become an acceptable topic of conversation in virtually every adult forum. In the more open climate of the late 1990's even a Church authorized Eddy biography could broach the subject. In her biography of the Christian Science Leader, Dr. Gillian Gill (a non-Christian Scientist) wrote,

> Mary Baker Eddy was in many ways a wise and open-minded woman on sexual matters, but socially she was also the product of a conservative Christian tradition. My guess is that homosexuality would be something she could neither understand nor countenance.(5)

Gill does not share with readers the basis of her "guess" apart from referring to Mrs. Eddy as being "the product of a conservative Christian tradition." What we do know is that the Christian Science Leader kept abreast of the news of the day.(6) Contemporary events relating to same-gender sexuality such as "Boston marriages" and the Oscar Wilde trial in the late 1890's were almost certainly known and possibly discussed even avidly in Mrs. Eddy's household. Speculation would have it that sexuality is one of those issues that kept Church archives closed tight to all but a chosen few. The archives include diaries and letters kept by those in daily contact with the Christian Science Leader. Who knows what someone near Mrs. Eddy might have quoted her regarding sensitive sexual topics, let alone what she herself may have written? Could it be that letters and/or other documents coming directly from Mrs. Eddy's pen might startle her followers even at the dawn of the 21st century? Startled or not, the resources could be highly revealing. As one who had unprecedented access to the archives, Dr. Gill notes,

> I am convinced that historians and theologians of many stripes will find a trea-sure trove of material once the doors of the Christian Science archives are opened wider to scholars.(7)(8)

Over the years changes of Church policy in sensitive areas were almost always handled quietly. While instances occurred of individuals having a dialogue with Mother Church authorities on delicate topics, the substance of these conversa-tions was not normally made public.

In the late 1950's, the *Christian Science Journal* eliminated its decades-old practice of labeling African-American practitioners and those branch churches with a majority of African-American members, as "colored" in its monthly direc-tory. This was also done without a general announcement. The Church of Christ, Scientist then quietly began to dismantle discrimination policies and practices toward racial minorities. It appears the Church is now following the same low key path in discarding discrimination policies against sexual minorities.

In spite of the enormity of the decision in 1990 to end discrimination against lesbians and gays in its broadcasting activities (chapter ten), there was likewise no known announcement of this development to the membership. Church officials likely see a no-win situation. It appears Church officials have been buffeted by those wanting a change in discriminatory policies, as well as from those who insist they remain. In a Church where membership has slipped considerably, it is understandable that officials would want to avoid controversy by keeping the issue out of the limelight. As mentioned above, Church authorities may also have been affected by the anguish and divisiveness the issue has caused in other denominations.

Since 1983, there have been no organized efforts by lesbian/gay Christian Scientists to work collectively to change the Church's discriminatory position. Individual efforts, however, continued.

Many individual lesbian, gay and bi-sexual Church members were disclosing their sexual orientation to their teachers with whom they came together annually at their association meetings. (See chapter 9, note 2) In local branch churches, members who were lesbian or gay seemed less afraid to divulge their orientation to fellow members who they deemed to be supportive. Many were also confiding their sexual orientation to their practitioner(s). Sexual minorities were slowly, but surely, building bridges of understanding and support. Rank and file Christian Scientists may have been more likely to respond positively to these quiet maneuverings than to the flamboyant demonstrations of times past. But there was at least one exception to the otherwise omission of activism on a wider scale. This was at Principia College.

Unlike many denominations, the Christian Science Church does not concern itself with education by either owning or supporting schools on any level. Nevertheless, over the years, various private independent schools were set up restricting their enrollment to Christian Scientists or children of Church members. None had formal ties to the Church of Christ, Scientist. By far the largest and the only one in the world to include college level education is Principia in Elsah, near Alton, Illinois.(9)

In 1993, alumnus Chandler Burr organized an unofficial college alumni group: "Gay and Lesbian Principians (GLP)." The first project of GLP was to identify as many Principia lesbian/gay alumni as possible. Chandler contacted those alumni members he knew to have a same-gender sexual orientation. Some of those, in turn, knew of others. Before long, Chandler had put together the first list of lesbian and gay alumni ever assembled. These graduates were asked to allow their names to appear in a newsletter for Principia's lesbian/gay alumni. The newsletter would also include space for listing names of heterosexual supporters among alumni and faculty.

The work by Chandler Burr(10) was soon picked up and carried on by another alumnus, David White. Soon, GLP also saw itself as a venue for dialogue with the college administration. The administration would grant interviews to the group because they were Principia graduates. But apart from holding meetings with them, College officials would not comply with any request from the group that would show a pro-lesbian/gay position. This included denial of a request to recognize GLP as a bona fide College group.

One of the most significant activities of GLP was its sponsorship of a lesbian/gay alumni reception on campus on July 16, 1994. Although the reception was held without official permission, David White considered the get-together "a success."(11) Successful or not, it was a contentious experience both for members of the gay alumni group and the College. Kathelen Johnson, the reception's hostess, recalled the following:

> In the summer of 1994 at Principia College I hosted the first Gay and Lesbian Alumni of Principia (GLAP) party ever held at Principia. We met in the rec-room in the basement of Sylvester House. There were about six of us. Well, [besides the] two guys I met later in the Pub, the coffee shop in the Student Center building. Principia officials were furious, outraged, and tore down all the notices I thumb-tacked to bulletin boards. One official yelled at me at full volume in Holt Gallery, telling me to stop causing problems and instigating and doing illegal things…Most of the people at Alumni Week were probably not aware of any LGBT people on campus. One gentleman kept a very low profile; he came to the party, but he wasn't interested in activism or in making waves.

Colleges, not even a college for Christian Scientists, remain immune from social issues. So homosexuality, along with other important issues, have been discussed openly, and at times heatedly, among Principia College students. Principia's administration, could be considered a bastion of homophobia. Up to the time this book went to press, no openly lesbian, gay or bisexual student, faculty or staff was permitted to attend or be employed at the College even if they agreed to abide by the school's moral code. The moral code provides for no sexual activity outside of a legal marriage. Nevertheless, students on the Principia Campus would occasionally engage in activities trying to gain for lesbians and gays the freedom to be open about their sexual orientation. Such efforts were always squashed by the administration. College officials came to have zero tolerance for even an advocacy of a lesbian/gay lifestyle.

In the spring of 1996, the author's son became involved in a major effort to create change for sexual minorities. David Stores, a heterosexual, returned to Principia after two years absence to complete credits he was lacking to graduate. He arrived at the beginning of the last quarter in March and planned to graduate two months later.

What David found as he settled back into campus life surprised him. Lesbian and gay sexuality were hot topics, never far from the surface in campus conversation. More importantly, he learned some students earlier in the school year formed a group to combat discrimination. They called it "Students opposed to Bigotry and Discrimination" or "STOP BAD." Through STOP BAD, David got to know many of the lesbian/gay students on campus. David soon became active in the pro-gay organization.(12) Lesbian/gay students came to trust David. They had no fear in revealing their sexual orientation to him.

The gay women and men David met shared problems they faced living on a homophobic campus. All had to go about their daily routine knowing Principia forbade self-declared lesbians and gays from enrolling and if discovered, must be expelled. Some were concerned their parents might discover their sexual orientation. For racial, ethnic and religious minorities, families are a bastion of support, while facing an intolerant world. For lesbian and gay children, however, parents are sometimes their biggest concern. Some would cut off all support upon learning their child is gay. Gay bashing by other students was yet another concern.

David felt strongly something should be done. Therefore, he would seek out opportunities to bring up gay issues. The gay issue first emerged for him back in 1993 when a student in his anthropology class made a homophobic remark. David challenged the other student and a shouting match ensued. According to David, "as the teacher was unable to handle the situation she insisted the subject be dropped." On his return to Principia in 1996, he continued to bring up gay issues in the classroom, as well as in conversations among fellow students and "in whatever way I could."

During this time another student drafted a questionnaire to learn about actual student beliefs and behavior. This would be in contrast to the idealized concept held by the administration. Topics ranged from vegetarianism to sexuality. Subjects included drugs, alcohol, tobacco, petting, sexual intercourse, even naked-hugging. Students were also asked "Should openly gay students who abide by the Principia pledge [no sex prior to marriage] be allowed to enter Principia?"

The number of replies received totaled 200 out of a campus population of 550, a remarkable return for a survey. Of the 200 replies, 70 % marked the "yes" box on allowing openly gay students in the College. This would imply that a progressive thought prevailed among the students, if not the administration.

Through STOP BAD gay and straight students worked together to create a greater awareness of lesbian/gay issues. This included having a booth at the College's Whole World Festival, which displayed copies of Principia's Gay and Lesbian Alumni Newsletter, *Emerge!* magazine and many pro-gay books. The booth reportedly drew a lot of attention from the students. A few students complained to the administration. A letter was sent to the President and Chairman of the Board regretting that a group exists on campus with such "low moral standards." In time, as the visibility of STOP BAD increased, so did repression from the administration. STOP BAD was deemed an improper group and it was declared illegal before the end of the school year.

In a last ditch effort to make valid the work that had been accomplished, David Stores drew up a petition for the right of STOP BAD to continue. In less than a week he received 120 signatures including a few faculty and staff. Meanwhile, his house counselor met with him to pass on a message from the administration that if he didn't stop his activism, David would be dismissed from Principia. He would not be permitted to graduate. The petition was not turned in. Materials, including the petition, were left with students who would return in the fall. Plans were made for STOP BAD to go underground the following academic year and continue its work.

Perhaps the most significant discussion of same-gender sexuality at Principia in this period came in the aftermath of a Christian Science lecture. Jill Gooding C.S.B., a member of the Christian Science Board of Lectureship, gave a Church sanctioned lecture at Principia College. Lecturers who come to Principia often hold open discussion meetings with students in addition to their lecture. In this context, Gooding asked various students what they felt was the major concern on campus.

The reply overwhelmingly was, "homosexuality."

"O.K." Gooding reportedly said, "We'll discuss that." The subject of Gooding's meeting was pre-announced all over campus, though many signs were taken down. Normally a lecturer could count on 30 to 50 students attending such a meeting. At this time, Gooding's meeting brought about 200, the equivalent of two-fifths of the student body to discuss lesbian/gay issues. Also present were house parents, the Dean of Students, and the Chairman of the Board.

In her opening remarks Gooding quoted Mrs. Eddy: "In Christian Science mere opinion is valueless" (S&H page 341, line 11) and reportedly told everyone "Homosexuality is something that needs to be healed." The meeting then, according to David Stores, became "explosive." David estimated that well over half of the attendees were pro-gay.

Arguments supporting the need to heal a same-gender orientation maintained that sex should be only for procreation. All Bible quotes against homosexuality were brought out.

David said,

We were well prepared for that. We had done our homework and simply astonished those, including the lecturer, who tried to use the Bible as a basis for discrimination. If that was an official debate, we'd have won bigtime.

Probably the only sanctioned place on campus where students may find information from a pro-lesbian/gay viewpoint is Principia's Marshall-Brooks Memorial Library. A visit to the library shelves by the author in 1989 showed a modest collection of pro and anti-lesbian/gay books. A glance at the check-out cards showed some students had borrowed a few of the pro-gay books. The author has learned that more current titles have been added since then. These have largely come through donations from the unofficial lesbian/gay alumni group. Principia Alumnus, Kathelen Johnson recalled:

> I donated a set of about 12 gay and lesbian fiction and non-fiction books to the Principia College Library. I had an appointment with the librarian, went in, and gave her the books and a donation list, and she gave me a written donation receipt. I often wonder if gay and lesbian books, my donations or others, are still on the shelves.

Interestingly, the library also includes a number of books the denomination had labeled *un*authorized due to their real or perceived bias against Christian Science. In view of The Mother Church's intense efforts over the years to suppress books supporting negative views of the denomination, including efforts to remove them from public libraries, it is remarkable the College had allowed these books as part of its collection.

The only time Emergence International (EI) became involved with Principia's sexual minority students was in 1997. That year EI held its annual conference 35 miles south of the College, October 16–19, near St. Louis, Missouri. A member of EI helped arrange for six currently enrolled Principia students to secretly attend a portion of the conference. These students were able to hear an address given by a *Christian Science Journal*—listed practitioner, the conference keynote speaker. The practitioner was billed ahead of time as one who is examining

> what impedes healing today, and what is producing it among unexpected places and peoples. He is not gay, but is doing research on the involvement of Christian Science practitioners in the healing of AIDS and is researching a variety of issues affecting the Christian Science movement, including self-knowledge, tolerance, reconciliation, medicine, and the law.(13)

At the conclusion of his address to EI, one Principia student referred to the meeting as "a life-changing experience."

In spite of the College's close, albeit informal, relationship with the Christian Science Church, the school did not appear ready to change its anti-gay policies, even when The Mother Church began to allow sexual minorities into its fold.

> "Principia does not knowingly admit or hire homosexuals," said Philip Riley, Principia Director of Personnel. "It is really a policy about extramarital and premarital relations, both heterosexual and homosexual. It comes under the category of community standards. Principia views homosexuality as something worthy of healing."(14)

Nevertheless, it is the hope of lesbian/gay students and alumni that the school will someday soon adopt a more humanitarian position. The root of continued exclusion of openly lesbian/gay students, however, may not be homophobia. David White explained what might be the cause of continued anti-gay policies.

> A major reason Principia remains steadfast in its discriminatory policy is because the College is dependent on private funding. There isn't going to be any [pro-gay] movement, until a major donor decides there will be.

Meanwhile, sexual minorities were watching with fascination as their Church opened dialogues in new arenas. This came following a disastrous decade for the Church in the 1980s.

The Church's image suffered greatly following indictments of parents whose children died when medical care had not been employed. Although most cases were reversed on appeal, the public relations fallout was catastrophic. Even Principia College had to temporarily close in 1985 following student deaths from a measles epidemic.(15)

This had a stirring effect on the Church. Discussions of such problems by employees at the Mother Church were frowned on by officialdom. Yet, this was a reality at the Church Center. As one former Church employee said,

> People gossiped constantly at the Church Center, about gays, about children dying, etc., etc. the entire time I worked at The Mother Church. I felt that it was an extremely unhealthy atmosphere, but it was an unspoken rule that you were not allowed to complain about anything—that you should just pray. This rule was emphasized and repeated at my Association meeting every year as well.

Another disaster for the Church was an ill-fated attempt to launch a media empire. This would include a nationwide cable TV network, a radio network, and a glossy-covered *Monitor* magazine perhaps to rival *Time* and *Newsweek*. The project not only was a financial failure, but also caused great dissention within the ranks of the Church. *U.S. News and World Report* put the cost of the failed media adventure at over $300 million. Apparently there were many minor flaws in the media project as well as the better known major ones. One employee who worked on the media project recalled,

> I was closely involved in the media project, working for Monitor television and all the rest of it—radio, short wave radio, etc. I watched as the broadcasting division was gradually taken over by people who didn't have a clue about Christian Science. My band was hired to play for a traveling TV special with political comedian Mort Sahl. I couldn't believe the money people were spending on this project, for things that were entirely unnecessary, in my opinion. It was always fancy lunches, fancy meetings, etc., etc. I had the impression that the people running these programs believed that The Mother Church was a bottomless source of cash.

Could these "disasters" have induced a humbling effect, which in turn helped precipitate changes in attitudes by Church authorities? Perhaps. It was on the heels of these events that doors began to open in many areas. As it turned out, the Church was rewarded in different ways for its new posture.

In the 1990's top Church officials were attending medical conferences at frequent intervals, especially those exploring mind-body relationships. There was also a real or perceived increase in interest in Christian Science among professionals in theological professions. Christian Science Board of Directors Chairperson Virginia S. Harris told the evangelical magazine *Christianity Today*, "Nary a day goes by that I don't hear from a minister or a doctor that says they're using [*Science and Health*]."(16) But medicine and mainstream theology weren't the only arenas where the Church was opening new doors.

The Church had long been at odds with the greater metaphysical movement outside its denomination. The common Church belief has been that these "offshoots" have stolen their ideas from Mrs. Eddy and never gave her credit. They also seemed to believe they are but a watered-down version of Christian Science. For their part, many of these churches claimed Mrs. Eddy stole her ideas from others, especially Phineas Parkhurst Quimby, and that she went on to malign the metaphysical pioneer. Such positions on either side did not foster mutual respect, much less friendship. But, even here there has been a breakthrough of sorts. The

October 2000 issue of *Science of Mind*, the official magazine for the Religious Science denomination, included a full-page advertisement for the *Christian Science Sentinel*, apparently approved and paid for by The Mother Church.(17)

With new thinking going on in so many areas, it may have been only a matter of time until The Mother Church looked favorably on lesbian/gay Christian Science groups.

What appeared to trigger positive action towards the lesbian/gay groups was a newspaper article. Following publication of an in-depth article on the New York City Group of lesbian/gay Christian Scientists, the Committee on Publication Manager for the State of New York contacted the organization. In their conversation, Bob McCullough, one of the facilitators, invited her to a Group meeting. Following the meeting she attended, Bob wrote and posted the Group's reaction on its website. Excerpts include the following:

> Was this really happening—the Christian Science Committee on Publication for New York at our meeting?....
>
> Members who had over the years been active in confronting homophobia in the Christian Science movement were understandably thrilled by the attendance of such an upbeat, supportive church official as our Committee [on Publication Manager for the State of New York]. One sat almost speechless. Another took furious notes, wondering whether any of it could be shared with our internet friends. Then there was the one who had a touch of bitterness in his voice as he launched into a description of some of the old battles. A member who came to Christian Science long after the really wounding thunderbolts landed, cajoled the others with talk show shtick, "Now, I'm still not hearing the love."...[W]e all burst into laughter and the mesmerism was broken. Recovery is solidly underway.
>
> As the meeting drew to a close we talked to the Committee about her duties, how she discovered us and what our interaction can be....
>
> She tracked us down after the article about our group appeared in the *New York Press* causing a stir in Boston and New York. Both she and officials at headquarters felt the article gave a fair impression of Christian Science.
>
> She was appalled at the treatment of Gay people in our movement, as depicted in the article but also based on some of the telephone messages she received about it from around the state, and has done some really good work in directing this release of bilge to its proper place. She emphasized that we too are members of the Christian Science community and may call upon her at any time.

New doors were opening continually for sexual minorities. While it seemed that progress might take longer to reach branch churches, advances were also seen at this level.

Sexual minorities were reporting a new acceptance by branch churches. Some reported they were able to be fully open about their sexuality in their local church without fear of reprisal. One applying for membership on the West Coast revealed his sexual orientation during his formal membership interview and was unanimously accepted into the Church.

In December 1999, a branch church in the Washington, D.C. area advertised a lecture in the local gay newspaper, the *Washington Blade*. This was the first known instance of the gay media being used by a Christian Science Church.

Another known instance of this new acceptance involved a previously ex-communicated member who received a formal invitation to return to his former branch church.

Emergence International (EI) member Hugh Key was asked to leave his Association along with his partner at the time, in 1981. They were told they could not be re-admitted unless they "split up and forsake this vile lifestyle." Just prior to his expulsion, Hugh had opened a practitioner's office with two others engaged in the healing practice of Christian Science. Meanwhile, Hugh continued being active in his branch church. At the beginning of 1982, he was elected First Reader. Before he could begin his term, however, a complaint from his Teacher resulted in the Branch Church asking Hugh for his resignation. Hugh lamented, "In less than nine months I lost my Association, my lover, and my branch church because of her [the Teacher's] actions." In Hugh's words, "I didn't hear from the Church [again] until April of 1996, when the clerk wrote me and stated:

> At a recent meeting of our membership, your association with this church was discussed. It was the thought of all present that a great wrong had been done [14] years ago and we feel it was an unfortunate incident. Would you consider meeting with one of our members who will be calling on you soon?

In spite of the harshness and stigma of the excommunication experience, Hugh replied graciously to the Clerk's letter. He did this without any sense of bitterness or harboring ill feelings.

> Please convey to your membership my deepest appreciation for the stand they have taken. Over the years I have come to realize that the incident to which you refer provided me with a huge blessing. It caused me to dig deeper in Science and to truly begin to discover for myself the full scope of our beloved

Leader's revelation to the world. As she states so clearly in our textbook, "…we find that whatever blesses one blesses all…." (*S&H* page 206, lines 15–16), so that we can all share in this blessing of spiritual progress.

Most interestingly, the same branch Church that took Hugh back into its fold went far beyond admitting to a past mistake. It showed its new feelings in one of the most positive ways possible. The branch Church went on to formally welcome lesbian/gay Christian Scientists to its city for EI's 2001 Annual Conference. The branch Church also arranged for a lecture from The Mother Church's Board of Lectureship to be held in conjunction with EI's Conference. The branch Church had been unable to sponsor a lecture for many years due to financial reasons. This time a few members of EI underwrote the lecture expense. The speaker, who lectured on the rooftop of one of the community's most fashionable hotels, was introduced by the city's mayor. Then, two years later, as if trying to outdo itself, the same branch Church opened its facility for use by EI's members. They came from around the USA and two foreign countries, to plan their organization's future at this three-day conclave. This was the first time meetings by and for openly lesbians and gays took place anywhere in a branch church edifice, all of which appeared a fulfilling of, "whatever blesses one blesses all."

While some situations such as the above became known, there is no way to learn how most branch churches are dealing with sexual minority issues. No such statistics are kept. But sexual minorities now found themselves in an easier position. No longer did they have to wander from church-to-church to find out where they might fit in. Lesbians and gays were now using the Internet to share information. When one of them moved to a new area, s/he could learn rapidly which branch churches not only proclaim, but actually practice, "All are welcome."

What was considered progress by some, no doubt caused grievance for others. For those who grieved, the momentous changes in the Church of Christ, Scientist might've reminded them of Lewis Carrol's classic, *Through the Looking Glass*. Here, everything suddenly appeared upside-down and backwards. Nonetheless, there appeared to be no turning back. Chief concerns among members on all sides of the issues centered more and more on what might happen next.

Predicting the future of any organization is never easy. In what may've seemed an anomaly, the number of people purchasing and studying *Science and Health* was spiraling upwards at the very time the number of members and churches were plummeting. This caused some observers and even some members to ponder whether Christian Science could become something other than a religion.

According to Mrs. Eddy's thought, the answer just might be "yes." Was the time approaching that the Church's Founder predicted, "when the religious element or Church of Christ [Scientist] shall exist alone in the affections and need no organization to express it?" (*Misc.* page 145, lines 3–5) Such was either the fear or desire of many students of her writings. Equally unclear was the future role of lesbian/gay groups supporting sexual minority Christian Scientists.

It appears safe to say lesbian and gay Christian Scientists will continue providing resources for sexual minorities in their faith to meet challenges of new times. And there was no void of challenges. As this book went to press, these seemed to be: 1) continuing hostility toward further liberties sought by the lesbian/gay communities fueled in no small part by religious zealots, 2) continuing challenges from acquired immune deficiency syndrome (AIDS), 3) the wider recognition (and obstacles) for same-gender marriage, 4) a continuing decline in Christian Science teachers, practitioners, churches, and members(18), 5) a continued unsettled world situation, particularly terrorism, and 6) an increasing exacerbation of adverse effects from environmental abuse.

Some lesbian/gay Christian Scientists believed the time may come when organizations supporting sexual minorities in their denomination will no longer be needed. This is a real possibility. It would require, however, a degree of concern toward sexual minorities by The Mother Church, branch churches and private schools for Christian Scientists far exceeding what has been heretofore practiced. The author has seen many devout Christian Scientists with a same-gender orientation, including practitioners, leave their Church for a more supportive environment. To stem the exodus, the Church might begin to address sexual minority concerns in the Church's religious periodicals, public lectures and other denominational forums. It would also require the greatest possible openness by the denomination. This would not only respect, but encourage individuals to follow their own spiritual leanings. This would not be inconsistent with Christian Science teachings. To discover Truth individually is what Mrs. Eddy asked her followers to do. The sixth tenet of the Church's teachings is an affirmation for members to "...solemnly promise to watch, and pray for that Mind to be in us which was also in Christ Jesus;..."(19) She never advised, "Let that mind be in us which is also in the Christian Science Board of Directors."

In the last month of the 19th century (December, 1900), a reporter for the *New York World* asked the Discoverer and Founder of Christian Science what she felt to be "the most imminent dangers confronting the coming [20th] century." Mrs. Eddy went on to identify five "imminent dangers." Could it be that any or all of same these five "dangers" still lay before us in the first decade of the 21st century? In trying to come to terms with "the most imminent dangers confronting the coming [20th] century" we in the 21st century have the advantage of hindsight. As it was, the 20th century produced two world wars, the Korean, Vietnam, and Persian Gulf wars, the depression, the holocaust, the rise of fascism, communism and Islamic terrorism, nuclear weapons, environmental catastrophes, concerns of over-population, and others.

Part of the intent in writing *Christian Science: Its Encounter With Lesbian-Gay America* was to provide an historical perspective of a small segment of the Christian Science movement, and in particular, how that segment responded to ecclesiastical authoritarianism and homophobia. The narrative concludes with Mrs. Eddy's response to the *New York World*. Under the title "Insufficient Freedom," the Christian Science Leader identifies "the [five] most imminent dangers confronting" the 20th Century.

To my sense, the most imminent dangers confronting the coming century are:

1.   the robbing of people of life and liberty under the warrant of the Scriptures;

2.   the claims of politics and of human power,

3.   industrial slavery, and

4.   insufficient freedom of honest competition; and

5.   ritual, creed and trusts in place of the Golden Rule, 'Whatsoever ye would that men should do to you, do ye even so to them.'(20)

End

PART VII
NOTES AND APPENDIXES

NOTES

Preface

1. *S&H* page 497, lines 24–25

2. From *U.S. News and World Report*, "*Healing an ailing church*," by Jeffery L. Sheler, Nov. 6 1989, page 76. Copyright © 1989 U.S. News and World Report, L.P. Reprinted with permission.

3. "A U.S. Judge has ruled unconstitutional the extended copyright on Science and Health. Judge Thomas Penfield Jackson wrote that the 75 year copyright extension granted by Congress in 1971 was in violation of the U.S. Constitution, which states: 'Congress shall make no law respecting an establishment of religion....'" *Christian Science Monitor*, August 22, 1985

4. "The Church of Christ, Scientist does not have an exclusive right to the 'Christian Science' name and a splinter congregation may continue using it, the [New Jersey] state Supreme Court ruled. The court upheld the Union County congregation's right to continue calling itself the [Plainfield, NJ] Independent Christian Science Church, saying the phrase is generic and cannot be protected as a trademark." *USA Today*, Feb 24, 1987 page 2.

5. "The most controversial move occurred a year ago when the Board ordered the redesign of its venerable daily newspaper, which, despite its worldwide reputation for excellence, has lost nearly $200 million over the past 30 years. Plans were announced to cut the staff, trim the number of pages from an average of 32 to about 20 and add color graphics to make the paper more visually appealing to a younger audience. The move prompted a wave of resignations among *Monitor* employees, including three of the newspapers top editors, who interpreted the redesign as a weakening of commitment to the newspaper by church leaders more interested in broadcast technology." *U.S. News & World Report*, Nov 6, 1989 Copyright © 1989 U.S. News and World Report, L.P. Reprinted with permission.

6.   From *Time* October 14, 1991 page 57. © TIME Inc. Reprinted by permission.

7.   The Church does not release membership figures. "Numbering the People" is prohibited by Article VIII, Section 28 of the Church *Manual,* page 48.

"...[S]ome Christian Scientists estimate there are fewer than 170,000 members worldwide, compared with about 270,000 just before World War II. Meanwhile the number of practitioners has plummeted from more than 8,000 in the early 1960's to about 2000 today." From "*In Mrs. Eddy's House: The Church of Christ, Scientist tries to heal its division*" by Jeffery L. Sheler, *U.S. News & World Report*, Feb. 16, 1998 page 61. Copyright © U.S. News & World Report L.P. Reprinted with permission.

A directory of all churches in the world is updated monthly in the *Christian Science Journal*. According to the *Banner* "A Newsletter for Christian Scientists" (*Un*authorized by the Church) Issued quarterly, (Editor: Andrew W. Hartsook) the Winter, 2000 edition calculated "Since the count [of the USA branch churches in the *Journal* listings] began in February, 1987, 503 churches/societies have closed and 36 have formed." That averages approximately 38.69 church/society annual closings from 1987 to 2000 with an average of 2.75 new churches/societies added per year in the same period. (With that rate of attrition continuing into the future, there would be no Christian Science churches remaining in the USA by 2050.)

8.   See: *Christian Science Sentinel*: February 17, 1962 page 281, November 18, 1972 page 2051; March 20, 1976 page 457; and March 5, 1979 page 377. *Christian Science Journal*: February 17, 1962 page 281; October 1978 page 609; April 1979 page 211; October 1973 page 6077; and November 1980 pages 591–593. *Christian Science Monitor*: November 8, 1977 (editorial page).

9.   *S&H* page 141, lines 20–21

Introduction

1.   The history of Metropolitan Community Church (MCC) and the autobiography of its Founder, Reverend Troy D. Perry Jr., are described in *Don't Be Afraid Anymore* by Rev. Troy D. Perry Jr. with Thomas L. P. Spicegood, St. Martin's Press, N. Y., 1990.

2. While membership in the National Council of Churches may have been elusive for the new denomination, many MCC churches were gaining admission to similar councils in their local communities. As evangelical/fundamentalist churches generally do not aspire to belong to ecumenical organizations, the chief opponents to MCC's admission, both locally and nationally were Eastern Orthodox churches.

3. Dignity was organized in 1971 in Los Angeles "to give witness to the [Roman] Catholic Church that it is possible to be both Catholic and gay." As such, Dignity was the first denominationally identified organization for lesbians and gay men. Its first national conference was held in Los Angeles, September 1973. For an in-depth view of Dignity's early years from a liberal Roman Catholic perspective, see *"Gay Catholics," Commonweal,* Feb. 15, 1974, page 479.

Chapter One—Craig Rodwell

1. See *S&H* 468:9–15

2. Kay Tobin and Randy Wicker, *Gay Crusaders,* Paperback Library, New York 1972 page 66

3. *Ibid* page 67

4. Personal interview with author.

5. Tobin, Kay *Op Cit* page 71

6. On learning of his terminal illness, Craig Rodwell sold his bookstore to William Offenbaker in March 1993. (Craig died June 18, 1993 in New York City at age 52.) The book store was sold to Larry Lingle in 1996. The bookstore did not prove profitable to Lingle, so much so that he lost $250,000. He then decided his only option was to close the business. On hearing the announcement of its soon-to-be closure in January 2003, Deacon Maccubbin decided to purchase the book store. Maccubbin was already the owner of Lambda Rising (lesbian/gay) bookstore in Washington, D.C. All store owners have retained the original name, "The Oscar Wilde Memorial Bookshop."

7. From *"Policing the Third Sex," Newsweek*, October 27, 1969 © 1969 Newsweek, Inc. All rights reserved. Reprinted by permission.

8. Andrea Weiss and Greta Schiller, *Before Stonewall;* Naiad Press, Tallahassee, FL 1988, Page 67

9. The *Village Voice;* New York July 3, 1969. Front page.

10. Teal, Donn *Gay Militants;* Stein and Day, New York, page 22

11. Interview with author

12. *Newsweek;* October 27, 1969, *Op Cit*

13. Interview with author

14. Mary Patterson [Mrs. Eddy's name from a previous marriage] was on her way to a local organization of Good Templars walking with a party of lodge members. "In the midst of apparent light-hearted social gaiety she slipped on the ice and was thrown violently. The party stood aghast, but soon lifted her and carried her into a house, where it was seen she was seriously injured…When the physician arrived he said little, but his face and manner conveyed more than his words. It was apparent to the watchers that he regarded her injuries as extremely grave and they believed him to imply that the case might terminate…On the third day, which was Sunday, she sent those who were in her room away, and taking her Bible, opened it. Her eyes fell upon the account of the healing of the palsied man by Jesus.

    "'It was to me a revelation of Truth,' she has written…'The miracles recorded in the Bible, which had before seemed to me supernatural, grew divinely natural and apprehensible.' (*Retrospection and Introspection* page 26)

    "Mrs. Patterson arose from her bed, dressed, and walked into the parlor where a clergyman and a few friends had gathered, thinking it might be for the last words on earth with the sufferer who, they believed was dying. She quietly reassured them and explained the manner of her recovery…." Sibyl Wilbur, *The Life of Mary Baker Eddy,* Christian Science Publishing Society, Boston 1907 pages 123–124.

15. See Don Clark, Ph.D., *Loving Someone Gay*, New American Library, Signet Book, 1977 for a detailed account of the successful effort to change the anti-gay position within the APA.

16. *S&H*, page 109, lines 11–12

17. Teal, Donn; *Gay Militants*; Stein and Day, New York, 1971 page 61

18. The resolution was made by Gay activist Rt. Rev. Michael Itkin.

19. Teal, *Op Cit*, page 61

20. Tobin, Kay and Wicker, Randy, *Gay Crusaders*, Paperback Library 1972, page 72

21. Teal, *Op Cit* page 61

22. John Boswell in his masterful work *Christianity, Social Tolerance and Homosexuality*, (University of Chicago Press 1980) makes the following observation on this verse: "It would have been difficult to justify the imposition of only those portions of Leviticus which supported personal prejudices, and even with circumcision it is difficult to imagine the wholesale adoption by the Graeco-Roman world of Levitical laws which prohibited the consumption of pork, shellfish, rabbit—all staples of Mediterranean diet—or of meats containing blood or fat. Thorough reaping and gleaning of fields, hybridization, clothing of more than one type of fabric, cutting of the beard or hair—all were condemned under Jewish law, and all were integral parts of life under the [Roman] Empire. Viewed through the lenses of powerful modern taboos on the subject, the prohibition of homosexual relations may seem to have been of a different order: to those conditioned by social prejudice to regard homosexual behavior as uniquely enormous, the Levitical comments on this subject may seem to be of far greater weight than the proscriptions surrounding them. But the ancient world...knew no such hostility to homosexuality. The Old Testament strictures against same-sex behavior would have seemed to most Roman citizens as arbitrary as the prohibition of cutting the beard, and they would have had no reason to assume that it should receive any more attention than the latter." Pages 102–103

(For Mrs. Eddy's viewpoint on the book of Leviticus, see chapter 6, note 12)

23. Speaking of this editorial 19 years later, Carl Welz said, "All I can say in defense of myself for writing it is that it was based on information I thought was authentic, but which later was disproved by further studies. If I were to write another article on the subject now, I would probably entitle it, '*We're all God's Children.*'" (Keynote Address, Emergence International Conference, Houston, TX, October 11, 1986) For a detailed discussion on why the late Carl Welz resigned his membership in The Mother Church, including his correspondence with the Christian Science Board of Directors, see Kerry Letter number nine, pages: 1–6 issued February, 1985. Copies of all Kerry Letters are available from "The Bookmark." See chapter 3, note 9.

Chapter Two—Ernest Barnum

1. In 1969, Black militants crashed the Annual Meeting of The Mother Church and demanded a right to be heard. They were given permission to address the gathering from the Reader's platform and read a list of demands to the congregation. (See Chapter 4)

2. From "*Gays Petition Christian Scientists,*" *The Boston Globe;* June 5, 1974. Copyright 1974 by Globe Newspapers Co., (MA) Reproduced with permission of Globe Newspaper Co. (MA) in the format Trade Book via Copyright Clearance Center.

3. *Gay Community News,* Boston, June 1, 1974, reported:

The building where BCOA has its offices is owned by the Christian Science Church, an institution that owns large amounts of property in the Fenway. If the Christian Science Church has its way, Fengay will never again meet in BCOA's offices. The Church has even threatened to kick BCOA out of the building if Fengay meets there again.

Why? Officially, the Church said it objected to the Fengay meetings because Fengay did not offer direct services to the elderly of the community. Therefore, argued Church public affairs director John Selover, BCOA violated its charter by permitting the meetings. But Selover admitted that he has not contacted Fengay, and does not know whether they may offer or be planning services, which are beneficial to the Fenway area elderly.

The Christian Science Church has no official policy regarding gays, according to Selover, who said that he sought understanding of the issues. He emphasized that the reasons for the Church's objections to Fengay meetings did not hinge on the fact that the group is homosexual. But it should be pointed out that other groups that are not directly offering services to the community's elderly have met in BCOA's offices with the full knowledge and implicit approval of the Church.

4. Boston's *Gay Community News* began publication as a weekly in 1973. The paper claimed to be the oldest "queer weekly newspaper" in the United States.

5. Under the headline *"Gays Petition Christian Scientists"* the *Boston Globe,* June 5, 1974, reported:

    "A gay activist group in Boston's Fenway section last night petitioned Christian Scientists who are ending an annual international meeting, to 'take a stand now on our human rights.'

    "A leaflet distributed to church members entering the Mother Church and the Hynes Auditorium for a final service deplored condemnation of gay persons by church groups and asked Christian Scientists to 'listen to us with your hearts.'

    "'It is totally consistent with Christian Science philosophy for them to help us debunk the old attitude of homosexuality being a sin or a sickness' said Thomas Nylund, a member of a group called Fen-Gay. 'We want them to say we have dignity as persons and stand beside us and tell the world that,' he added.

    "A church spokesman said only individual members take stands on social, political or economic issues.

    "'The church does not take positions, period,' said Douglas Russell, the church's communications supervisor."

    Boston *Globe,* June 5, 1974. Copyright 1974 by Globe Newspapers Co. Reproduced with permission of Globe Newspapers Co., (MA) in the format Trade Book via Copyright Clearance Center.

6. On June 15, 1974, *Gay Community News* (Boston) printed a personal account of the event by Sheri Barden:

FENGAYS DEMONSTRATE "THE TRUTH"

It was a warm spring night as a group of Fengays strolled over to the Christian Science Complex to hand out leaflets to the thousands of Scientists gathered for their Annual Meeting. Nostalgia filled the air as they remembered demonstrations of the past, but in their hearts they knew that this one would be different.

Christian Scientists had come from all over the world, 10,000 strong. They all wore name tags, but that really wasn't necessary for they all looked pretty much alike. Nice pastel dresses with white shoes and neatly coiffured hair, nothing flashy. The nice thing about them is that they all have that wonderful look of euphoria about them, as though their thoughts were on a much higher plane than the rest of the world.

So the Fengays handed out their leaflets in the hopes that perhaps they could enter their thoughts. No way, baby 'cause they "know the Truth" about us. "Christian Science cures this," said one nice woman. While another said, "That's nice."

The peaceful demonstration was planned by the newly formed Fengay Organization. One member, Bernie Danoff, was escorted from the property. Tom Nylund, heading the group, was told he must leave the premises. When Tom told them it was a public sidewalk and would they care to speak to the press that was standing by, they backed off.

There appears to be one tiny crack in The Mother Church facade: they cannot stand to be embarrassed. Any adverse criticism sends shivers up their spines.

Because they don't believe in sickness and they know there is no sin, they thought they'd hit them with the truth. "We are neither sick nor sinners," was the plea. "Listen to us with your hearts," they asked, but their pleas fell on deaf ears.

Elaine Noble put on her pastel suit and white shoes and for awhile they thought she was one of them until the word got around.

"The church does not take a stand on any social, political or economic issues. The church does not take positions on anything, period," said Douglas Russell the Christian Science Church's Communications Supervisor....

The reception given the Fengays last Tuesday evening was more like a sheet of ice rather than the blanket of love that you would hope to get from 10,000 supposed Christians. Somehow we must show them the "Truth." There is a great big world of reality beyond that reflecting pool and homosexuals are a living, breathing part of it.

7.   Letter from the Christian Science Board of Directors, November 13, 1974.

8.   "...[W]hat danger lurks in decriminalizing consensual adult homosexual behavior, a proposal made by William Buckley in 1970? And what evil is to be found in forbidding discrimination against homosexuals by government agencies...?

"...[T]he maltreatment of homosexuals, including the psychologically debilitating sense of shame and guilt *imposed* by heterosexuals, is...scandalous, unnecessary, and should offend sensitive conservatives as well as liberals and radicals." Brudnov, David and Van Den Haag, Ernest. From "*Reflections on the Issue of Gay Rights*," From *National Review*, July 19, 1974, © 1974 by National Review, Inc.,. 215 Lexington Avenue, New York, NY 10016. Reprinted by permission. Page 802

9.   For a discussion of Elaine Noble's election and her service in the Massachusetts State House see *Ms* Magazine, August 1975, pages 58–60.

Chapter Three—The Kerry Letters

1.   Kerry Letter # 2, Exhibit E: "[I] applied for a *Journal* listing at the suggestion of the Board of Directors, but Mr. [William] Lee [C.S.B., Manager of the Practitioners Division] said consideration of my application would be deferred until after I had completed my work in Boston and returned to my home base of Santa Barbara. I was also invited to become a Christian Science teacher and also to lecture which I turned down. At my last meeting with the Board, Mr. [Otto] Bertschi, [Chairman] assured me that I had never been refused *Journal* listing."

2.   *Manual of the Mother Church*, Christian Science Publishing Society, page 17, lines 10–13.

3.   Kerry Letter # 2; page 26

4. Reinhardt, Madge—*The Voice of the Stranger*, Back Row Press, St. Paul 1982, page 404

5. Kerry said original estimates were $8 million; actual costs were nearly $80 million. Letter # 1; page 2.

6. The *Time* article said,

    "Last December a curious nine-page letter landed in the mail boxes of Christian Science practitioners and local church leaders. It warned that the faith's Boston headquarters was rife with 'gross mismanagement, inexperience and lack of Christian ethics.' Unless 'the Field' demanded a housecleaning, the letter said, the religion could virtually disappear within a decade. In the serenely authoritarian world of Christian Science, rarely had such a challenge been issued against officials of the Mother Church. Its author is Reginald G. Kerry, 62, a straitlaced former restauranteur and police and fire commission member in Santa Barbara, Calif and devout Scientist for 40 years. In 1973, Kerry came to the Boston headquarters as a consultant on security. He learned about other matters, however, and decided to tell all.... The directors' cautiously crafted reply to recipients of the Kerry letter ignored some charges and insisted that others 'verge on conscious dishonesty.' They said their annual incomes were 'far less' than Kerry's $100,000 estimate, but granted that financial reserves had been 'seriously depleted' in order to build the Boston church center. Last week a spokesman added that the Kerry figures on membership and failing churches were distorted. Apparently undeterred, Kerry wants his fellow Scientists to demand a special investigation and insist on 'an honest and thorough account' of church conditions at the annual June meeting in Boston."

    From *Time*, March 15, 1976, page 44. © TIME Inc. Reprinted by permission.

7. Copies of all Kerry Letters are available from "The Bookmark." See note number eight.

8. Ann Beals' cassette tape: "*The Spiritually Organized Church*" c/o The Bookmark, P.O. Box 801143, Santa Clarita, CA 91380. Reprinted by permission from Ann Beals. Ms. Beals, Founder of the Bookmark, collects and sells a vast collection of Christian Science material, most of which, is not available from Church ("authorized") sources. Also available are copies of Reginald

Kerry's letters. Internet home page: <http://www.thebookmark.com> E-mail: <order@thebookmark.com>

9.   From author's interview with Chris Madsen.

Chapter Four—Save Our Children

1.   Anita Bryant *The Anita Bryant Story*; Fleming H. Revell Co., Old Tappan, NJ 1977 pages 14–15.

2.   Ibid page 15

3.   *Ibid* page 17

4.   *Ibid* pages 28–29

5.   *Newsweek,* March 13, 1978

6.   Anita Bryant, *Op Cit* page 13

7.   From *"Enough! Enough! Enough!" Time*; June 20, 1977, page 59. © TIME Inc. Reprinted by permission.

8.   Ibid page 59

9.   From *"Affectional Preference" Commonweal*; July 7, 1978 page 435

10. Bryant, Anita and Green, Bob *At Any Cost*; Fleming H. Reville Co., Old Tappen, NJ 1978 page 27

11. "Our community could become a haven for practicing homosexuals, lesbians, prostitutes and pimps," said one pamphlet distributed by the Concerned Citizens for Community Standards of Wichita, KS. Another warned, "There is a real danger that homosexual teachers, social workers or counselors, simply by public acknowledgment of their life styles, can encourage sexual deviation in children." These and other fearful concerns—widely circulated in a $50,000 publicity campaign—helped produce a dramatic result last week in Wichita voting booths. From *Time;* May 22, 1978, page 21. © 1978 TIME Inc. Reprinted by permission.

12. *Ibid* page 22

13. From *"Political Ceremony in California"* by Joseph R. Gusfield. Reprinted with permission from the December. 9, 1978 issue of *The Nation,* page 633. For subscription information, call 1-(800) 333-8536. Portions of each week's Nation magazine can be accessed at http://www.thenation.com.

14. *Ibid* page 637

15. From *"A California Travesty,"* *The New Republic;* Oct 28, 1978 page 8. Reprinted by permission.

16. From *Seattle Gay News;* Seattle, WA, March 30, 1979 page 8, article by Bruce Stores

17. Source: *The Christian Science Monitor,* November 8, 1977. Reproduced with permission. Copyright © 1977 The Christian Science Monitor (www.csmonitor.com). All rights reserved.

18. Calling attention to the "serious sin of omission" in the following letter to the editor may have accurately gauged the sentiment in sexual minority communities across the United States as to the media's indifference about their role in American life.

Homosexuals in the "Me" decade

Gay People in the U.S. measured by nearly every researcher since Kinsey constitute approximately 10 per cent of our population. The *Monitor's* feature ["Activism in the 1970's"] ignored the decade's unprecedented gay movement, a movement which resulted in significant changes in legal, psychological, religious, and media treatment of homosexuality, and marked by unheralded development of lesbian/gay subcultures, organizational networks, and lifestyles.

The historical changes effected by this movement have affected millions of people and are sure to affect millions more.

In an article that featured the important activism of the preceding decade, the omission of the gay movement must be considered a serious sin of omission to the *Monitor's* comprehensive journalism.

Michael K. Hughes, Seattle, WA, "Reader's Write" Column, *Christian Science Monitor,* Jan 15, 1980. Reprinted by permission from Michael K. Hughes.

Chapter Five—Beginning of Lesbian/Gay Christian Science Groups

1. Bob Mackenroth's military service in World War II began in the Army Signal Corps. He was later transferred to the Army Air Corps. He went to the European Continent "just behind the first wave on D-Day." He later fought in Holland and Belgium. There, he played an important role in capturing a number of Germans during a combat mission. At one point his guard buddy just a few feet from him was killed by a bomb. At the war's end, he was awarded a metal by the Prince Regent of Belgium for participating in the liberation of his country.

2. Kay Tobin and Randy Wicker, *The Gay Crusaders*; Paperback Library 1972., page 66. (Chapter devoted to Craig Rodwell pages 65 to 76.)

3. *S&H* page 226, lines 5–6

4. Francis Bernard, Robert Mackenroth, and Ray Spitale

5. *Christian Science Hymnal* # 298

6. Boston's *Gay Community News* reported on June 14, 1980, page 6:

   When several thousand Christian Scientists from around the world convene here in early June, gay Christian Scientists will for the first time be visible among them. A group of about 20 gay Christian Scientists and some straight supporters within the church will be distributing their pamphlet, "Gay People in Christian Science?" in an attempt to change the widespread unacceptance of gays by the Christian Science Church. They stress that their activity at this annual meeting of church members, held each June at the church's world headquarters in Back Bay [Boston] will be orderly, legal, and peaceful. The nucleus of the group is about ten gay men from New York City who will be joined in Boston by Christian Scientists, both gay and straight, from several other cities. In addition to leafleting, the group plans a silent protest in the church itself in the event that anti-gay remarks are made during the meeting. The New York group, Gay People in Christian Science, authored the pamphlet which has been mailed to every Christian Science church and practitioner in the world....

Although lesbians and gay men have always been active in the Christian Science church, rarely have they been open about it. There have been many instances, especially in the last ten years, where gays have been forced from the church, been denied employment, or been fired at the church headquarters.

The various Christian Science publications…have carried numerous articles condemning homosexuality, stressing that it can be 'healed'—that gay people can become heterosexual by studying the teachings of Mary Baker Eddy…While Gay People in Christian Science do not doubt the ability of Christian Scientists to heal through prayer, they challenge the notion that homosexuality should be healed, and scoff at the idea that 'becoming' heterosexual is an improvement, given the generally negative view of Christian Scientists towards any sexuality.

Gay People in Christian Science hope to reach the Christian Science Board of Directors, the governing body of the church, with their actions at the meeting. The board has for the past several years refused to meet with gays to discuss their place in the church. The group, which is committed to working within the church, and in accord with the principles of Christian Science, wants to appeal to all Christian Scientists to re-examine their thoughts on sexuality.

7. Homosexuals were forced to wear pink triangles in Nazi Germany and Nazi occupied Europe to identify themselves as Jews were required to wear the star of David.

8. Smaller leafleting activities took place at various branch churches by GPICS in New York City. In Seattle, WA., Glen Hunt (deceased) and the author handed the pamphlet *"Gay People in Christian Science?"* to many attendees at First, Third and Twelfth churches on the Sunday prior to Annual Meeting. Interestingly, the activity revealed a bit of the nature of different congregations. Attendees at First Church were overtly friendly. Ushers pleaded with us to come inside and attend the service. Attendees at Third Church were hostile to the point of anger. Several screamed at us. One man yelled, "Why are you trying to destroy us?" Virtually all attendees at Twelfth Church were indifferent though many accepted the pamphlet.

9. As a reaction to the anti-gay article, the late Jim Bradley, a member of Gay Christian Scientists in the Northwest, was one of those who put his feelings

on paper and mailed them to the *Journal's* Editorial Department. He also sent a copy to Neil Bowles, author of "*Only One Kind of Man*," and also to the Christian Science Board of Directors. His letter was shared with all lesbian/gay Christian Science groups. It soon became a manifesto for many against Mother Church homophobia. The letter was re-printed in newsletters of most local groups. Salient passages from Bradley's letter include the following:

The article's chief flaw is that it never substantiates its guiding premise. Mr. Bowles bases his entire argument on the premise that homosexuality is an error or evil that needs to be healed. He calls it "abnormal," "unnatural," "a perversion," and an "aberration." He labels homosexuals as "second class," "deviates," and "outcasts from society." Today's scientific community tells us that homosexuality is natural and healthy for at least ten percent of the population and has been a normal part of human sexuality throughout history. Because the article's premise is opposite to these findings, it is very important that Mr. Bowles back it up with something other than his own opinion…

Mr. Bowles does offer us some of his own opinions on why we should think of homosexuality as error. When analyzed in the light of the *Bible* and *Science and Health*, these opinions become just that—one person's opinion.

He claims that 'the physical structure of male and female bodies indicates what is humanly normal in matters of sexual relationships.' He never states what it is about gay relationships that do not come naturally for the body. Many would dispute his claim. But, more importantly, it is hardly appropriate for the *Journal* to be telling us to look to our physical bodies for guidance on what is good and normal for our lives. Christian Science teaches us not to be limited in any way by 'the physical structure of male and female bodies.' Would mankind ever have walked on water, beaten the four-minute mile, flown to the moon, or healed diseases if we had followed Mr. Bowles' advice?

He complains that homosexuals do not marry, and marriage is "the standard for Christian Scientists." Does this mean that all single people, heterosexuals included, are leading unnatural lives, that only once we are married are we good people? Neither Jesus, his disciples, nor Paul were married. Many homosexual couples, however, do get married. The bonds of love between gay couples can be just as deep and lasting as the ones between heterosexuals. Perhaps Mr. Bowles has never met such couples. I have. He calls being gay a "lustful practice." How is it any more lustful than being straight? Furthermore, when one discusses homosexuality or heterosexuality, one is not talking primarily about sex, but about love…. The *Journal* is on shaky ground when it tries to judge what is and isn't lust between two people who love each other. A stronger position would be to give couples the same instructions Mrs. Eddy gave. On page 287 of *Miscellaneous Writings,* she states that her advice to couples who would come to her with 'important questions concerning their happiness' was quite simple: "God will guide you."

Mr. Bowles tells us that gay people do not contribute to society. "Everyone has a responsibility to society and an obligation to aid in the betterment of the human race. But homosexuality leaves to the institution of the human family no legacy of improvement." I can only conclude that Mr. Bowles has met very few gay people. I know lawyers, heads of corporations, bankers, civil servants, politicians, ministers, soldiers, and teachers who are gay and leading productive lives. Historians tell us that Alexander the Great, the emperor Hadrian, Leonardo da Vinci, Michelangelo, Peter the Great, Walt Whitman, and many others were homosexuals. Did Socrates contribute nothing to society? Mrs. Eddy refers to his teachings in her chapter on "Marriage" (*Science and Health,* page 66). On page 215 of our textbook, she describes him as a man who "understood the immortality of good," who "sought man's spiritual state," and who "recognized the immortality of man." Socrates was openly gay all his life. Plato and other writers discuss his love for other men in depth. By being well read in the classics, Mrs. Eddy could have been quite aware of his orientation, but perhaps she realized that whom Socrates loved and slept with were irrelevant to the good he accomplished.

Mr. Bowles' final argument for the unhealthiness of homosexuality is that it causes unhappiness. He describes it as a "perversion" that leads "to an unfulfilled, isolated existence." Once again I can only wonder how many gay people he actually has met. I know many who are open, well adjusted, surrounded by friends, and involved in loving, fulfilled relationships. Even the most superficial research into the topic would have taught Mr. Bowles the same.

The most disturbing aspect of this article for all Christian Scientists, regardless of sexual orientation, is the author's view that "normalcy" is the great goal of Christian Scientists. He writes, "In this present sense of life, we best serve and glorify Him with normalcy—for normalcy in the human, rather than deviate tendencies, more nearly tends to pattern the fact of spiritual perfection." Not only is this a very awkward sentence, but it is not backed up with a reference of any kind from our textbooks. Neither Mrs. Eddy nor Jesus advocated that their followers fit into the norm. On page 238 of *Science and Health*, Mrs. Eddy writes, "To obey the Scriptural command, 'Come out from among them, and be ye separate', is to incur society's frown, but this frown, more than flatteries, enables one to be Christian."

Jesus was considered so abnormal by society that it crucified him. As a woman lecturing, writing, and founding a religion in the unliberated nine- teenth century, Mrs. Eddy was not considered normal by her contemporar- ies, either. She was accused periodically of being avaricious, senile, or insane, and ultimately she was brought to trial. If our Leader had followed Mr. Bowles' advice, I am afraid that there would be no Christian Science today…

I hope that some of my suggestions will help you in future articles on human relationships. Thank you for taking the time to consider them. I support the healing mission of the *Journal* and look forward to future issues. On one point Mr. Bowles and I do agree. There is indeed 'only one kind of man'—a man in whom human sexuality has no real role, a man who is the image and likeness of God.

(signed) Jim Bradley, Joseph, Oregon

Bob Mackenroth of Gay People in Christian Science, New York City also wrote to Mr. Bowles re: his article "*Only One Kind of Man.*" His letter ended with the words: "Mr. Bowles, there is no legitimate reason to attempt to 'heal' *any* human relationship if it does not break the Golden Rule. Those who accuse, condemn or 'throw stones' are the ones who need healing."

10. Soon after Chris Madsen's court settlement with The Mother Church, in October 1985, GPICS/New York did die out. About a year later, a lesbian/ gay Christian Science study group was begun by Bob McCullough. As the name suggests, this group has been study only and not involved in activism of any sort. This has been the most successful local group in the country and continues to this day.

11. See Chapter 8, note 5.

12. The Plainfield Church was de-listed as a branch church. Following a long dispute The Mother Church asked Plainfield's membership to vote out of

office the members of its Board. The members refused. This resulted in the branch's excommunication by The Mother Church in 1977. When the Plainfield Church insisted on using the words "Christian Science" as part of its name, ten years of litigation followed. This ended in a victory by the Plainfield Church, but at a cost to them of $250,000. In a visit to the independent Church in April, 1993, the author found an active membership well represented by all age groups. Eighty to ninety per-cent of their spacious auditorium was full at this mid-week service. (For more information, see author's article "*A Journey to Plainfield*," *Emerge!* May/June 1993, pages 17–19)

13. Reginald Kerry's letters to the Church field were discontinued in the mid-1980's. A similar work, The *Banner*, began in 1987 by Andrew W. Hartsook. The quarterly newsletter carries news and analysis about the Christian Science denomination from a non-authorized point of view. The *Banner* appears to be a far less sensational publication then were the Kerry letters. The newsletter discusses matters most Christian Scientists would be unable to glean from Church sources. Subscriptions to the *Banner* may be obtained by writing: Mr. Andrew W. Hartsook, 2040 Hazel Avenue, Zanesville, OH 43701-2222

Chapter Six—The Chris Madsen Affair

1. One of the most remarkable achievements by Mary Baker Eddy was founding the *Christian Science Monitor*, which she did at age 87 in 1908. As a Church sponsored international daily newspaper there is nothing comparable to it in the world. In his book *Commitment to Freedom*, then *Monitor* Editor-in-Chief, Erwin D. Canham put it this way:

"Half a century ago a lone woman, in her eighty-eighth year, foresaw the service a newspaper could perform…In all the history of journalism, surely there is no more extraordinary and unexpected phenomenon."

These views are somewhat shared by many who are not Christian Scientists. The *Christian Century*, an ecumenical magazine for Protestants, once told its readers: "The *Christian Science Monitor* is a unique journalistic institution, a church publication with worldwide circulation and the competent staff and resources necessary to make it excellent by secular as well as religious standards…. Many non-Christian Scientists are glad that God told Mrs. Eddy to establish a daily newspaper." From *"The Monitor is Unique"* by Nathanael M. Guptill, pages 1017–1019, Copyright 1955, Christian Ministry. Reprinted by permission from the May 7, 1955 issue of the *Christian Century.*

In addition to reviews from religious publications, the secular press also gave high marks to Mrs. Eddy's newspaper. In 1958, the year of the *Monitor's* 50th anniversary, *Time* magazine told its readers, "The *Monitor* has no truck with trivia, concentrates instead on solid, staff written interpretative reporting…. For this reason the *Monitor* gets the ultimate tribute of the news profession: its subscribers include 4,000 editors and newspapers throughout the world, some of whom pay as much as $1,000 a year to have their copies airmailed" [worldwide surface mail rate in 1958: $18]. *Time*, like many *Monitor* observers, brought out what some feel are its most unusual peculiarities: "…the 115 *Monitor* staffers…work in its cathedral-hushed city room…turn out prose unpolluted by cigar smoke, gin fumes or profanity. Working at the *Monitor*, therefore, is more than a job for many of its employees. It's a mission. And one could imagine news and editorial writers who believe in the paper's mission approaching assignments with a zeal unmatched by counterparts from other papers." From *Time*, Jan. 27, 1958, pages 42–43 © TIME Inc. Reprinted by permission.

2. According to Ray Spitale, GPICS/New York had already learned that two of the five members of the Christian Science Board of Directors favored a change in the Church's discriminatory bias towards same-gender sexuality. Peritin confirmed this fact to Chris Madsen.

3. Sitomer later wrote an article titled *"Discriminating Against Homosexuals."* In it he wrote: "Understanding and compassion as well as a clear grasp of individual rights will take us a lot further than ostracism." The article was reprinted in *Emerge!* May/June, 1988. Page 21.

4. *GPICS/New York Newsletter*—June 30, 1982, page 3.

5. One of the letters received by the newspaper was from former *Monitor* reporter Allen Young. Young (not to be confused with Alan Young the former Church lecturer and Communications Director) who wrote over 100

articles for the *Monitor* in the 1960's, sent a letter to Personnel Manager Karen H. Gould. In it, he said in part:

"I was certainly not surprised at the recent spate of nasty firings of gay employees. I think it is shameful. I won't pretend to get involved in the theological aspects of what you are doing. A group called 'Gay People in Christian Science' can take care of that. But on a strictly human level, I think the homophobia of the church is a terrible thing, and my thoughts go out especially to Christine Madsen, a fellow journalist, who has been so devastated by the firing. I hope that the good people in the Christian Science community will prevail over those who are narrow-minded and bigoted, and that this shameful persecution of gay people will cease." (Reprinted in *GPICS/NY newsletter*)

6.   *GCN* (June 19, 1982) in a front page story reported:

Shouting, "Stop the witch hunt," about 50 people marched through the grounds of the world headquarters of the Church of Christ, Scientist on Monday, June 7.

In the cold drizzle, protestors carried signs demanding justice and job security for lesbian and gay male employees of the church. They leafleted hundreds of the 8000 rank and file church members who had come from around the globe to attend the annual meeting of the Mother Church last week. Reporters from most of the major television and radio stations were at the scene. "Their coverage of the demonstration was sympathetic to us," said [Chris] Madsen.

"We held the rally in hopes of getting publicity to put more pressure on the Board of Directors to change their policy regarding gays in the church," she said. "We chose this date specifically so we'd get the word out to Christian Scientists at the annual meeting about the fact that the Mother Church is firing competent, loyal employees for no good reason. I have faith in the ability of Christian Scientists to think independently."

However, most of the church members leafleted on the grounds were unreceptive to the leafleters and a few were hostile, "Ignorance makes you do this," said one elderly woman. "Yes, I know why you're here and you shouldn't be," said another church member. And Madsen herself reported that she and three other Christian Scientists who attended that day's meeting wearing pink triangle buttons were ostracized by other conferees.

7.   Text of A.W. Phinney's statement:

"There aren't any witch-hunts for homosexuals in this church. There plainly isn't the time or inclination for such a thing in the face of the suffering and the needs of the world today. The topics of which we are trying to bring a spiritual perspective at our annual meeting are subjects of everyone's concern. The church's basic position on homosexuality is well known. It isn't based on isolated passages, but on the whole Bible, specifically New Testament Christianity. Society hasn't always agreed with Christian moral standards. But the standards remain. The church can't change every time a social trend changes. The denomination's position on homosexuality isn't that different from many churches today. It emphasizes healing and compassion. But it is straightforward, open, not secretive. The church simply believes that society doesn't make rules for Christians. Therefore, if you believe otherwise, it probably doesn't make sense in the first place to want to work for the denomination and its activities, including the *Monitor*."

8.   Writing in the *GPICS/New York Newsletter*, June 7, 1982, Bob McCullough wrote:

"Over the years of struggle with the sin of homophobia in the Christian Science movement we have heard from a number of Gay and non-Gay Christian Scientists who feel that while there is no conflict involved in being Gay and as Christian Scientists we should not organize or engage in any 'human activities' to fight this deadly sin, but should simply pray for the lifting of the problem. Let us say first that all people should most fervently pray for the lifting of the sin of homophobia in ourselves and others. Prayer is certainly the essential part in destroying sin but it is not the only part.

"Gay People in Christian Science are basically involved in pointing out and fighting the sins of homophobia, racism and sexism still clinging to our Movement in a number of ways. It should be noted that it is not only heterosexuals who suffer from homophobia. Many Gay/Lesbian Christian Scientists, for instance, continue to search for the 'easy' way of acceptance through passing as non-Gay—thus distorting their human lives, rather than working to evangelize and spiritualize them. This tragic misperception and all the others based on homophobia, racism and sexism need to be whipped from the temple."

From the other side of the Country, a member from Emergence/Los Angeles, identified only as Daryl, wrote in its newsletter of June, 1982 as follows:

"...Most of us who have grown up in Christian Science tended to be raised with a rather passive attitude: 'Turn the other cheek,' 'See what works out,' etc. However, the first definition of militant in the dictionary says, 'to serve as a soldier.' A soldier is alert to defend and resist all transgressors.

"We in the gay community find ourselves in an awkward position with regard to The Mother Church and Boston. Far be it for us to advocate any 'civil' disturbances or demonstrations regarding our beloved church. However, there seem to be rather self-righteous members of the governing church structure that dearly love to condemn, stoop to name calling. We may say 'Sticks and stones....' yet these names can hurt because they are lies about God's true man. As soldiers we must reject the bombardment of lies directed toward us by a nameless foe...."

9. "One of the early cases that came before [the Christian Science Board of Directors] was a charge of immoral conduct against a First Member who was a student of Mrs. Eddy's. From the evidence submitted, the Directors were convinced that the charges were sustained. They, therefore, removed the individual from membership in the church, and took his practitioner's card out of the *Christian Science Journal.* That punishment in no wise healed the individual, but made him so rebellious that he threatened a lawsuit in revenge.

"When Mrs. Eddy heard of this case, she asked the Directors to restore her student to full church membership, including his office as a First Member, and to replace his card in the *Journal.* This resulted in a complete healing of the individual; but it was a shock to the Directors' idea of church discipline." *Ira Oscar Knapp and Flavia Stickney Knapp, A Biographical Sketch,* by Bliss Knapp; Plimpton Press, Norwood, MA. [c1925] Page 140

In a letter to all Mother Church members (April 23, 1992) the Board outlined their reasoning as to their place in Church affairs:

"In the Church *Manual,* Mrs. Eddy states that the business of her Church is to be conducted by a Board of Directors...The Board...is entrusted with the learning experience—often humbling—of securing the Church's position in a changing world. The *Manual* compels them to minister to the needs of all mankind. Mrs. Eddy's years of counsel to her Board of Directors trained them to study her works constantly and to turn radically to God for direction in all their endeavors. She admits in her writings that the Board at times made mistakes. (See *Miscellaneous Writings* [by Mary Baker Eddy] page 130, line 17). Yet Mrs. Eddy's lasting demonstration of love for her Church was shown in her placement of the actual government of her Church, under its Church *Manual* provisions.

"The Board of Directors would be the last to claim any mantle of infallibility...Building on our Leader's demonstration, we feel that the prayers, individual and collective, of all the members provide the workers of this Church with the ability to exceed their ordinary capacities. Current difficulties should not be allowed to make us lose sight of the significant good that is being accomplished every day as each member contributes to this Church's healing mission. Our Leader requires us all to conform to God's ways and not to human usage. We make these points because all who love this Church need, at this time, the greatest alertness and devotion to prayer."

10. The following account of the Houston group was discussed as follows in *Identity Newsletter*, San Francisco, September, 1984:

"Several gays in Houston meet *weekly* to read and discuss the Lesson-Sermon. This is not new. But what has given cohesion to this group for a year and a half is the *purpose* they meet. Each participant to the meeting comes prepared to discuss the results of his study as it relates to himself and his world.

"Meetings are tightly structured, and are no more than 90 minutes long. Each member may discuss any problem he is working on, and ask for help. Then, during the following week, every member keeps in touch with all other members in an outreach of concern and love. This group demonstrates caring in a tangible form.

"Through individual members the group makes an outreach to others in the New Thought or metaphysical movement—Unity, Science of Mind, Religious Science, *et al*. Contrary to the Boston Directors' exclusionary stance, the Houston people find more room for agreement than disagreement with these 'fallen' people, many of whom have left the CS Church because of its rigidity. And nowhere in the broader metaphysical movement is there any stigma on being gay except in the CS Church."

Emergence/Houston went on to host the third national lesbian/gay Christian Science conference, (October, 1986). This was the first conference sponsored by the newly formed national organization, Emergence, Inc. The Conference included speakers that once held high positions in the larger

Christian Science movement: Carl Welz and Robert Doling Wells. The Houston conclave was the first time a conference included its own Sunday Church service. This marked the beginning of experimenting with variations of the Sunday Church service which is identical in all branch churches in the world. Instead of using the prescribed Lesson-Sermon from the *Christian Science Quarterly,* readings became tailored to the organization and the Conference. At the 1986 Houston Conference, the spiritual interpretation of the Lord's Prayer was taken from the first edition (1875) of *Science and Health,* (page 295). Testimonies were added to services at future conferences primarily because they could include comments that were not likely to be appreciated at branch churches.

It was at the first service in Houston an event occurred which has become a legend in the annals of the organization. As the Sunday Church service drew to a close, Conference Coordinator John Scott told attendees substantially as follows: "As you all know this is the time when a collection normally takes place. We in Emergence/Houston, however, have learned that before we can receive, we must learn how to give. Therefore, instead of a collection we are going to have a distribution." Then, in a louder voice, John said, "Ushers, please bring the boxes in!" At that moment the ushers entered carrying large cardboard cartons. Inside each carton were stuffed teddy bears. They were distributed to everyone present. No collection was taken.

11. The history of the first lesbian/gay Christian Science group in the Old World can be traced to a business trip by Gordon Allen from Kent, England to San Francisco in 1987. There he first heard of Emergence International. He contacted Kentner Scott and was given basic information on the organization. Back in London, he took out ads in the sexual minority press about forming a lesbian/gay Christian Science support group. He received several replies. The first meeting of the London group was held in the Spring of 1988 with six persons present. Meetings were first held in members' homes. Later they would meet in London's Lesbian and Gay Centre. The Group published a newsletter and held monthly meetings. The Group was recognized as a formal chapter of Emergence International in 1989.

12. In her published writings, Mrs. Eddy makes no mention of the Book of Leviticus. Her only quote from this book in her published writings is Lev 19:18 "Thou shalt love thy neighbor as thyself." This verse she quotes on ten occasions. Official Eddy biographer, Robert Peel, however, gives us an opinion

she held about the third book of the Pentateuch: "Many years later she wrote that despite the stimulus of the Quimby period she had lacked 'the one thing needed' until the experience of 'the accident and injury called fatal, [when] the Bible healed me; and from Quimbyism to the Bible was like turning from Leviticus to St. John.'" *Mary Baker Eddy: Years of Discovery*, page 205.

13. *The First Church of Christ Scientist and Miscellany,* by Mary Baker Eddy; Page 266, lines 3–5

Chapter Seven—Chris Madsen's Trial

1. (Continuing) "To the contrary, Eddy wrote quite a few things about androgyny male and female combined in one human nature. 'Let the "male and female" of God's creating appear' (*S&H* 249:5), is a benediction. By their action, the Directors are attempting to thwart this divine appearing. The consequences of impeding right action is theirs. Then, there's that remarkable Boston allegation that heterosexual marriage is to be considered the norm in human experience. Even a cursory reading of Eddy statements on the subject shows 1.) she had precious little to say that was positive about marriage, and 2.) the institution was to be regarded as a concession to the times. Not exactly a standard to judge the gay lifestyle against!" Kentner Scott, "*Speaking Out*" *Identity* March, 1984, page 3.

2. As this book went to press, the following 14 states and the District of Columbia had laws banning employment discrimination on the basis of sexual orientation: California, Connecticut, Hawaii, Maryland, Massachusetts, Minnesota, Nevada, New Hampshire, New Jersey, New Mexico, New York, Rhode Island, Vermont and Wisconsin.

3. *S&H* page 563, lines 27–30

4. Chris Madsen: quoted on Yahoo Group's Internet Bulletin Board "cslesbigay" November 9, 2000. Reprinted with permission.

5. *Gay Community News*, October 13, 1984

Chapter Eight—The Christian Science Board of Directors

1. The following quotes on human organization are from Mrs. Eddy's published writings:

Miscellaneous Writings

Page 91: lines 4–12 "It is not indispensable to organize materially Christ's church. It is not absolutely necessary to ordain pastors and to dedicate churches, but if this be done, let it be in concession to the period, and not as a perpetual or indispensable ceremonial of the church. If our church is organized, it is to meet the demand, 'Suffer it to be so now.' The real Christian compact is love for one another. This bond is wholly spiritual and inviolate."

Page 144: lines 32–7 "The Church, more than any other institution, at present is the cement of society, and it should be the bulwark of civil and religious liberty. But the time cometh when the religious element, or Church of Christ, shall exist alone in the affections, and need no organization to express it. Till then, this form of godliness seems as requisite to manifest its spirit, as individuality to express Soul and substance."

Page 274: lines 1–2 "From the scant history of Jesus and of his disciples, we have no Biblical authority for a public institution."

Page 358: lines 20–22, 30–4 "Be it understood that I do not require Christian Scientists to stop teaching, to dissolve their organizations, or to desist from organizing churches and associations....

"When students have fulfilled all the good ends of organization, and are convinced that by leaving the material forms thereof a higher spiritual unity is won, then is the time to follow the example of the *Alma Mater* [the Massachusetts Metaphysical College]. Material organization is requisite in the beginning; but when it has done its work, the purely Christly method of teaching and preaching must be adopted."

Retrospection and Introspection

Page 45: lines 5–15, 23–25 "Despite the prosperity of my church, it was learned that material organization has its value and peril, and that organization is requisite only in the earliest periods in Christian history. After this material form of cohesion and fellowship has accomplished its end, continued organization retards spiritual growth, and should be laid off, in order to gain spiritual freedom and supremacy.

"From careful observation and experience came my clue to the uses and abuses of organization. I also saw that Christianity has withstood less the temptation of popularity than of persecution.

Page 50: lines 23–28 "I see clearly that students in Christian Science should, at present, continue to organize churches, schools, and associations for the furtherance and unfolding of Truth, and that my necessity is not necessarily theirs; but it was the Father's opportunity for furnishing a new rule of order in divine Science, and the blessings which arose therefrom."

Page 60: lines 25–27 "Material sense contradicts Science, for matter and its so-called organizations take no cognizance of the spiritual facts of the universe, or of the real man and God."

People's Idea of God

Page 1: lines 1–7 "The great element of reform is not born of human wisdom; it draws not its life from human organizations; rather is it the crumbling away of material elements from reason, the translation of law back to its original language,—Mind, and the final unity between man and God."

Science and Health.

The first edition of *Science and Health* and subsequent editions (over 400 in all) have many more passages showing Mrs. Eddy's displeasure with human church organization. One example: "We have no need of creeds and church organizations to sustain or explain a demonstrable platform, that defines itself in healing the sick, and casting out error." (*S&H*, first edition, page 166).

The current Church position is that the present edition of *Science and Health* reflects Mrs. Eddy's highest level of inspiration and should be the one used by Church members and all students of her writings. The current (authorized) edition of *Science and Health* makes no mention of human church organization, much less our need to have it.

On the other hand, there is much to be seen from Mrs. Eddy's writings in favor of organization. Her book, *The First Church of Christ, Scientist and Miscellany* contains 34 letters supporting the work of branch churches. To the branch Church in Salt Lake City, for example, she wrote, "It gives me great pleasure to know that you have erected a Church of Christ, Scientist, in your city." page 186: lines 27–1. And to First Church of Christ, Scientist in Pittsburg, she wrote, "My Beloved Brethren:—I congratulate you upon erecting the first edifice of our denomination in the Keystone State,..." *Ibid*, page 196, lines 1–3.

Still, a case can be made that Mrs. Eddy was only giving in to the vast majority of her followers not yet ready to give up human organization.

From the thousands of Christian Scientists in the world, she selected those few she felt to have the highest understanding of her Discovery to live and work in her household. At the very time she was writing the above mentioned letters to branch churches, she was giving the members of her household (those with the understanding closest to hers), a very different message.

"An outspoken message which she [Mrs. Eddy] delivered to her household at this period [circa 1902] reveals very clearly what lay at the heart of her concern:

The true Science—divine Science—will be lost sight of again unless we arouse ourselves. This demonstrating to make matter build up is not Science. The building up of churches, the writing of articles and the speaking in public is the old way of building up a Cause. The way I brought this Cause into sight was through healing; and now these other things would come in and hide it, just as was done in the time of Jesus. Now this Cause must be saved and I pray God to be spared for this work." From Peel, Robert, *Mary Baker Eddy, The Years of Authority 1892-1910*. Holt Rinehart and Winston, New York, 1977 page 226.

2.   Beasley, Norman, *The Cross and The Crown*; Duell, Sloan and Pearce, NY 1952, page: 629

3.   The quotation in context reads:

"All revelation (such is the popular thought!) must come from the schools and along the line of scholarly and ecclesiastical descent, as kings are crowned from a royal dynasty. In healing the sick and sinning, Jesus elaborated the fact that the healing effect followed the understanding of the divine Principle and of the Christ-spirit which governed the corporeal Jesus. For this Principle there is no dynasty, no ecclesiastical monopoly. Its only crowned head is immortal sovereignty. Its only priest is the spiritualized man. The Bible declares that all believers are made 'kings and priests unto God.'" *S&H* page 141, lines 10–21

4. (Continuing) Individually, the members of the congregation considered themselves fully equals with the bishop in spiritual affairs.... By the end of the second century the bishops were meeting together for the purpose of deciding controversy and issuing decrees, so that fairly early in the third century...a hierarchy was issuing commands and requiring obedience, not only in spiritual but in temporal affairs. Beasley *Op Cit* pages 628–629.

5. Until recently, the independence movement in Christian Science had little credibility. The Mother Church owned copyrights to the Christian Science textbook and exclusive use of the words "Christian Science." No rival movement within the Church ever had long-standing success. Branches that left The Mother Church had previously withered into oblivion. Americus, Georgia is known to have left in Mrs. Eddy's lifetime. Six months after her passing, the members of Fourth Church Minneapolis, Minnesota and Second Church, Duluth, Minnesota voted to leave The Mother Church. Around 1950, First Church, Watford, England and Fourth Church, Rochester, New York voluntarily left The Mother Church. Of the Rochester Church, *Time* magazine said:

"All of the Rochester church's approximately 50 members were in favor of the split. Actually they had been working up to it ever since 1943, when two Rochester board members published pamphlets under the pseudonym 'Paul Revere,' reviving an old controversy over whether the Mother Church should operate under the Deed of Trust left by Founder Mary Baker Eddy. The deed, they argued, would have had the effect of making branch churches independent of the Mother Church in Boston. When the authorship became known last year, the two board members were 'excommunicated' by The Mother Church's Board of Directors. This, the Rochester Scientists decided, was the final stroke in a pattern of 'increasingly despotic control' from Boston...." From *Time*, May 1, 1950. © 1950 TIME Inc. Reprinted with permission.

The largest competitive Church was engineered by a flamboyant Englishwoman, Annie C. Bill, which began in the teens and lasted until 1937. She changed the name of her Church many times, but it's probably best remembered as the "Christian Science Parent Church." At its height there were some 80 branches in the United States, Great Britain, and as far away as

Syria. None exist today. A detailed account of Mrs. Bill's Church may be found in Altman Swihart's *Since Mrs. Eddy* Henry Holt & Co. NY 1931. A collection of the *Christian Science Watchman*, the major periodical issued by Bill's Church, may still be found (with name changes) in the New York City Public Library. Its most recent copy, and likely the last one published, is dated Jan/Feb 1937.

Also an unknown number of branch churches in Germany and Switzerland left The Mother Church forming the German Church of Christ, Scientist in 1906. The separation was due to nationalistic reasons fearing adverse affects on their national heritage and the German language. These churches apparently continued until the end of the World War II. Source: *Christian Science Under the Nazi Regime* by William E. Stillman, unpublished bound manuscript, Marshall-Brooks Memorial Library, Principia College Library, Elsah, IL.

6.   In a letter to the *Christian Century* (October 29, 1958) an African-American Christian Scientist wrote in part:

"[A]lthough there are colored Christian Scientists in Boston, there are no colored ushers serving at the regular worship services in the Mother Church. In the higher echelons of the movement there is no colored person holding office. There are Christian Science radio and television programs sponsored by the Mother Church, but never is there a Negro participating in any of these programs.

"There are no Negro lecturers on the Board of Lectureship of the Christian Science movement, despite the fact that there are many Negroes who could lecture competently. There is only one colored C.S.B. authorized teacher of Christian Science. It is thought that she is permitted to hold office because the white teachers do not desire to accept colored pupils...I had to travel a thousand miles to Boston in order to get class instruction despite the fact that there are three teachers of Christian Science living in my city..."

From "Letter to the Editor" by African American Christian Scientist. Copyright 1958 Christian Century. Reprinted by permission from the October 29, 1958 issue of the *Christian Century*.

The label "colored" was removed from church and practitioner listings in the *Christian Science Journal* in 1959. During the 1960's The Mother Church and branch churches slowly assimilated African-Americans into the organization. All of this happened quietly. There was no known general announcement.

7. Ch*ristian Science Journal*; July, 1952 page: 346

8. See Allison Phinney's announcement: Chapter 6, footnote 7

9. Braden, Charles S., *Christian Science Today*; Southern Methodist Press, Dallas, 1969 page 288

10. Merritt, Robert (as told to Arthur Corey) *Christian Science and Liberty*; De Vorss., Los Angeles 1970 p: 157 ff. Some of Mrs. Eddy's views on pacifism and war can be found in *First Church of Christ, Scientist and Miscellany* pages: 277 and 286

11. Mother Church officials refer to estoppel clauses as "consent" clauses.

12. *Christian Science Journal*; April 1922, page: 6

13. Peel, Robert, *Mary Baker Eddy: The Years of Trial 1876–1891*, Holt, Rinehart and Winston, N.Y., NY, page: 292.

14. *Christian Science Journal;* July 1891 quoted in Beasley, Norman *The Cross and The Crown*, page: 220 and 221.

15. Also of interest regarding Mrs. Eddy's ideas on not controlling what her students read are these comments by Norman Beasley: "At the time [1886] there was a great deal of interest among Christian Scientists in all literature pertaining to metaphysics, including all manner of esoteric literature and in everything that was written about the life and times of Jesus…. Hoping the enthusiasm of her followers for other literature would subside, *Mrs. Eddy did not interfere.*" [Emphasis added] *The Cross And The Crown*, page 134

16. "The precise form and the conduct of the college society are left by the *Manual* of The Mother Church to be worked out according to the needs and state of progress of the individual organization." *Christian Science Journal*; January, 1918 page: 564

17. Eddy, Mary Baker *The People's Idea of God*, page 1, lines 1–7

18. *S&H* (Preface) page ix, lines 16–19

Chapter Nine—"That City of Ceaseless Enterprise"

1. Historically, Chicago was the most important city to the denomination outside the Boston area. Mary Baker Eddy made her influence known on Chicago in a very direct way. As her discovery moved into the 1880's, the challenges to the movement were as great as the opportunities. In many areas, but particularly in large cities, metaphysical systems of every description were using the name "Christian Science" to identify and advance their own cause. This was compounded by problems within the Church which were primarily problems of personalities and loyalties. It was one thing to contain these in New York and Boston, but quite another in communities far removed.

    The Church in Chicago was not immune to growing pains. "In the brash young Chicago which had risen less like a phoenix than a turkey cock from the ashes of its great fire, Christian Science had found a hearing, but was running a little wild." (Peel, Robert *Mary Baker Eddy: Years of Trial* Holt, Rinehart, Winston p: 140–141) Mrs. Eddy's students in the mid-west metropolis pleaded with their Leader to visit them and set Christian Science on the right track.

    "Their pleas did not fall on deaf ears. Mrs. Eddy's continual revision of rules and by-law changes in her Church *Manual* illustrated deep sensitivity on her part to troublesome elements in the fold. In this case she realized more than rules were necessary. The remoteness and strategically geographical setting of Chicago demanded more of a personal touch. Mrs. Eddy also perceived the City's potential as a bastion of great strength for her movement. For all these reasons, Mary Baker Eddy went to Chicago in 1884. In her words she described her visit: 'I went in May to Chicago at the imperative call of people there and my own sense of the need. This great work had been started by my students needed me to give it a right foundation and impulse in that city of ceaseless enterprise. So I went, and in three weeks taught a class of 25 pupils, lectured…to a full house.'" (Letter to Colonel F. J. Smith, June 25, 1884; Powell, Lyman P. *Mary Baker Eddy-A Lifesize Portrait* Christian Science Publishing Society, Boston 1950 footnote p: 302)

    In spite of the importance Mrs. Eddy gave to her visit, Chicago's response to the Founder of this radically different religious movement was hardly overwhelming. Christian Science had yet to make deep inroads in Chicago. But her visit must've paved the way for something far greater than the initial response to her first visit. The event, four years later, was the National Christian Scientist Association. In the *Christian Science Journal* Mrs. Eddy urged all Christian Scientists to "let no consideration bend or outweigh your purpose to be in Chicago…" (*Christian Science Journal,* June, 1888)

Mrs. Eddy's second visit to Chicago was significant in that it was the first planned gathering to bring Christian Scientists together from all over the country. For this reason, it was quite unlike her first visit. Those who came to see her speak at Central Music Hall, numbered nearly four thousand. She did not come to speak, but was told by organizers at the last minute, this would be the case. She gave an impromptu address that by every account had a stunning effect on her audience. So effective was she that day that even one of her harshest critics gave a glowing account of how she handled herself.

"It was an unprepared speech, delivered without notes, and poured out upon the audience like a stream of molten gold. She thrilled her hearers in words that have been described as 'Pentecostal.'

"When she came to an end the scenes enacted in that audience of four thousand were so amazing as to be utterly unprecedented. The whole throng arose as one man and started to sweep forward to the stage. Men surged up on the platform and pulled women and children after them. They fought to grasp her hand, to touch her dress. Women who could not bring their children near held the youngsters up calling for a blessing. Others shouted that they had been healed instantaneously.

[Here the writer quotes the Boston *Traveler*] "What wonder if the thoughts of those present went back to eighteen hundred years ago, when the healing power was manifested through the personal Jesus? Can the cold critic, harsh opposer, or disbeliever in Christian Science call up any other like picture through all these centuries?" Dakin, Edwin F., *Mrs. Eddy: Biography of Virginal Mind*, Freethought Press Association, NY 1929 page: 203.

While things went well in Chicago for the "Boston Prophetess" (as the midwest press was fond of calling her), the same cannot be said about her home turf. Back in Massachusetts, Mrs. Eddy was faced with defections, conflicting loyalties, and problems of personalities. So severe was her sense of failure on returning that she contemplated leaving Boston altogether and reorganizing her mission elsewhere with the new headquarters destined for Chicago. Norman Beasley writes,

"…[I]n a moment of despair, Mrs. Eddy confided in a pupil, 'I do not believe I have twelve loyal students left,' expressed herself as seeing little hope for her church in Boston, and indicated, most seriously, of moving to Chicago and continuing her work from there."

What a tribute to the outstanding work of the Christian Science pioneers in the mid-west metropolis that Mrs. Eddy never gave serious consideration to moving her headquarters anywhere outside Massachusetts, except Chicago! Even so that "wonder of the western hemisphere" did not prove a viable alternative.

For Mrs. Eddy, the darkest moments are the times given over to deepest prayer, and as in other such occasions, this brought new resolve. "A night of prayer turned her despair into determination not to be driven from the state where she began her teachings." (Beasley, Norman, *The Cross and The Crown* p: 185–186)

Chicago would command center stage one more time for Christian Scientists. Five years after Mrs. Eddy's triumphant visit, the Windy City would play host to the World Parliament of Religions. In accepting an invitation to participate, Christian Scientists generated deep respect toward themselves from the major organized religions. The President of the Parliament, Charles Carroll Bonney gave a ringing praise of welcome to the participation by Christian Scientists. Judge Septimus J. Hanna was selected by Mrs. Eddy to read several quotations from her writings.

The *Chicago Tribune* the next day made this comment: "The crowd in the Hall of Columbus yesterday morning was greater than at any time since the Parliament first opened. It was apparently the announcement that the cause of Christian Science would be presented, that attracted them….

"One evident result of the Parliament was the acknowledgment by other religious groups that Christian Science was not a thing of passing moment, but a vital force." (Beasley, Norman *The Cross and The Crown* p: 302–303)

Chicago produced some of the giants of the Christian Science movement around the turn of the century. Teachers like Judge William G. Ewing, Edward Kimball, and Bicknell Young (nephew of Mormon pioneer Brigham Young) significantly advanced the cause of Christian Science in the mid-west metropolis. So strong was their work, they helped stem the idea both in and outside the Church that when Mrs. Eddy would no longer be around, her movement might whither and die.

The growth of Christian Science in Chicago in the latter end of the 19th century and early 20th century was truly remarkable. Following the organization of First Church, Chicago in 1893, other branches quickly followed. Early *Christian Science Journals* bear witness to the dramatic increase in members and churches. Growth continued so much that by 1922 there were 16 churches. The denomination was to reach a zenith of 23 branches in Chicago before the numbers would level off and begin a slow decline. In 2004, the *Christian Science Journal* listed nine churches and one society in the Windy City.

2.   Students who have had class instruction by an "authorized" teacher of Christian Science are members of that teacher's association. The association meets yearly to hear addresses from their teacher and other students.

3.   The letter's purpose was to enthuse lesbian/gay Christian Scientists around the country to attend the conference on the 4th of July weekend, 1983.

"We've all thought about it wistfully for several years—now its going to happen! Fourth of July weekend in Chicago—festivities planned just for us: fanfares!…fireworks!…feasts!"

The letter announces the keynote speaker to be "Madge Reinhardt author/playwright, publisher of her own novels, and a former contributor to the Christian Science periodicals, who has spoken out in the national press against certain policies and practices of the Church." Also mentioned were the "special welcoming party on Friday night…on the roof-top deck of a condominium…" and the remainder of the Conference agenda.

4.   The full text of Madge Reinhart's address was printed in *Identity Newsletter*, San Francisco, September, 1983. (Madge Reinhardt went on to continue her writing career. She also remained a vocal supporter of lesbian/gay Christian Scientists up to her passing in 1987.)

Following Reinhardt to the podium was Francis Bernard., a member of GPICS/New York. He gave an investigative paper on the life and work of gay poet Hart Crane (1899–1932). He discussed the metaphysical influences in Crane's life and poetry.

After lunch, James Nelson Oglesby, a practitioner from Seattle and a member of Gay Christian Scientists of the Northwest, spoke on the subject, "Congratulations! You're a Perfect Child of God." *Identity Newsletter* said he "spoke tenderly and autobiographically, telling us poignantly of his emergence into Christian Science as a gay man, living with the statement, 'God knows I am gay.'"

5.   Richard Whittaker (GPICS/Chicago) wrote a report "Challenging the False Belief of Age." This addressed a major fear in the GLBT communities: getting old. Richard's paper was read by Dell Yarnell (GPICS/Chicago). Excerpts include:

"The fears and claims of age have been a part of world consciousness since the 'Lord God' of the fable of material creation made his Adam of the dust of Eden, left him vulnerable to temptation, and finally condemned him to till and eat of that same soil in sweat and sorrow the rest of his days...

"Sadly, the Adam man, 'whose breath is in his nostrils,' the man 'of few years and many sorrows,' the man who 'withereth as the grass' is the model which is constantly held up for us to pattern our lives by.

"Who is this Adam man? Do you know him?

"We all know him...and much too well!

"In short, we believe he is us!

"...The cynical acceptance of aging as inevitable is part and parcel of the gay expedience of the material world. In a segment of society in which youth is a prize, the unattractive evidence of advancing age is absolute anathema!

"...By using youth as one of the most important criteria for judging attractiveness and desirability, gay people do indeed generate their own social punishment—a harsher and uglier punishment than all the words and actions of bigots and antagonists could ever inflict.

"Friends, we have a blatant case of malpractice within our own community! We are our own worst enemies! We are malpracticing on our own thought!

"We don't have Jesus with us today to command us to release our tenacious hold on the false belief of age—to rouse us out of the mortal dream of decline, stagnation, and death...But we do have a record of his demonstrations over all the effects of life in matter...and over death itself.... To the students of Christian Science, Christ Jesus' promise, 'He that believeth on me, the works that I do shall he do also' [John 14:12 KJV] is literal."

The next day, Sunday, was an off day. No Conference activities were planned. Some opted to attend services at 17th Church of Christ, Scientist. As a downtown branch, 17th Church stood as an exception to urban churches that are often decaying. It had an active membership and a new building of modern design.

Identity Newsletter (San Francisco) discussed Sunday's events as follows:

"Several of us attended morning service at 17th Church, Chicago, followed by a midriff-blowing brunch at The Pinnacle, overlooking Lake Michigan. And Sunday evening some of us gathered at Grant Park for the annual 4th of July concert and fireworks. The 1812 Overture of our soul-brother P. Tschaikovsy, appropriately climaxed the concert, followed by a half-hour of extraordinarily orchestrated fireworks. A wonderful day!"

Before the Conference concluded mid-day Monday, July 5th, there were three events. The first was a report by Wayne Huff (Emergence/Los Angeles). *Identity Newsletter* said Wayne "presented a warmly received paper, based on his experience of the need for visibility of gay Christian Scientists in the branch churches—and doing this through example, courage and love."

The next speaker Richard Whitaker, gave "Remarks on Fear and Illness" The AIDS pandemic was very new at the time of this Conference. It was causing much fear in the gay community. No one could tell where it was going.

The final Conference event was a panel discussion on the subject "activism." Panelists were composed of three members of GPICS/New York: Francis Barnard, Bob McCullough, and Craig Rodwell. Joining them was Kentner Scott from Identity/San Francisco. No transcript was made of this event. After each panelist put forth his position, a general rap session followed.

According to *Identity*, "We adjourned the meeting at 1 PM by gathering in a large circle, holding hands, and repeating the 'Scientific Statement of Being.' And then we hugged and hugged."

6. Kentner Scott went on to play a formidable role in Emergence International's (EI) first decade. He served the organization as President, Treasurer, and Editor of *Emerge!* magazine, all at the same time! He also served as EI's first Executive Director after the Coordinating Council created that post.

His planning and organizing skills are largely credited with putting EI on a sound footing. He is affectionately known by many of the members who knew him as "the father of Emergence."

Kentner Scott stepped down from his work at the helm of Emergence International in 1994. No one person replaced all his positions.

7. The name "Emergence: Gay People in Christian Science" was a compromise between the names of the two most prominent names used for local groups. Within a year, "Gay People In Christian Science" was dropped. The name "Emergence" was seen by some as a rebuke (based on Mrs. Eddy's teachings) to those Christian Scientists who believed lesbians and gays must overcome their sexuality before heterosexuals, and also before they could become Church members. Mrs. Eddy wrote: "Emerge gently from matter into Spirit. Think not to thwart the spiritual ultimate of all things, but come naturally into Spirit through better health and morals and as the result of spiritual growth." (*S&H* page 485, lines 14–17)

An early (undated) pamphlet printed by Emergence International, explained the nature of the organization:

"*What is EMERGENCE International?*

Emergence International: Christian Scientists Supporting Lesbians and Gay Men is a world-wide association of Christian Scientists, their families and friends, who provide spiritual and educational support to gay men and lesbians as they deal with homophobia and heterosexism. Honoring the integrity of individual growth, EI is a resource for those searching for a change of perspective and spiritual growth through the leadership of Mary Baker Eddy in her writings, and by fellowship with similarly-minded Christian Scientists."

8. *S&H* (Preface) page vii, line 6.

9. The first edition of what became *Emerge!* was published in February 1986. The lead article in its first edition presented to readers what its Editor, Kentner Scott, believed to be its mission.

"*EMERGENCE*" [later renamed *Emerge!*] will try to focus on solutions, not problems. Its goal will be to inspire, to uplift, to heal. Re-fighting church battles will not be part of its mission, but diversity and respect for individual points of view will be. Its columns will be open to the discussion of controversial ideas."

10. The first edition of *Emerge!* Listed seven cities, all in the U.S., "with varying degrees of [local] activity." Fourteen years later the number of local groups reached ten. Two groups in the latter list were outside the U.S. (Toronto, Canada and London, U.K.), giving credibility to the organization's name, "International."

11. Major speakers at the 1986 conference in Houston included Carl Welz, a former Christian Science teacher and former editor of the Church's religious periodicals for eleven years, and Robert Doling Wells, former Christian Science teacher and lecturer for The Mother Church. The keynote speaker at the 1987 conference in San Francisco was former church lecturer and communications director, Alan Young. This is the same Alan Young who played a starring role in the 1950s TV sit-com "Mr. Ed," and "The Alan Young Show."

Chapter Ten—The Healing Begins

1. Charles Linebarger appears to have been the first person to have discovered NPR's inconsistency and acted on it. He saw the incongruity of the public radio station joining up for a news program with the Christian Science organization with its long record of discrimination. This is in spite of NPR's highly-touted policy of non-discrimination based on sexual orientation.

2. From the late forties to early seventies a 15-minute religious program was carried throughout the United States. The Church maintained that these programs were listened to by a conservative estimate of about ten million every week over more than 450 radio stations. The Church continued experimenting with various formats for religious broadcasting, including Spanish language programming, until the mid-1970's when regular radio broadcasting ceased.

3. A news program "*The Christian Science Monitor Views the News*" was broadcast over the ABC radio network in the 1940's and 1950's. The highly acclaimed program was well received even by the U.S. government. According to the *Christian Science Journal*, (July, 1949 page: 299) the U.S. State Department re-broadcast the program to many countries.

4. The *Monitor*'s circulation continued dropping dramatically. By 1997 it had decreased to 95,000 according to *Writer's Market 1998*; F&W Publications,

Cincinnati 1997, page 472. Two year's later, by its own admission, it had dropped to 73,000. Its edition for September 14, 1999, cited lower circulation in announcing a new plan to increase subscriptions: a morning doorstep-delivery program for 50 cities to be phased-in by the end of 2000. "Doorstep delivery is a key step in plans to increase the *Monitor's* circulation, which currently stands at 73,000." Source: *The Christian Science Monitor*, September 14, 1999, page 8. Reproduced with permission. Copyright © 1999 The Christian Science Monitor. (www.csmonitor.com) All rights reserved. According to *Business Week*, Nov. 30, 1998 page 42, The *Monitor* "has not made a profit since 1956. The loss for fiscal year ending April, 1999 is expected to be $18.1 million."

5. *Wall Street Journal*; Oct 3, 1988 page 33

6. *Wall Street Journal*; Oct 3, 1988, page 33

7. *BAR*; Sept 11, 1986. Excerpts from *Bay Area Reporter*. San Francisco, Reprinted by permission of BAR.

8. *BAR*; Oct 2, 1986. Excerpts from *Bay Area Reporter*. Reprinted by permission of BAR.

9. *BAR*; Feb 12, 1987. Excerpts from *Bay Area Reporter*. Reprinted by permission of BAR.

10. *BAR*; Jan 29, 1987. Excerpts from *Bay Area Reporter*. Reprinted by permission of BAR.

11. *BAR*; Jan 29, 1987. Excerpts from *Bay Area Reporter*. Reprinted by permission of BAR.

12. Fact sheet printed and distributed by KQED on the history of the relationship between KQED and Monitor Radio (Undated).

13. KQED fact sheet (*Ibid*)

14. *Bay Area Reporter*, April 23, 1987

15. San Francisco *Sentinel*; Aug 14, 1987

16. San Francisco *Sentinel*; Feb 12, 1988

17. Interview with Carol Pierson

18. *S&H* (Preface) page x, lines: 11–12

19. Passage of the lesbian/gay rights bill in Massachusetts was the culmination of 15 years of intense work by activists. Shortly afterwards, the *Christian Science Monitor* told its reader's how the non-discrimination law came into being.

Bay State Pushing Ahead on Gay Rights

by Catherine Foster

…The bill—written on former legislator Elaine Noble's kitchen table in 1972—has seen 17 years of fighting in the State House. Crucial to this year's passage, observers say, has been a low—key approach, with traditional lobbying replacing past year's civil disobedience. It is also not an election year for state legislators.

"In the last two years, the gay movement has developed the sophistication it takes to make the legislature do something its members might be disinclined to do," says Robert Schaefer, a public policy consultant. He says legislators found it less damaging to vote for the bill than to vote against it.

…Massachusetts has undergone an evolution of public thought and emerged favoring greater tolerance, some say.

"I simply don't think opponents of the bill understand that positive images of gay people are projected in the popular culture," [said] Sen. Michael Barrett (D) of Cambridge, a supporter of the bill.

"I simply cannot get a rise out of my constituents on the subject of gay rights,' Senator Barrett says.

"They aren't concerned…. They want to see traditional values strengthened, they abhor the generally permissive culture that seems afoot in the land. But they don't associate gay people living quietly with the kind of permissiveness they dislike."

Others say changing public attitudes have also reduced the political risk of voting in favor of gay-rights legislation.

Many "legislators are saying they feel comfortable going back to their constituency and saying I do not personally approve of homosexuality, but I don't believe it should be legal to discriminate against them just because they are gay," says Arlene Isaacson, co-chair of the Massachusetts Gay and Lesbian Political Caucus. "The bill has had a majority of votes for years," contends Isaacson. "But it has been stalled by delaying tactics." One senator, she says, "held it in committee for 45 days, long enough to avoid a vote. Homosexual activists then chained themselves to Senate gallery chairs and 14 were arrested."

The Massachusetts homosexual community is now left to ponder the next step. Isaacson says the bill does not address foster care by gays, survivor rights, bereavement leave, and "all the legal rights between gay partners that weren't known 17 years ago when the bill was designed." Source: *The Christian Science Monitor*, November 8, 1989, page 7. Reproduced with permission. Copyright © 1989 The Christian Science Monitor (www.csmonitor.com). All rights reserved.

20. From *San Francisco Chronicle*, Jan 27, 1990, Editorial Page. Copyright 1990 by San Francisco Chronicle. Reproduced with permission of San Francisco Chronicle in the format Trade Book via Copyright Clearance Center.

21. Interview with KQED Station Manager, David Hosely.

22. "'Some 64 cities and 16 counties have passed a spate of 'human rights' ordinances containing clauses prohibiting discrimination against individuals because of their sexual orientation,' Mr. [Robert] Bray [a spokesperson for the National Gay and Lesbian Task Force] says." Source: *The Christian Science Monitor*, Nov 8, 1989, page 7. Reproduced with permission. Copyright © 1989 The Christian Science Monitor (www.csmonitor.com). All rights reserved.

Epilogue

1. The Mother Church's Internet website, which began in 1996, is: <http://www.tfccs.com> A second website operated by The Mother Church is <www.spirituality.com>

2. [Continuing] Next, let us suggest that focusing on homosexuality can easily lead one to miss the larger issue, sexuality itself and our actual identity. Christian Science, based squarely on the Bible, teaches that each of us is in reality the image and likeness of God (see Genesis 1:26). Therefore, we all no matter what our perceived sexual orientation, need to see ourselves and oth-

ers not as sexual beings at the mercy of sensual impulses but as the purely spiritual idea of God. This is an issue that must be faced at some point by homosexuals and heterosexuals alike. What's really needed is spiritual progress leading away from the mortal condition and toward redemption. God and His Christ will support us in that.

Different people, whether homosexual or heterosexual, will be at different points in their consideration of sexual matters. But, no matter where we find ourselves in the quest to overcome mortality, we can have the utmost compassion for others and their wrestlings.

Experience shows that people are sometimes all too willing to trade real progress for pat answers, blithely condoning some behaviors and vehemently condemning others. Perhaps it is only fair to say that as we advance beyond sexuality, we are responding to a real stimulus, expressing a genuine love for our fellowman, and helping society move Spiritward from its imprisonment in materiality....

3. Also expressing her thoughts on androgyny are the following passages written by Mrs. Eddy:

"The lamb's wife presents the unity of male and female as no longer two wedded individuals, but as two individual natures in one; and this compounded spiritual individuality reflects God as Father-Mother, not as a corporeal being...." *S&H* page 577, lines 4–8.

"Let the "male and female" of God's creating appear." *S&H*, page 249, line 5.

"Look high enough and you see the heart of humanity warming and winning. Look long enough, and you see male and female one—sex or gender eliminated; you see the designation *man* meaning woman as well, and you see the whole universe included in one infinite Mind and reflected in the intelligent compound idea, image or likeness, called man, showing forth the infinite divine Principle, Love, called God,—man wedded to the Lamb, pledged to innocence, purity, perfection." *First Church of Christ, Scientist and Miscellany*, page 268, lines 29–5

Mrs. Eddy taught that God possesses both masculine and feminine qualities while S/He is Father/Mother to Her/His creation. "Spirit duly feeds and clothes every object, as it appears in the line of spiritual creation, thus tenderly expressing the fatherhood and motherhood of God." *S&H* page 507, lines 3–6

As part of her spiritual interpretation of the Lord's prayer, following "Our Father which art in heaven," she wrote "*Our Father-Mother God, all-harmonious,*" *S&H*, page 16

"Love, the divine Principle, is the Father and Mother of the universe, including man." S&H page, lines 256:7–8

4.   The *Sentinel* article was written by Laura Matthews C.S., a *Christian Science Journal*-listed practitioner. Matthews told the author:

"I was actually asked to write the article by the associate editor. I don't know that I would have come up with it spontaneously…But when the idea to write an article addressing homosexuality was presented to me, it seemed like a worthy opportunity for standing up and being counted.

[It is quite common in the Church's periodicals that when a writer discusses sensitive areas about her/his own life that the writer remains anonymous.]

"I was asked at one point if I wanted the article to be 'name withheld,' but I knew that usually detracts from the credibility for me, so I went ahead and put my name on it.

"The point of the piece, of course, was not being judgmental. Not everyone understood that point, primarily because the mention of homosexuality was inflammatory. But I did get one lovely letter from a grandmother in the heartland who said my article helped her to know how to respond to her grandson who had just revealed to the family his homosexual orientation. She said she now knew she could just keep on loving him, and showing that love. That made it worthwhile, even with the highly charged aftermath I had to face.

"It was a long time before I wrote another article, but the overall experience is one I wouldn't replace." (Excerpts of e-mail from Ms. Laura Matthews C.S. to the author, November 22, 1999) [The article "*Homosexuality: how do I respond?*" is from the *Christian Science Sentinel*, December 15, 1997, pages 24–27]

Matthews' article was the subject of a letter to the *Sentinel*, published in February 9, 1998. The letter praised the *Sentinel* for printing the article, mentioning how well written it was, and wishing it could be read by every Sunday school teacher.

5.   From *Mary Baker Eddy* by Dr. Gillian Gill, Perseus Books, Reading, Massachusetts 1998, page 207. Reprinted with permission by Dr. Gillian Gill. Dr. Gill includes in her book an intimate letter written by Mary Baker Glover [Eddy] to her student and landlord, Sarah Bagley, dated November 8, 1868. Page 627, note 32. The degree to which the overtones in the letter carry lesbian feelings in Ms. Glover's thought has been a matter of intense speculation by some. Perhaps the issue will be clarified when the entire Glover/Bagley exchange of letters have been made public. Sarah Bagley died in August 1905.

6.   "During these years [prior to establishing the Monitor] she [Mrs. Eddy] had subscribed to a number of newspapers and magazines, annotating them in her usual fashion and marking items she particularly wished the members of her household to read." Peel, Robert; *Mary Baker Eddy: The Years of Authority*, Holt, Rinehart and Winston, New York NY 1977 page 308.

7.   Gill, *Op Cit*, (Preface) p: xix

8.   A greater degree of public access to The Mother Church archives may be forthcoming in the near future. In a letter to all members of The Mother Church, dated June 6, 2000, the Christian Science Board of Directors announced the creation of "The Mary Baker Eddy Library for the Betterment of Humanity." Their letter reads: "It is a not-for-profit corporation, under a Board of Trustees appointed by The Christian Science Board of Directors. This new Library will fulfill the requirements of copyright law by providing for the orderly, contextual, and publicly accessible presentation of Mrs. Eddy's unpublished writings. As a result, The Mother Church will have the full protection of the copyright laws for these writings through the year 2047.... Maintaining the collection within The Mary Baker Eddy Library—under protection of copyright—will give The Mother Church the opportunity to place her notes, writings, and correspondence in their context and thus help ensure that they are more accurately understood. Exhibits, trained docents, and ongoing programs that encourage intelligent inquiry and public discussion of Mrs. Eddy's ideas and accomplishments will also

provide an appropriate environment for inquiring more deeply into Mrs. Eddy's life."

The library opened its doors to the public in September 2002.

9. Principia began as an elementary school in 1898, founded by Mary Kimball Morgan in St. Louis. A junior college opened in 1910 on the same St. Louis campus where the four-year college opened 22 years later. The College moved to its present campus in Elsah, IL, March 1, 1935. The present College campus is comprised of 3,000 acres overlooking the Mississippi River some 40 miles north of St. Louis. The college prepares students for four-year B.A. and B.S. degrees. With approximately 50 plus full-time faculty and 500 plus full-time students, the student/faculty ratio is about ten to one.

10. Chandler Burr authored, *A Separate Creation: The Search for the Biological Origins of Sexual Orientation*, Hyerion Press, NY 1996

11. The unofficial campus lesbian/gay alumni group's reception on campus was reported in the lesbian/gay newspaper, *St. Louis-Kansas City News Telegraph*, September 9, 1994.

Prin [Lesbian/Gay] Alumnus Meet For First Time

ST. LOUIS—Though the school has an official stance that bans Gay or Lesbian staff, faculty or students; homosexual alumnus of Principia College in Elsah, Illinois, held an alumni reception on the campus on July 16 [1994] as part of alumni week.

The Gay and Lesbian Principians, with about fifty members nationwide, formed about a year ago. Because of the school's "standards of Christian Science," which considers homosexuality as a sin to be healed, "being 'in the closet' was the safest choice" for students who attended Principia. Now as alumni they are out and are vocally working to change school policy.

David White, an organizer of the Gay and Lesbian Principians, said that alumni from as far away as Stockton, California and Boston, Massachusetts and representing classes from 1959 to 1988, attended the recent reunion. As part of the gathering, the organization donated books on Gay and Lesbian themes to the college bookstore.

12. A fuller discussion of David Stores' activism, particularly at Principia College, may be found in the newsletter "*In Between Times,*" a publication of Emergence International, March 1997, pages 1–3.

13. The Conference Information sheet for prospective attendees (undated) was prepared by Emergence International.

14. *The PILOT* [Principia's student newspaper] May 28, 1999 *Principians Divided on Gay and Lesbian Issue* by Grant Adams, staff writer. For more information re: Principia College and its policies toward lesbian/gay students, see the author's articles: "*A Visit to Principia College*" *Emerge!* Oct/Nov/Dec 1989 p: 10–13 and "*Gay Rights at Principia*" *In Between Times*, a newsletter from Emergence International, March, 1997 pages 1–3.

15. Of all positions taken by Christian Scientists, perhaps none is more widely known than their perceived proclivity to avoid medical treatment. Public obsession with members' avoidance of doctors seems, unfortunately to adherents, to have prevented many outsiders from taking note of what the devout believe are Mrs. Eddy's truly revolutionary, even radical teachings. In a nutshell, some of these teachings include:

a) A view of God as universal correct thought; not a personal Being. "…God is all true consciousness…" "…Spirit [God] is *spiritual* consciousness alone." (*Unity of Good,* by Mrs. Eddy, page 4, lines 12–13 and page 35 line 24)

b) Responsibility for healing rests *entirely* with the individual. It results from harmonizing one's thought with the Principle (Law) of universal consciousness (God). It does not come from requesting or pleading for a cure with a personal Supreme Being. When thought arrives at the point of conviction, healing results. "But the fact remains in metaphysics, that the mind of the individual only can produce a result upon his body." (*Christian Healing*, by Mrs. Eddy, page 6, lines 20–22)

c) There is an essential oneness of God and man. "Principle [God] and its idea [creation] is one…." (*S&H,* page 465, line 17)

d) Heaven and hell are not localities, but states of consciousness. "Heaven is harmony, infinite boundless bliss." (*First Church of Christ, Scientist and Miscellany*, page 267 lines 16–17) "Hell[:] Mortal belief; error; lust; remorse; hatred; revenge; sin; sickness; death; suffering and self-destruction; self-imposed agony; effects of sin; that which "worketh abomination or maketh a lie." (Rev 21:27) (*S&H* [Glossary], page 588, lines 1–4)

e) Perfection is not only obtainable in our experience but it is mandated by God. "God requires perfection, but not until the battle between Spirit and flesh is fought and the victory won." (*S&H*, page 254, lines 6–9)

f) Mrs. Eddy did not shirk from weighing in on the most raging controversies of her day. She took a strong stand for temperance, gave a positive nod to Charles Darwin's theory of evolution and supported the rights of women. As to Darwin's theory, she said, "May not Darwin be right in thinking that apehood preceded mortal manhood?.... Darwin's theory of evolution from a material basis is more consistent than most theories." (*S&H*, page 543 lines 20–21 and page 547, lines 15–17)

g) As to believers avoiding medical treatment, Mrs. Eddy wrote, "Christian Scientists are harmless citizens that do not kill people either by their practice or by preventing the early employment of an M.D." *Message for 1901*, pages 33–34, lines 29–1.

16. *Christianity Today*, October 5, 1998, page 28

17. Dr. Stuart Grayson, Pastor Emeritus of New York City's prestigious Church of Religious Science, wrote the author, "I was shocked to see [the *Sentinel* ad]. The fact that they acknowledge us [the Church of Religious Science] and our place as a metaphysical movement worthy of respect and a certain acceptance is most remarkable. That is a history-making connection with our Religious Science institution. I wonder if it hints at anything more." [The late Dr. Grayson was a co-founder of "The Christian Science Monitor Youth Forums," an international social/educational organization for young adult Christian Scientists which began shortly after World War II. It was disbanded by The Mother Church in 1959.]

18. Local Christian Science churches continued to disband through the 1990s at the rate of forty or more a year in the United States alone. Another casualty of the 1990s was Monitor Radio. Its last broadcast was aired on June 28, 1997.

"'The Church has heavily subsidized Monitor Radio over the years, keeping costs to stations extremely low. In recent years it was spending about $9 million and getting less than $1 million back,' said David Cook, who edits the

Christian Science Monitor and heads Monitor Radio." *Current* June 23, 1997 by Jacqueline Conciature.

19. *S&H* 497:24–25

20. *First Church of Christ, Scientist and Miscellany* p: 266: 3–9

APPENDIX A

Text of the Pamphlet "Gay People in Christian Science?"

NOTE: The text below is from the pamphlet that was distributed to many attendees at the Annual Meeting of The Mother Church in June, 1980, as well as some branch churches before or after services and lectures in New York City and Seattle that same year. The previous year it was mailed to all Christian Science churches, practitioners and college/university organizations in the world as listed in the *Christian Science Journal.*

Gay People in Christian Science?

Today, many Gay women and men are active in the Christian Science move-ment—serving as Readers, practitioners, branch members, employees at head-quarters, and workers in the Field. The purpose of this pamphlet which is being distributed at the Annual Meeting of The First Church of Christ, Scientist, in Boston, Massachusetts in June, 1980 is an appeal to all Christian Scientists and especially to The Christian Science Board of Directors to re-examine their thought on the subject of human sexuality in the light of Christian Science; and to take whatever loving and practical steps are necessary to rectify the present wrongs being done to Gay people in the name of Christian Science.

Incorrect Literature

(Please refer to *The Mother Church Manual*, p.43:21)

To many loyal Christian Scientists, April 22, 1967 was a day of great sadness. It was on that day that the first article on the human expression of love between people of the same sex appeared in one of our periodicals. In that piece ("Homosexuality Can Be Healed," *Christian Science Sentinel*, p.681), a particularly uninspired quote from Leviticus (Lev.20:13) was used to suggest that homosexuals be put to death.

Since then similar pieces have appeared in the Christian Science periodicals. (See *Christian Science Sentinel*, November 18, 1972, p.2051; *Christian Science Sentinel*, March 20, 1976 p.457; *The Christian Science Monitor*, November 8, 1977, editorial page; *The Christian Science Journal*, October, 1978, p.609; *Christian Science Sentinel*, March 5, 1979, p.377; *The Christian Science Journal*, April, 1979, p.211; and especially *The Christian Science Journal*, October 1973, p.607.)

In the above-cited examples of incorrect literature which mis-state Christian Science and violate the Golden Rule, Gay women and men are depicted as "promiscuous," "bizarre," "abnormal," "immoral," "unseemly," "unhealthy," "unnatural," "cursed," and "perverted." Nowhere is there even the slightest recognition that the basis of same-sex relationships is love, the exact same human need for love and mutual respect that is the basis for heterosexual relationships. Indeed, not one of the articles has in any way shown how same-gender relationships are unacceptable in the light of Christian Science. In the negative and hostile atmosphere created by our periodicals, it should come as no surprise that so-called "healings" of homosexuality should appear. This, naturally, prompts one to ask what exactly has been "healed"? Has the person been "healed" of love, companionship or friendship?

Incorrect statements of Christian Science are the most obnoxious and damaging kind of literature in the world today because they blind the reader to the applicability of Christian Science to every human situation. They would foist upon us the notion that Christian Science is a cult to which only those who subscribe to a certain regimented lifestyle need apply. And when a form of mental malpractice is directed at a group of people—in this case, Gay women and men—in the Christian Science periodicals, it is time to speak out and keep speaking out.

Spirit and Letter

I Corinthians 14:34,35. The New English Bible: "As in all congregations of God's people, women should not address the meeting. They have no license to speak, but should keep their place as the law directs. If there is something they want to know, they can ask their own husbands at home. It is a shocking thing that a woman should address the congregation." What a tragic loss to the world, had our Leader, Mary Baker Eddy, considered the above citation as inspired! She could not have been the Discoverer and Founder of Christian Science. If a literal interpretation of the Bible had been enforced as it had in centuries past, she would have been silenced and even severely punished for having dared to speak out and start her own church.

Many scriptural prohibitions and injunctions were merely social and political conveniences of the time. Mary Baker Eddy states in the Tenets of The Mother Church that "As adherents of Truth, we take the inspired Word of the Bible as our sufficient guide to eternal life." (*Science and Health* p.497:3) In *The First Church of Christ, Scientist and Miscellany* on page 266 in an article called "Insufficient Freedom", Mary Baker Eddy warns that the most threatening danger that we are faced with in this century is the using of the Scriptures as authority to strip people of their very lives and liberties—substituting creed and ritual for the Golden Rule. Certainly, an example of this, is the mass extermination of thousands of homosexuals by the Nazis. In addition, thousands of Gay people in Europe were interned in concentration camps and were forced to wear patches with pink triangles on them to denote their homosexuality. Hitler's justification for this action was that it was necessary to maintain the "morality" and "Christian environment" for the youth of Germany.

Many passages in the Old Testament as well as the one quoted above from the New Testament can be used to justify the oppression of women. Racists quote the story of Ham as proof that Black people were "cursed" by God to eternal inferiority. In short, there is something in the Bible that every zealot can use to justify every prejudice imaginable.

Today, in the Christian Science church, new applicants are not accepted into the membership if they are openly Gay. Members of long standing who are openly Gay are being thrown out of branch churches. Others who have concealed their homosexuality and are members of the church, would not be permitted to work in any capacity at The Mother Church Center if their orientation were known. Although Christian Science recognizes the place of sexuality in the human experience, on what grounds is the Gay person asked to be "healed" immediately or refrain from any intimate relationships while heterosexuals have freedom to express their affectional orientation?

Mary Baker Eddy's forceful reminder in *Miscellaneous Writings,* p.223:15 speaks of this kind of cruel hypocrisy that ignorantly or maliciously breaks the Golden Rule.

How does one determine morality in the spirit of Christian Science? Our Leader quotes from Shakespeare at the beginning of *Science and Health,* "There is nothing either good or bad, but thinking makes it so." This quotation does not imply that one can justify immorality. However, in the practice of Christian Science, we learn that the First Commandment and the Golden Rule are the all-in-all of Christian Science. (*The First Church of Christ, Scientist and Miscellany*, p.5:12). It is the application of the First Commandment and the Golden Rule which determines whether "something is either good or bad" or moral or immoral. In the case of Gay people as well as heterosexuals, it is the quality of the love in their relationships which is the prime consideration.

Can we be responsible Christian Scientists and at the same time demand of Gay people the relinquishment of their affectional orientation in order for them to be worthy of church membership? Is this not a violation of the "all-in-all" of Christian Science?

Morality, Love and Sexuality

Christ Jesus taught his followers to work faithfully within their own human circumstances to understand Truth and from that basis to achieve salvation. This point is shown clearly in his teachings and in his own life. In the parable of the talents in the twenty-fifth chapter of Matthew, those servants who worked to increase their human understanding of the divine idea received increased harmony in their lives and then found heaven, i.e., at-one-ment, with divine Mind. The servant who failed to use or understand his human gift in a meaningful way lost it and delayed his eventual salvation. In Jesus' own experience he rebuked Peter soundly for suggesting that as Saviour of the world, he, Jesus did not need to go through the crucifixion. (Mark 8:31–33). Jesus knew that it was precisely through living out his own God-established mission that he would find his resurrection and ascension.

This teaching and actual demonstration by the Master has an important message for Gay women and men. Simply stated, it is: Make use of the gift you have, love as only *you* can, for in so doing you have embarked on the road to heaven, harmony.

Our Leader, Mary Baker Eddy, also her counsels her students to start working with what they understand. On page 288:13 of *Miscellaneous Writings*, she says "Wisdom in human action begins with what is nearest right under the circumstances, and thence achieves the absolute." On page 234 of the same book, she says in substance that the *only* way to find the Love which is God is through love for man.

Furthermore, Christian Science teaches that the individuality of man is eternal and unique, unabsorbed in matter or stereotyped by mortal mind. Science promotes the flowering of our individual gifts and condemns attempts to reduce them to bland theological posturings.

The human expression of love is indeed subject to healing, not through the obliteration of one's affectional orientation but through the operation of divine Truth and Love, bringing enrichment and refinement to one's affections. Homosexuality and heterosexuality may be positive or negative depending upon the degree of spirituality and the demand upon each of us is to relinquish whatever blocks the realization of our highest selfhood. For both Gay and non-Gay, the standards with which to judge and elevate motives and actions are the First Commandment and the Golden Rule, as both Christ Jesus and Mary Baker Eddy have taught.

Conclusions

Our dear Leader, Mary Baker Eddy, was far in advance of human thought. Her revolutionary discovery that the real nature of God's man is not divided into males and females—but rather each of us is the full reflection of our Mother-Father God—is beginning to dawn on world thought.

She challenges us to grasp the full import of our real spiritual nature—to combine the best of femaleness and maleness in each of our characters.

It is clear that in our daily application of Christian Science to all human needs, we must understand and acknowledge that the full human expression of divine Love is not limited in any way to people of mortal mind's two sexes, male and female. Rather we have the responsibility to be examples to the world in demonstrating the completeness of creation by practicing the wonderful truth of our reflection of God as Mother-Father.

Just as racism had a strong hold on the Christian Science movement until very recently, today heterosexism appears to be thriving. (Heterosexism is the erroneous concept that only people of the so-called opposite sexes can or should express the full range of love.) Heterosexism is a devise of mortal mind to enslave us into thinking that creation originates from an egg and sperm.

Christian Science challenges us to throw off this yoke of mortal mind and to demand of ourselves and the world a higher and more real concept of our being as the image and likeness of our Creator.

Mary Baker Eddy counsels us in "*The First Church of Christ, Scientist and Miscellany*, p.268:24–5: "Truth canonized by life and love, lays the axe at the root of all evil, lifts the curtain on the Science of being, the Science of wedlock, of living and of loving, and harmoniously ascends the scale of life. Look high enough, and you see the heart of humanity warming and winning. Look long enough, and you see male and female one—sex or gender eliminated; you see the designation *man* meaning woman as well, and you see the whole universe included in one infinite Mind and reflected in the intelligent compound idea, image or likeness, called man, showing forth the infinite divine Principle, Love, called God,—man wedded to the Lamb, pledged to innocence, purity, perfection."

APPENDIX B

A Response to the GPICS Pamphlet

The following letter was received by GPICS/New York shortly after the pamphlet with the above text was mailed to Christian Science practitioners and churches throughout the world.

Dear Ones, dear spiritual ideas of God,

Is God's perfect man ever *really* oppressed? Could it be that gay people misunderstood that true freedom is within? To imagine that others' views of you can limit you is a sad misapprehension at best.

I firmly believe (and years of practice bear this out) that once feelings of guilt are permanently set aside and true individuality—whatever its expression—is recognized, can continue making demonstrations of Christian Science in our daily lives without the false or backward steps collective humanity predicts for us.

Overcoming discrimination was a long, hard struggle for me. One little word—colored—beside my name in the *CS Journal* clouded my thinking and tried to tell others that my race was inferior—that members of my race couldn't practice Christian Science healing with the same degree of success as others whose mortal bodies were another color—that we should confine our practice and the sharing of the Truth and Love to "our own people." The prayer of the Pharisee (Luke 18:11), "God, I thank thee, that I am not as other men are...," if never spoken aloud, was sadly evident in many hearts during those years when we begged and pleaded, reasoned, and prayed to free Mrs. Eddy's "structure of Truth and Love" from the evil grip of racial discrimination. Children of Ham—or children of God? Indeed!

What a travesty on the spiritual Truth on which the teachings of Christian Science are based!

If the time for thinkers has indeed come, then you be those Christian Scientists who think us out of this rut of conflict over sexual lifestyles. Don't dwell too long on mortal evidence and social theories. Your answer will never be found there. Instead cast your anchor into the Shekinah which Mrs. Eddy mentions in *Science and Health* (page 40, lines 31–7) where gender and sexuality and the pleasure and pain of belief in sentient flesh are no more.

Live out your human experience of life lovingly and fully, guided by the "still, small voice" which speaks to every listening heart "all the rugged way."

Children of Sodom—or children of God? To imagine that you are ever separated from God, or that at any time man does not reflect God, would be like trying to puncture a hole in the "seamless garment" of divine Principle—an impossibility.

We are all constantly and dearly loved.

(Signed)

A *Journal*-listed practitioner (no longer colored)

I hesitate to add my name—scars of past battles are still healing. I am comforted by the fact that the name of seekers after freedom are forever "writ bold" in the sight of God alone.

APPENDIX C

Chronology

April 27, 1967—First article to appear in Christian Science periodicals devoted to same-gender sexuality, *Homosexuality Can Be Healed* by Carl Welz, *Christian Science Sentinel.*

Thanksgiving Day, 1967—Craig Rodwell opens the first bookstore in the United States for serious LGBT literature in New York City. He names the bookstore "Oscar Wilde Memorial Bookshop."

October 6, 1968—In what would become Metropolitan Community Church, the first church service ever conducted by and for sexual minorities is held in Los Angeles.

June 2 1969—African-American militants crash The Mother Church Annual Meeting and give demands to Church members.

June 27–July 1, 1969—Stonewall Riots in New York City mark the beginning of the modern lesbian/gay rights movement.

June 27, 1970—First annual LGBT Pride Marches in New York City and Los Angeles commemorate uprising at the Stonewall Inn.

May 1974—Mother Church evicts gay group "Fengay" from one of its rental properties in Back Bay, Boston.

June 4, 1974—Lesbian and gay activists in Boston protest Fengay's ouster from a building owned by The Mother Church by distributing leaflets to attendees at the denomination's Annual Meeting.

November 1974—Elaine Noble becomes the first openly lesbian or gay person elected to state-wide political office in the United States. Her legislative district encompasses The Mother Church and its administrative offices.

December 11, 1975—Reginald Kerry mails his first letter to Church field.

June 7, 1977—In the nation's first referendum on gay rights, voters in Miami/ Dade County, Florida overturn local ordinance protecting sexual minorities from discrimination in employment.

1978—"Gay People in Christian Science" New York is organized, the world's first-ever support group for lesbian/gay Christian Scientists.

November 1978—Voters in California and Seattle defeat anti-gay ballot measures.

1979—GPICS/NY mails its pamphlet "Gay People in Christian Science?" to all Christian Science churches, practitioners and college organizations in the world.

October, 1979—First National March on Washington D.C. for Lesbian/Gay Rights.

June 1980—GPICS/NY distributes its pamphlet to members attending their denomination's annual meeting over a three day period.

November 1980—The article *Only One Kind of Man* appears in the *Christian Science Journal.* It is considered by many as the most homophobic and pejorative tirade against sexual minorities to come from the Christian Science Church.

January, 1982—Wisconsin becomes first state to ban employment discrimination based on sexual orientation.

January 4, 1982—Chris Madsen, reporter for the *Christian Science Monitor* is fired after admitting she is a lesbian. Chris Madsen hires a lawyer and plans to sue the *Monitor.*

June 7, 1982—Members of GPICS/NY protest Chris Madsen's firing at The Mother Church's Annual Meeting.

June 19, 1982—Members and friends of GPICS/NY march in Boston's lesbian/ gay Pride March. Chris Madsen speaks to rally that follows.

June 20, 1982—GPICS members and friends attend Sunday Service at The Mother Church and stage another protest afterwards on Church property.

Fourth of July weekend, 1983—First national conference of lesbian/gay Christian Scientists held in Chicago.

October 13, 1983—Supreme Judicial Court of Massachusetts upholds right of Christian Science Church to fire Chris Madsen.

October/November 1983—Chris Madsen sues the Church a second time based on invasion of privacy. A settlement is reached, but its conditions remain confidential.

June, 1984—City of Boston outlaws employment discrimination based on sexual orientation.

1985—Representatives for Monitor Radio and radio station KQED begin negotiations re: the Monitor's discrimination policy based on sexual orientation. Meetings would continue for five years.

October 1985—National organization of lesbian/gay Christian Scientists formed in Chicago.

November, 1989—Massachusetts becomes the second state to ban employment discrimination based on sexual orientation.

February 5, 1990—Monitor Radio publicly announces sexual orientation is no longer a bar for employment in hiring.

1993—Unofficial alumni group for Principia College alumni "Gay and Lesbian Principians" organized.

July 16, 1994—Lesbian/Gay alumni hold unofficial reception at Principia College.

1999—It was learned (in answers given to questions on its official web-site) that The Mother Church no longer bars openly lesbians and gays from membership.

August 2, 2001—A State Manager of The Mother Church's Committee on Publication attends local meeting of lesbian/gay Christian Scientists. She emphasizes the "Group" is part of the larger Christian Science community.

June 26, 2003—Sodomy laws nationwide are overturned by the United States Supreme Court.

October 10–12, 2003—Lesbian/gay Christian Scientists hold historic first-ever meeting in a branch Church.

February 24, 2004—The President of the United States announces his support for a constitutional amendment banning same-gender marriage.

May 17, 2004—The first state-sanctioned marriages in the United States for same-gender couples take place in Massachusetts.

APPENDIX D

Web-Sites for Lesbian/Gay Christian Scientists and Their Supporters

The Mother Church, The First Church of Christ, Scientist in Boston, Massachusetts, Official Web-Sites

http://www.tfccs.com   http://www.spirituality.com

Emergence International

http://www.emergence-international.org

New York City Area Activities

http://www.nycsgroup.com

Principia College Lesbian/Gay Alumni Group

http://www.gaylesbianprincipians.org

Women's Activities

http://www.christiansciencewomen.org

For specific information contact: Kathelen Johnson <kathelen2001@ hotmail.com>

APPENDIX E

About the Author

Bruce Stores was a reporter for *Seattle Gay News* from 1979 to 1984 and an occasional contributor after that time. He was also a frequent contributor to *Emerge!* magazine. He was active in several gay political and social organizations in Seattle, Washington from 1979 to 1995.

Prior to his activism in the gay community, he was a Peace Corps Volunteer in Guatemala working in community development programs while also teaching English and literacy. He was a community development officer involved with refugee resettlement in Vietnam at the height of that war with the U.S. Agency for International Development. Later, he served the YMCA as youth director in Vineland, New Jersey and branch director in Midland, Texas. He left the United States again to serve as Recreation Coordinator for American employees and their dependents with Bell Helicopter/Textron in Esfahan, Iran, prior to that country's revolution. Back in the United States, he worked with self-help housing projects in Washington state and was later employed several years with the *Seattle Times*. He moved to Mexico in 1995. Since then he has devoted much of his time to teaching English, translation work, traveling and writing.

Bruce Stores is a life-long Christian Scientist. During his college years he helped create the Christian Science Organization at Springfield College in Massachusetts and served as its first President. Later he was a member of local Christian Science churches in Vineland, NJ, Midland, TX, Guatemala City, Guatemala and Seattle WA. At various times he served as Board member, First Reader, Lecture Committee Chair, Treasurer, and taught in the Sunday school. His membership in Fourth Church of Christ, Scientist, Seattle, WA was terminated when his sexual orientation became known. After hearing about lesbian/gay Christian Science support groups in New York and California, he helped organize Gay Christian Scientists in the Northwest in 1980. He became a founding member of Emergence International in 1985 and has served on its Coordinating Council (Board) for most of the organization's existence.

Bruce Stores is a graduate of Wesley College, Dover, Delaware (A.A. degree in liberal arts) and Springfield College, Springfield, Massachusetts (B.S. and M.Ed. degrees in humanities).

He was married in 1967 and divorced in 1980. He has one son and one grandson.

Christian Science: Its Encounter with Lesbian/Gay America is his first book.

0-595-32620-X

Printed in the United States
21511LVS00001B/166